"The Reverend H. B. London Jr. and I are both 'only children' and cousins who grew up like brothers. We were college roommates and nearly killed each other before we decided that it wasn't working. Now we have grown to enjoy a collegiality and mutual admiration like none other I have known. He is one of the finest men ever to grace a church pulpit. 'H,' as I call him, has been my pastor, my confidant, and my beloved friend through the many storms and seasons of life.

"After H. B. had served for 32 years in various pastorates, the Lord opened the door in 1991 for him to join us at Focus on the Family. He has been our 'pastor to pastors' through the intervening years, and God has blessed his ministry with us in remarkable ways. After we had been working together for about a decade, we received a letter from a well-meaning woman who wrote, 'It is wonderful that you are able to spend your declining years together.' We both still thought of ourselves as 'Joe College,' and were shocked by the implications of her letter. After reflection, I decided that H. B. was definitely declining, but I was not.

"Some of my most treasured memories have been with my Cuz. I hope you enjoy his book. It contains a lifetime of encouragement, ideas, and inspiration. I might even show up on several pages. Greetings to you all."
—Jim Dobson
"The brains" of the family

"Encouragement seems to be the fuel for our spiritual enthusiasm. With that being said, H. B. London is bringing a great service to the spiritual leaders of this country in reminding us to pause, recharge, and refresh. If we are to be for Christ what He has called us to be, and to His body that which we need to be, these three principles will have to be a reality in our lives. Read and be refreshed. Blessings!"
—Dr. Johnny Hunt
Senior Pastor of First Baptist Church of Woodstock, GA
President, Southern Baptist Convention

"I have had the privilege of working alongside and observing H. B. London for more than 17 years as he has served as 'pastor to pastors' for Focus on the Family's Church & Clergy outreach. From a lifetime of personal experience, as well as his unique vantage point of 'sounding board' for thousands of pastors and their spouses, H. B. understands the day-to-day ups and downs of fulltime ministry. He is able to address those challenges and opportunities in a practical and encouraging manner that few others can match. This new book offers devotional insights that will benefit anyone who has heard and accepted Christ's call to serve His body in a leadership position. I heartily recommend *Pause, Recharge, Refresh*."

—Jim Daly
President and CEO, Focus on the Family

"Pastors must win the war over burnout and discover a rhythm of life that will strengthen and sustain them. We are called to nurture and shepherd the people of the local church while remaining dependent on the Good Shepherd ourselves. Pastor London gives all of us practical insight and proven ideas to do just that."

—Brady Boyd
Senior Pastor of New Life Church, Colorado Springs, CO

"I enthusiastically recommend that every pastor and family member not only read H. B. London's inspirational and encouraging book *Pause, Recharge, Refresh*, but that you study and meditate and pray through it. I am sure it will lift you up in the same way it did me."

—Dr. Walt Kallestad
Senior Pastor of Community Church of Joy, Glendale, AZ

PAUSE

RECHARGE

REFRESH

Devotions to Energize a
Pastor's Day-to-Day Ministry

H. B. LONDON JR.

AMERICA'S PASTOR TO PASTORS

Tyndale House Publishers, Inc.
Carol Stream, Illinois

In reality this book has taken 17 years to write,
and it most likely will be my last.

I am indebted . . .

To Dr. James Dobson for the opportunity he gave me in 1991 to serve as a pastor to pastors. He has accepted me as a brother and colleague.

To Beverley, my wife, for her love and encouragement through 31 years of pastoral ministry and now 18 years at Focus on the Family.

To my sons, Brad and Bryan, who were great PKs and are even better husbands and fathers.

To Sue McFadden, my assistant for more than three decades, for her valuable input and support.

To Jim Daly, President of Focus on the Family, for his friendship and ongoing confidence to serve our ministry and God's church.

To my staff in Church & Clergy who have held up my arms as Aaron and Hur did for Moses. We have traveled long and effective miles together.

To these and the tens of thousands of clergy families it has been my privilege to serve . . .

I dedicate this book as an expression of my love, genuine admiration, and appreciation.

H. B. LONDON JR.

Acknowledgments

Thank you to all my coworkers at Focus on the Family who encouraged me during the writing of this book. Kathy Davis, my editor at Focus, you were so diligent in spending hundreds of hours wordsmithing my prose to make it a far better book than I ever imagined it would be. Thank you to Tyndale House Publishers for recognizing the value of this book to pastors and for your good communication and guidance in making it more effective. Special thanks, too, to Josh Shepherd, Cami Heaps, Jane Terry, and Shari Martin for your contributions to marketing and packaging. Many others gave their time and talent to making my dream for this book come true. I wish we could list everyone.

Thank you and bless you all!

H. B. London Jr.

Contents

How to Use This Book

Dear Pastor,

We have designed this book to be different from most other devotionals. We believe that at least two distinct differences merit an explanation so you can use it to your greatest advantage.

In addition to a devotion for each ordinary day, we've included special devotions for some of the significant days of the year that pastors often like to recognize, meditate upon, and pray for. Special attention is given to national holidays such as Independence Day and Mother's Day, as well as such noteworthy days as Sanctity of Human Life Sunday and National Day of Prayer. You'll find a devotion for every day of Holy Week, including the day after Easter, and for each day of the Advent season through Christmas Day. Since many of these observances do not consistently fall on the same day each year, you'll find them at the back of the book in a section titled Devotions for Special Days.

The second distinctive is that we have purposely left the regular days of the week undated so you can pick up this book anytime and find day-to-day encouragement.

It is our prayer that this devotional book will bring great encouragement to you and recharge and refresh your everyday experience as a pastor.

Be blessed and be a blessing!

H. B. LONDON JR.

Introduction

One thing we know for sure: Life is very unpredictable. That is especially so for those of us who serve the body of Christ as pastors or undershepherds. In Proverbs the writer cautions, "Do not boast about tomorrow, for you do not know what a day may bring forth" (Proverbs 27:1). In other words we live life day to day.

In some ways this is what our book is all about: day-to-day living. Making the most of every day. Counting each day as a gift. Entering every day with the echo of the Psalmist: "This is the day the LORD has made; let us rejoice and be glad in it" (Psalm 118:24).

I have served the church—and you, its leaders—for some 48 years, 31 of them as a pastor, the other 17 as a pastor to pastors staff member at Focus on the Family in Colorado Springs, Colorado. I have loved and highly valued my assignments. I have learned from you and from my experiences some valuable lessons. One that stands out is to hold very lightly those things that are of greatest value to you. Why? Because those things are most likely God's gift to you—not so much to possess as to protect, to surrender if need be, ever hoping that what He has given you has been invested properly to His satisfaction. There is not one of us who does not want to hear our Father's affirmation: "Well done, good and faithful servant!" (Matthew 25:23). How do we achieve that affirmation? By investing our gifts and opportunities day to day as though it will be our final opportunity to satisfy or fulfill the Master's expectation. That is what I call day-to-day living.

I was sailing along just fine in 2008. I had more triumphs than failures, more acceptance than criticism, many more good days than bad, until November 27th when I was admitted to John F. Kennedy Memorial Hospital in Indio, California. It was early (3:00 A.M.) on Thanksgiving morning when I realized I was in distress. I was unable to breathe normally, and the pain in my chest was severe. I was in trouble. I woke up Beverley, my wife, and asked her to take me to a place where I could find help.

When we arrived at the ER, they could tell I required immediate attention. The receptionist ushered me into an area where I could be examined.
The first diagnosis was that I was critical and suffering from heart failure. The
second, and correct, diagnosis was that I had an advanced stage of pneumo-
nia. My left lung was, for all practical purposes, so infected that it was basically useless.

For the next several days my doctors did everything they could to stem
the infection, but to no avail. Finally they decided, since the antibiotics were
not working, to do a surgical procedure called thoracotomy. They would go
into the area between the lung and the chest and clean out the infection that
was blocking the medication's access. This they did, and for a total of 13 days
I was in the intensive care unit under very close attention.

In a somewhat dramatic way I came to understand the meaning of day-
to-day living. One physician told my family I was very fortunate to be alive.
I believe that.

It was sobering to learn that when you become very ill, it is difficult to
pray for yourself. But later I found out that thousands of people—maybe
you were one of them—were praying for me, for my recovery, and for my return to ministry.

I'm not sure why God has chosen to give me more days to serve Him,
but I do know this: I plan on doing just that. Doing whatever I can in every
opportunity I am given, knowing that for me and for you it is all day-to-
day. Each day is a gift.

I hope that as you have time to read these pages, you will find encouragement and strength to face each and every day with excitement and expectation.

The devotionals contained here are dedicated to you and your family. May
you know each day His guidance, and may you sense His power to complete
your task. May you experience grace to show His love to those you meet along
the way and have His patience to bloom where He has planted you.

In the words of the Psalmist, "Wait for the LORD; be strong and take
heart and wait for the LORD" (Psalm 27:14).

When you stop to think about it, it really is day-to-day, isn't it?

DEVOTIONS

·

FOR

·

EVERY

·

DAY

God's Great Expectations

I would imagine that when you entered the ministry you were filled with great expectations. I know I was. In time, reality sets in, and those expectations are tempered by many variables—namely people, places, and chemistry between you and those you were called to serve. In some ways, your great expectations are at the mercy of others' expectations for you. I didn't like that part very much, but let me encourage you with a few timely passages from God's Word.

"If the LORD delights in a man's way, he makes his steps firm" (Psalm 37:23).

The Lord spoke through Jeremiah, "For I know the plans I have for you, plans to prosper you and not to harm you, plans to give you hope and a future" (Jeremiah 29:11).

Paul wrote, "Now to him who is able to do immeasurably more than all we ask or imagine" (Ephesians 3:20).

Paul quotes from Isaiah 64:4, "No eye has seen, no ear has heard, no mind has conceived what God has prepared for those who love him" (1 Corinthians 2:9).

It's all about God cheering you on! He has great expectations for you!

Sometimes I think we forget how much faith God has in us, and we give in to our own self-doubt and challenges. Don't do that! His hopes and dreams for you are great—even more so than what you believe for yourself. You are a winner—live like it!

In John 14:12, Jesus startled Philip with the promise, "I tell you the truth, anyone who has faith in me will do what I have been doing. He will do even greater things than these."

My Hopes for You

Here are my hopes for you and your family. Specifically . . .

- I pray that your intimacy with God will be even closer and that your motivation for doing what you do will be influenced by your conversation with Him rather than the latest fads and programs.
- I covet for you a really close friend—someone you can trust to hold you accountable and one who allows you the privilege of genuine honesty.
- I ask God to remove those roadblocks in your ministry that would prohibit you from finding the fulfillment you desire, and to bring about healing in any relationships with your parishioners that cause you to be anxious or fearful.
- I challenge you to "speak your word with great boldness," and I long for you to experience within your labors "miraculous signs and wonders through the name of your holy servant Jesus" (Acts 4:29, 30).
- I envision a multitude of you pastors falling in love with your call all over again, and finding great satisfaction in a servant/shepherd relationship with the people you pastor. Love them!
- I beg you to let your own family know how valued they are by you . . . and, from time to time, to ask them how they are doing.

"Not that we are competent in ourselves to claim anything for ourselves, but our competence comes from God. He has made us competent as ministers of a new covenant—not of the letter but of the Spirit; for the letter kills, but the Spirit gives life" (2 Corinthians 3:5-6).

God's Healing Balm
for the Hurting

In Isaiah 61, and again in Luke 4:18, the Bible speaks of freedom and recovery and release. It could refer to those within your congregation who are in a prison of drugs, perversion, and addiction. When Jesus read from the scroll of Isaiah, He identified Himself as one who had been sent "to proclaim freedom for the prisoners [those in bondage] . . . to release the oppressed." What a calling!

As you walk among your people, you are confronted every day with those who desperately need the freeing, healing balm that only God can provide. The problem is that such folks are troubled, they take your time, and they often fail in their attempt at whatever. Then you have to begin all over again.

Jesus felt the effort was worthwhile, and He spent a great deal of His time with those on whom others had simply given up. Who in your care desperately needs "to be free"? What are you willing to invest in that person? When was the last time you knelt in the dust to minister to a needy person— one with whom you must take the risk of loss before you win? I really believe it's worth a try. God will bless you.

"On hearing this, Jesus said to them, 'It is not the healthy who need a doctor, but the sick. I have not come to call the righteous, but sinners'" (Mark 2:17).

When Our Children Go into Ministry

What do you think of your child or grandchild being in ministry?

Despite the negatives we want our children to avoid, the ministry is a great calling, one that your children can and should consider. Let me offer a few suggestions that can cast a more positive light on your daily walk and make it shine more brightly for your children:

1. Be positive about the role God has called you to fill.
2. Help your family understand your calling.
3. Live your private life as a mirror of what you say and do in public.
4. Encourage any inclinations your children and grandchildren have toward ministry.
5. Pray daily that God will work in the hearts of your family, that they will be sensitive to His voice.

It really is a great thing God has given us in ministry, isn't it? God in His wisdom put His hand on you and me from among more than six billion people. Unbelievable! And He might have something just as special in mind for our children and grandchildren.

"You did not choose me, but I chose you and appointed you to go and bear fruit—fruit that will last" (John 15:16).

Accountability

Each of us is just one decision away from failure, and none of us is immune to temptations and weaknesses. I am no paragon of virtue, so I built several habits into my life as a pastor that helped me stay accountable:

1. I met every Tuesday morning with a group of men who cared for me. We held each other accountable as a fellowship of Christian brothers who cared enough about each other to ask the big questions.

2. During my three decades as a pastor, in each ministry I found a man who was willing to enter into a covenant with me. Like Jonathan did with David, this friend "made a covenant . . . because he loved [me] as himself" (1 Samuel 18:3). We promised each other to meet once a week, pray for one another by name every time we prayed, and ask each other the big questions.

3. The third point of accountability was Beverley, my wife. She asked me the big questions. She also addressed little weaknesses or concerns along the way that were potentially dangerous to us and to my ministry.

"Therefore confess your sins to each other and pray for each other so that you may be healed. The prayer of a righteous man is powerful and effective" (James 5:16).

Accountability—Second Verse

Being accountable means asking ourselves some hard questions, searching our hearts, and being honest with ourselves and our Lord. It requires taking the time to think deeply about where we are in our spiritual walk.

Here are the hard questions you should ask yourself often, according to Chuck Swindoll:

1. Have you been with a woman anywhere this past week that might be seen as compromising?
2. Have any of your financial dealings lacked integrity?
3. Have you exposed yourself to any sexually explicit material?
4. Have you spent adequate time in Bible study and prayer?
5. Have you given priority time to your family?
6. Have you fulfilled the mandate of your calling?
7. Have you just lied to me?

We deal every day with members of the clergy and their families who are facing their own dilemmas . . . forced terminations, unrealistic expectations, false accusations, moral failures, doubtful calling, mistakes in judgment, and spouses who just do not want to be in the ministry any longer. The list seems endless. We listen to these folks when they call. We pray with them, but we know each person must face his own issues in his own way. Asking yourself the hard questions can help you gauge where you are in your walk with the Lord and where you need to pay extra attention. Ask yourself the hard questions often and answer honestly. They may just spare you and your family some pain.

"But when he, the Spirit of truth, comes, he will guide you into all truth. He will not speak on his own; he will speak only what he hears, and he will tell you what is yet to come" (John 16:13).

He's Still There

It's a beautiful winter day in Colorado Springs, but our weather can change dramatically from one day to the next (or one moment to the next). We, in our city, are blessed by a sight we sometimes take for granted—Pikes Peak. It stands majestically along the Front Range of the Rocky Mountains. When you look to the west, it is nearly always visible. But there are days when the clouds hang low and the 14,000-foot peak is hidden.

It seems strange when you can't see "The Peak," but I am reminded of a truth I heard from an old pastor years ago. He said, "Remember, son, even when the clouds hide the beauty of the mountains . . . the mountains are still there, and that is what makes the difference."

What a comforting thought for folks like you and me. Sometimes trouble, distress, setbacks, or sickness overwhelms us to the point where we feel separated from God. During those times, behind the clouds of despair, beyond the fog of doubt, we know God is there, and that is what makes the difference. That is what we call faith.

"Now faith is being sure of what we hope for and certain of what we do not see" (Hebrews 11:1).

Having a Healthy Family

You know how hectic our schedules can be. Several years ago a leadership survey reported that 81 percent of ministers said insufficient time with their spouses was a problem, by far the most common concern. Likewise, when we at Focus on the Family ask ministers about the greatest danger facing them and their families, the overwhelming answer is lack of time.

What would happen if you asked your spouse and children how they feel about your schedule? Do they ever feel they take second place to your profession? Find out whether your children think being a PK is a positive or negative experience.

Do you engage in activities that strengthen the bonds between you and your children? Why not surprise them when they get home from school today with a special activity together. Or, if your kids are grown, just give them a call and tell them how much they mean to you. Or, if you and your children have been at odds over something, use this day as an opportunity to clear the air.

Does your family know how you feel? I pray that, without a doubt, they realize you love them more than anything. And I pray they know it because of your actions, not just your words.

"I guide you in the way of wisdom and lead you along straight paths" (Proverbs 4:11).

A Reason to Get Up in the Morning

I heard someone say one time that "to live your life to the fullest, you really need a reason to get up in the morning." I believe I have found that reason in a renewed passion: I want to see ministerial couples and families thrive. I want pastors to know how blessed they are to be chosen by the same God who called the disciples more than 2,000 years ago. I pray that I can assist the clergy couples I meet to find balance in their lives and to realize that the most important people in their congregations are their spouses and their children.

Further, I want to become a part of a movement to awaken a slumbering church. The church is in chaos right now. We need a new vision for every congregation, be it large or small. We need to learn again that God's truth is the greatest message we can teach a person. If we are simply attempting to entertain our flocks, we need to remember that the world can do that much better than we can.

As long as I am allowed to serve at Focus on the Family, I want to increase the reach of our efforts throughout the world—to impact pastors in developing countries, stagnant nations, and disillusioned Christian leaders wherever they may be found.

"He said to them, 'Go into all the world and preach the good news to all creation'" (Mark 16:15).

It's His Church

In my work with pastors and church boards, unfortunately, I too often find colleagues who see themselves as bigger than the churches they pastor and more important than the causes they represent. They are intolerant of their peers, disrespectful to leadership, and more interested in building their kingdoms than THE Kingdom. Their behavior is devastating to the integrity of the body of Christ. In nearly every case, there is heartbreak.

Your church belongs to Christ. God has merely allowed you the privilege of being a custodian of His body—a bride that, in time, He will send the Groom to collect. Are you and your congregation ready?

Sometimes I worry that some of us might think for a moment that we are in charge. Please don't fall captive to that kind of thinking. The church is still God's church, and for a little while, we are blessed to serve His church—not because of our power or talent, but through the power of His Holy Spirit.

As clergy, we too are admonished to "walk humbly with your God" (Micah 6:8) and to "live in peace with each other" (1 Thessalonians 5:13). Just a reminder: it's not about you—it's about HIM, the Christ we serve and the church HE birthed.

"Pride goes before destruction, a haughty spirit before a fall" (Proverbs 16:18).

Leading Your People

I am thinking of you right now, and how blessed we are as a nation to have you in Christian leadership. Your role is not an easy one, but so essential as you help lead your people into a mentality of praise and reflection. We have so much to thank God for!

The Psalmist penned, "Praise the LORD, O my soul; all my inmost being, praise his holy name. Praise the LORD, O my soul, and forget not all his benefits" (Psalm 103:1-2).

There are a lot of things out there that might cause you to forget if you're not careful—but forget not! Surround yourself with positive people for the next several days. Forget not, and fret not! Count your blessings. Take long walks with those you love. Journal a bit—jot down the specifics of your praise, and include them in your sermon.

"Great is the LORD and most worthy of [your] praise" (Psalm 145:3).

Resurrection Preaching

Jesus said, "I am the resurrection and the life. He who believes in me will live, even though he dies; and whoever lives and believes in me will never die. Do you believe this?" (John 11:25-26).

I choose to believe that our Lord Jesus Christ's remains are not in a box in Jerusalem with some of his so-called family members. I have chosen with the apostles "to testify to the resurrection of the Lord Jesus" (Acts 4:33). I pray you have, as well.

The apostle Paul said it very well: "And if Christ has not been raised, your faith is futile" (1 Corinthians 15:17) and "our preaching is useless" (1 Corinthians 15:14). How sad.

Question: Do you practice resurrection preaching? In a "feel good" world, it is not popular to mention sin and its consequences, and we can fail to do justice to the truth of our Lord's resurrection. "He is not here; he has risen!" (Luke 24:6). What a marvelous opportunity we have to underscore the reason for Christ's life on earth—a sacrifice for all mankind . . . yet without the resurrection, simply a life well lived. Resurrection preaching can become a catalyst for resurrection living.

Proclaim the real truth that Jesus Christ "was declared with power to be the Son of God by his resurrection from the dead" (Romans 1:4).

Giving Thanks in All Things

I remember the remarks of a wise colleague after I had been complaining about what I believed to be unfair treatment by a church member. He said, "It could have been a lot worse. If I were you, I would be thankful." I have never forgotten those words: It could have been a lot worse.

You may have had it tough lately, but I urge you to be thankful, for it could have been worse. Sure, the attendance at church has not been all you had hoped for, but just think how many *have* attended. You probably should have been recognized more often for the things you did for your people, but think back to those who did affirm you. I would imagine there have been some lonely times, but what about those encouraging telephone calls that came at just the right time?

In ministry, we all look for the obvious, often at the expense of His grace and mercy. I know I do! His blessings come in many forms. Be thankful!

"Give thanks to the LORD, call on his name; make known among the nations what he has done" (1 Chronicles 16:8).

Remembering the Blessings and Victories

"I have not stopped giving thanks for you, remembering you in my prayers" (Ephesians 1:16). You and your family are very important to me. Even in the midst of massive challenges, you—who are called of God—are a favored person.

Too often we in the ministry forget the blessings and victories of the past and concentrate on the challenges of the present. You can very easily discount God's goodness because of a setback of some kind. So, count your blessings. Live by the words of the apostle Paul: "Whatever is true, whatever is noble, whatever is right, whatever is pure . . . think about such things" (Philippians 4:8).

For instance, quickly think of five ways God has worked His will in your ministry, your family, or your own personal life. See? I told you—the blessings are bountiful.

"I do all this for the sake of the gospel, that I may share in its blessings" (1 Corinthians 9:23).

Living in Peace

Many years before Jesus came, the Old Testament prophet Isaiah wrote that a child was to be born who would be called the Prince of Peace. Jesus would later say, "Peace I leave with you; my peace I give you. I do not give to you as the world gives. Do not let your hearts be troubled and do not be afraid" (John 14:27).

In a world like ours, I doubt if peace among men will ever be a reality—especially in these last days—but personal peace is possible and attainable through our faith in Jesus Christ. We live in a fallen world controlled on the human level by sinful men. That combination rejects the peace that Jesus offers, but there is the promise of perfect peace. It comes by emptying our minds of fear, anxiety, and bitterness, by allowing the presence of God to fill us where dismay and doubt exist.

We become instruments of His peace as we pray the prayer of St. Francis: "Lord, make me an instrument of your peace. Where there is hatred, let me sow love. Where there is injury, pardon. Where there is doubt, faith. Where there is despair, hope. Where there is darkness, light. Where there is sadness, joy."

"Let the peace of Christ rule in your hearts, since as members of one body you were called to peace. And be thankful" (Colossians 3:15).

Living with Integrity

I wish all of us in the clergy would react positively to the call to live with integrity. What is integrity? Let me define it for you with the help of Merriam-Webster: "firm adherence to a code of especially moral values . . . INCORRUPTIBILITY." It really speaks of a lifestyle—a code of conduct, if you will.

In the King James Version of the Bible, Paul uses the words *corruptible* and *incorruptible* in relation to athletes running a race. He tells us that the prize they receive will decay but the crown we seek will "last forever." Paul says he lives in such a way that after he preaches, he will not be disqualified for the prize or, as the KJV says, become a "castaway" (1 Corinthians 9:25, 27).

As Paul wrote to Timothy, "Set an example for the believers in speech, in life, in love, in faith and in purity" (1 Timothy 4:12), and "Keep yourself pure" (1 Timothy 5:22). Pretty straightforward.

Do you know what typically happens to the clergy I work with who find themselves in tough, compromising situations? They begin by "flirting" with the questionable, and it nearly always ends in moral shipwreck. Don't let that happen to you. Guard your heart and soul, my colleague!

"But among you there must not be even a hint of sexual immorality" (Ephesians 5:3).

Prizes of True Value

What if we win the race but it is the wrong race, or we have the applause of people and it rings hollow? What if all we have to show for what we do is a room full of trophies that will in time decay?

Dr. Dobson tells a story about someone finding his prized college tennis trophy in the trash can. That is what the world can do to us—it can "trash our trophies." In ministry, there are those times when we feel "down by three" and the odds are against us. We sometimes wonder if we should even play the next game, but we do because we are on the winning team. We have Calvary on our side, and "if God is for us, who can be against us?"

We have every reason to believe in ourselves. Yet, the problem we face, beyond a lack of confidence, is the tendency to listen to the naysayers. Don't do that!

No one receives the victor's crown unless he competes. Don't ever quit, my colleague! The smile of God validates that which has eternal value. That is the prize we should run for. And even if we do not come in first in men's eyes, we do in our Father's eyes. That's what counts.

"I press on toward the goal to win the prize for which God has called me heavenward in Christ Jesus" (Philippians 3:14).

Be Bold and Courageous

When was the last time you stepped out of your comfort zone in your assignment? If there is to be renewed attention on the church, its leaders must be strong and courageous. We need men and women who will take some risks, who will preach with great authority.

It seems that the church is often lulled into complacency. It appears we can turn a blind eye and a deaf ear to the crises around us. Please don't be guilty of that, my colleague. Equip yourself with facts and figures. Be compassionate—but never compromise on the critical issues. Refuse to tolerate sin in your leadership. Take a stand on cultural issues that might be unpopular. Refuse shortcuts. Maintain a high level of prayer and study. Serve as a servant-shepherd. And most important, never compromise your call.

You have been called, equipped, anointed, and assigned. You are God's spokesperson and, in many ways, His only avenue to the people who desperately need to know how much He loves them.

I hope that we as clergy around the world are constantly motivated by the words of the Great Commission: "Therefore go and make disciples of all nations, baptizing them in the name of the Father and of the Son and of the Holy Spirit" (Matthew 28:19). The world grows smaller, but the urgency is ever greater. Share God's love, my colleague, both at home and wherever man is found. Do it with boldness and courage.

"Have I not commanded you? Be strong and courageous. Do not be terrified; do not be discouraged, for the LORD your God will be with you wherever you go" (Joshua 1:9).

Taking on New Challenges

I want to challenge you to think outside the box. Dream a bigger dream, and risk a bit where before you have chosen to play it safe. Only a small percentage of our colleagues will go out on a limb. When I ask them why, they always say there is too much at stake . . . too much to lose.

Many of us just continue along the same old trail, looking at the same scenery and encountering the same people day after day, settling for what is rather than striving for what might be. I admit that stepping farther out on the ledge is often chancy, but the pastors I know who seem most fulfilled are those who test the limits and trust God for His guidance and protection.

When you dream of ministry and those things you have always wanted to accomplish, what do you see? What excites you? If the Lord is the Author of your new adventure in faith, then go for it! It is not about throwing caution to the wind; rather, it is about continuing to grow, stretching your courage, and moving beyond the norm to keep your dreams alive.

I challenge you to stretch yourself beyond the realm of the comfortable, to live life on the cutting edge. Be courageous. You will be amazed at what you can do with God's power and might as your source and a courageous spirit as your motivator.

The Psalmist declares, "Sing to the LORD a new song" (98:1). The Lord said to Isaiah, "Do not dwell on the past. See, I am doing a new thing!" (Isaiah 43:18-19).

Caring Enough to Confront

Speaking the truth in love is a learned talent. Avoiding the truth is more the norm. Why? Because caring enough to confront not only takes a lot of courage; it also takes time.

When it comes to conflict, we are always ahead if we consider these questions:

1. Why is this happening? Think about it. Most conflicts arise when our "turf" is threatened. What will need to be given up? What will be required of me? Am I being taken advantage of? Does the person in conflict feel minimized? Do I understand his or her position? Is the conflict really necessary?

2. How have I contributed? In times of disagreement, we must all be honest enough to ask ourselves if we have been creating an atmosphere conducive to conflict.

3. Has my Christian attitude been evident? Isn't it interesting that so many of our petty differences are complicated because we cannot act as Christians? In the last heated issue in which you were involved, would the Lord have been pleased with the way His children behaved and showed honor and love for each other?

Remember, "Do not let any unwholesome talk come out of your mouths" (Ephesians 4:29).

Living Out Forgiveness

We want to! We try! We think we give it our best effort, but many of us just can't rid ourselves of that painful feeling that comes from being wronged by another.

The remedy? Forgiveness.

If there's a message we must continue to preach, and a sermon we must constantly live, it's that we must drop all charges against people who have done us wrong. If we don't, we will never live in peace or be free to live victoriously. So many clergy I know hang on to an offense they have suffered at the hands of a parishioner or colleague until it becomes like a festering sore in their lives. My colleague—let it go! Surrender your issue to God.

How can we forgive? We are granted the same power to forgive others that Christ uses to forgive you and me—His blood. We must be compassionate and ready to forgive, even as Christ has forgiven us (Ephesians 4:32). I urge you to ask God to give you strength and courage to tear every page from your little black book and hand it over to Him. Our burdens become His burdens; He takes responsibility for them. By faith, commit to God each day your hurting heart and your damaged emotions. Allow Him to ease your pain.

Intimacy with the Lord is possible only through a willingness to forgive as Christ has forgiven us.

"And when you stand praying, if you hold anything against anyone, forgive him, so that your Father in heaven may forgive you your sins" (Mark 11:25).

Worshiping with Your Family

Would it hurt if every now and again you sat with your family on a Sunday morning? It would be wonderful for your family and would send a powerful signal to those in your congregation who look to you for leadership.

Leading or just "being in charge" is a far cry from actual worship, as I learned in my years as a pastor. I was often consumed by what was happening around me rather than by what God was doing in me. So I started occasionally to sit in the front row with my back to the congregation. Then I could concentrate on worship. When it was time to deliver the sermon, I did so with a clear mind—because I had not been distracted but had truly participated in worship. And, just as important, I had worshiped with my family.

Become one of those who is lost in the wonder of genuine worship. While you're at it, take a look at the family beside you. What's that smile you see? It's only a happy bunch of people enjoying the company of one they love very much—you!

"God is spirit, and his worshipers must worship in spirit and in truth" (John 4:24).

Loving Your Family

I once heard a pastor say that we in ministry often treat our parishioners with more tenderness and affirmation than we do our own families.

My experience leads me to ask you: Are your expectations for your family as unrealistic as some that your congregation has for you? Or do you give yourselves the permission and the opportunity to be real? Do you praise your spouse and children as often as you can, or do you tend to take them for granted?

I remember another minister who told me without shame that he and his family were like actors in a play. They went so far as to match their clothing for Sunday morning!

But if we succeed in our congregations and alienate those in our homes, what will we have accomplished? We are human, not perfect.

Please—love the people in your home for who they are and not for what you and they are perceived to be. You can express this love in a number of ways: Praise each other regularly. Be patient with one another. Hesitate before you express a negative opinion. Take time for one another. In big and small ways, honor each other as the people God created you to be.

"If anyone does not provide for his relatives, and especially for his immediate family, he has denied the faith and is worse than an unbeliever" (1 Timothy 5:8).

A Recipe for Ministry Success

As the old saying goes, "Nothing succeeds like success."

As I travel about the country from church to church, I see the same phe-
nomenon: "Success breeds success." When a church is doing what it does
best, people flock to it. When a body allows contention, indecision, staff
problems, uncontested sin, and arrogance to sneak into its hallways, people
drift away.

When pastors ask me how to jump-start their churches, I tell them first
to pray. Then, I tell them to encourage unity with the leadership, and have
a vision. Do what you do best and don't try to be like everyone else. Just be
yourself! That's how you please God.

With God on your side, a healthy self-image, and a renewed vision for
your ministry, you can become all that God has planned for you to be. But
with an attitude of arrogance and pride, the "slide" could be just around the
corner.

The pastors I see succeed (and I'm not talking attendance numbers) are
those who are assured of their call, cast a proper vision for themselves and
their ministry, stay focused on the main thing, appreciate the success of their
colleagues, don't take themselves too seriously, maintain good health, love
their family foremost, and walk humbly with their Lord. That's a recipe for
success.

"Whatever you do . . . do it all in the name of the Lord Jesus" (Colossians 3:17).

Finding Fulfillment

Many pastors struggle as they grasp for the elusive feeling of fulfillment in their ministries. They complain about the low level of affirmation that comes from their congregants. It affects their morale, they say. Well, read what Neil Wiseman and I wrote on that very subject in our book *The Heart of a Great Pastor:* "Unless ministers find a high level of meaning in their work, they almost never have a significant impact on a congregation or a community. . . . No pastor can depend on anyone else to feed his feelings of fulfillment. It is an inside job, but anyone can achieve it. . . .

"Genuine fulfillment is rooted in knowing what ministry is and then doing it energetically and creatively. You know better than anyone else when your ministry is vibrant and satisfying. You know what pleases God. This is what matters most in measuring meaning in ministry."

Real fulfillment comes from knowing that you are where God wants you to be, doing what He desires you to do, and when possible, receiving from a group of people who lovingly acknowledge your leadership. Stay the course, my friend!

"But you, keep your head in all situations, endure hardship, do the work of an evangelist, discharge all the duties of your ministry" (2 Timothy 4:5).

Only the Lonely

Some of the loneliest times during my 31 years of pastoral ministry occurred when the heaviness of the moment seemed to rest on my shoulders, when it seemed I was the only one who could make the decision. And, sometimes, I didn't know what to do.

The issue is not so much whether we will become lonely. That is a given. It happens to us all. The real question is, "What do we do when we are lonely?"

Here are some guidelines that I have used during my ministry and continue to use today. They have helped me clarify the cause of my loneliness and have often led me out of it.

1. Examine the events, motives, and attitudes that have led to loneliness.
2. Determine whether you should share your condition with a significant spiritual brother or sister.
3. Get away for a while.
4. Rest.
5. Allow the Lord to provide the comfort He desires to shower upon you.
6. Review and modify your spiritual habits.

There will be times of loneliness and isolation in your life, but they need not cause you damage that cannot be repaired. The psalmist has written, "Hear my cry, O God; listen to my prayer. From the ends of the earth I call to you, I call as my heart grows faint; lead me to the rock that is higher than I. For you have been my refuge, a strong tower against the foe" (Psalm 61:1-3). May that be your prayer as well.

The Necessity of Dreams

A wise old preacher was right when he told two young beginning pastors, "A pastor never achieves more than his dreams."

That's an important starting point for ministry in every generation. Every pastor needs dreams that are passionately focused on the gospel and its supernatural effect on people who make up the congregation he or she serves.

So much depends on the combined dreams of pastors around the world. Think of the needs: perplexed persons, dysfunctional families, indifferent churches, deteriorating neighborhoods, and a rotting society. Think of the possibilities: thousands of ministers representing an incredible force for setting direction, restoring purpose, and calling the world back to God.

You know what it will take? A positive attitude—a belief in God with whom all things are possible—discipline of thought, prayer, preparation, and a dream.

What is the impossible dream you think about, pray about, and talk about? Begin to live that impossible dream. Reveal it to someone. Write it down in your Bible, and believe God for it!

"You may ask me for anything in my name, and I will do it" (John 14:14).

Living a Life of
Personal Holiness

"But among you there must not be even a hint of sexual immorality, or of any kind of impurity, or of greed, because these are improper for God's holy people. Nor should there be obscenity, foolish talk or coarse joking, which are out of place, but rather thanksgiving" (Ephesians 5:3-4).

A life of personal holiness is not easy. But it is important—for the Christian himself, for those he encounters today, and for those whose lives he might someday touch.

Even the best and the brightest of our colleagues often fall prey to the attacks of Satan. When that happens, precious lives are left in ruins, promising ministries are destroyed, and priceless future opportunities for sharing God's love are lost. The cost is too high.

There is only one preventative course to take: Stay very close to our Lord. Admit to Him your weaknesses and surrender to Him your fears . . . and then flee. Flee every form of evil, and take yourself out of harm's way.

"You were taught, with regard to your former way of life, to put off your old self, which is being corrupted by its deceitful desires; to be made new in the attitude of your minds; and to put on the new self, created to be like God in true righteousness and holiness" (Ephesians 4:22-24).

Healing Depression

How do you help the sorrowful or depressed person? For sure, pray for them and help them trace back to the cause of the situation. If the condition is ongoing or persistent, they will need to get professional assistance. Offer emotional support, and, whatever you do, please do not just sweep their feelings under the rug. They most likely are not faking and in time will get better. But you can't just say, "Snap out of it!" and, like the wave of a magician's wand, expect everything to be better.

I have had bouts of depression. Many type-A personalities do. I have prayed for that veil of sadness to lift. I have carried on a schedule that was filled with smiles and joy on the outside while, on the inside, I was dying. When the veil lifted, it was wonderful.

So, my colleague, please do not overlook those under your care who live their lives in sadness. Here's a list of scriptures that might help you as you guide people touched by your ministry back to wholeness:

- "The LORD is close to the brokenhearted and saves those who are crushed in spirit" (Psalm 34:18).
- "A cheerful heart is good medicine, but a crushed spirit dries up the bones" (Proverbs 17:22).
- "We are hard pressed on every side, but not crushed; perplexed, but not in despair" (2 Corinthians 4:8).

Facing Disappointment

To borrow a line, "The best-laid schemes of mice and men oft go awry." It happens, and in many cases there is absolutely nothing we can do about it. Imperfect expectations!

Very few of us live our lives as members of the clergy without disappointments and heartbreak. I think the question is, "What do you do when your dreams lie on the office floor like a scattered stack of newspapers?" I don't have a fail-safe response, but one that I ask you to think about.

The sun will come up tomorrow. How you face the new day depends on how you finish this one. Consider the following suggestions:

1. Confide in reliable people.
2. Search your heart for any motivations that might appear selfish.
3. Remember your ministry does not rise or fall on one isolated event or circumstance.
4. If you have made a mistake, apologize to the proper people or group.
5. Don't allow a perceived failure to drive a wedge between you and your family.
6. Make your next move only after you have had some time to recover.

Bottom line: To those who love the Lord first and foremost, there will always be God's way . . . a better way. As Stan Toler and I said in *The Minister's Little Devotional Book*, "He has chosen you to spread His Word! And whenever you do stumble, He will pick you up, brush you off, and set you back on track—brighter and smarter than when you started."

"He heals the brokenhearted and binds up their wounds " (Psalm 147:3).

Divine Healing

I have always believed in healing. I have prayed for and anointed the sick. Wonderful things have happened, but I am certainly no healer. My simple, childlike faith takes God at His word.

James talks about the "prayer of faith" in James 5:15 (KJV). In verse 16, he continues, "The prayer of a righteous man is powerful and effective." Faith and righteousness! Power and effectiveness!

Why has divine healing taken on such a circus feel? Why is it that we do not exercise our rights in Christ, making healing a regular part of our worship? I am not trying to be naïve, but practical. We believe the heaven portion of John 14, but do we believe in the miracle portion that says, "You may ask me for anything in my name, and I will do it" (John 14:14)?

I once spoke at a church where they prayed for healing and deliverance during worship time. I wish the subject of healing were not so sensational. I wish it were more of a normal practice in the church—when man backs away and lets God take center stage.

"Therefore I tell you, whatever you ask for in prayer, believe that you have received it, and it will be yours" (Mark 11:24).

Your Identity

Our lives in Christ are identifiable. People can see what our values are—how we face a crisis, the way we treat our families, how we relate to the awesome commands of God, and where our priorities are placed. So what would others say of you? "He is faithful! Moral! Full of integrity! Prayerful! Humble! Obedient! Devout! Committed to his family!" Or maybe a combination of these things.

Or would they describe you in less flattering terms? "He is arrogant. Prideful. Stubborn. Difficult." Regardless, you have identifying characteristics and a "great cloud of witnesses." My colleague—what name will you leave behind?

I am moved by the one who wrote, "Since we are surrounded by such a great cloud of witnesses, let us throw off everything that hinders and the sin that so easily entangles, and let us run with perseverance the race marked out for us. Let us fix our eyes on Jesus, the author and perfecter of our faith, who for the joy set before him endured the cross, scorning its shame, and sat down at the right hand of the throne of God" (Hebrews 12:1-2).

Seeking Wellness

I know for a fact that childhood hurts lead to adult misbehavior. At Focus on the Family, we see this proven over and over again through calls from clergy couples on our toll-free "care line." Everything from sexual perversion to abuse has been confessed to us, and in nearly every situation our colleagues are crying out for help. They realize they are damaged goods, and their ministries will never be as effective as God wills unless they begin to take steps toward wholeness. You might be one of those.

If you are struggling with this kind of issue, get help now, my friend. Don't wait until sin has destroyed your ministry and your family. Turn to a trusted mentor or counselor and confess your sin. Seek the help of a professional who deals with your specific problem. Seek wellness, my colleague.

"Then I acknowledged my sin to you and did not cover up my iniquity. I said, 'I will confess my transgressions to the LORD'—and you forgave the guilt of my sin" (Psalm 32:5).

Don't Give Up in Hard Times

The work that you and I have been called to is filled with disappointments and "emotional speed bumps." But our directive is to continue loving and serving God and His children in spite of setbacks and missteps. We are never the healer—God is. We are neither the judge nor jury—God is. But we are His agents for change, and we must never grow weary of trying. Why? Listen to the apostle Paul: "Let us not become weary in doing good, for at the proper time we will reap a harvest if we do not give up. Therefore, as we have opportunity, let us do good to all people, especially to those who belong to the family of believers" (Galatians 6:9-10).

I can honestly tell you there have been times when I have been weary in welldoing in spite of the scripture's admonition not to give up. I have wondered, as you have, if there was strength sufficient to complete the journey. But I labored on, resisting the temptation to give it up, knowing inside I could not reject the call that our Lord had placed upon my life.

No doubt you have used the familiar phrase in Matthew 11:28 many times: "Come to me, all you who are weary and burdened, and I will give you rest." Have you read that passage lately? What does it mean to you? May I expand that question and provide you with at least a glimpse into the words of Jesus? To me, it says: When faced with the pressures and challenges of our assignments, the Lord asks us to surrender to His loving yoke and experience His perfect rest, His strong arm around our shoulders.

So, hold your head high. You're doing a great work, and there will be many who join you around God's throne because of your faithfulness.

"Take my yoke upon you and learn from me, for I am gentle and humble in heart, and you will find rest for your souls. For my yoke is easy and my burden is light" (Matthew 11:29-30).

Do You Need a Social Concern Committee?

A social concern committee can be of great assistance to any pastor for understanding and addressing cultural issues.

In my first years as a pastor, I believed that openly opposing societal ills would create problems for me from people who felt uncomfortable with their pastor talking about "news" subjects. And I was right. I was hammered from all sides, and I became reluctant to speak my conscience. I eventually worked myself out of that corner and took stands on public policy. Had I not done so, I would have felt less than honest.

There were also many occasions when I felt lonely and exposed because it was difficult for me to know where I stood with those who mattered most to me—my congregants. Then it dawned on me that I should not stand alone, nor take the abuse for my well-intentioned convictions. That was the genesis of a social concern committee.

Every congregation has a nucleus of people who care deeply about the signs of the times. They are concerned when society begins to move in a direction that could be detrimental to the institution of the family, the church, and our children. Call them together around a cause and you will have the simple beginnings of a social concern committee.

"May the favor of the Lord our God rest upon us; establish the work of our hands for us—yes, establish the work of our hands" (Psalm 90:17).

What Does a Social Concern Committee Do?

A social concern committee can be used as a research and information source for the whole church body. Committee members can attend meetings of the city council, school board, library board, and so on. They can gather pertinent information related to social issues. They can meet each month to discuss whether or not an issue is worthy of further action. They can make telephone calls and visits to the significant players in the community who influence policy matters. They can compile lists of names and telephone numbers of those who need to be contacted and whose opinions can be influenced by the public. They can write letters. Further, they can provide pertinent material with issue-related information for those in the church body who need to become better informed. In short, the social concern committee is like Nehemiah on the wall—a watchman on behalf of the church and the community it serves.

You can't be everywhere in the community and do everything in the church. So you need concerned individuals to act as your eyes and ears, collecting information, informing your congregation, being a liaison with the community, praying for you. It's a wonderful way to get individuals involved and is a great help to any pastor.

"Brothers, choose seven men from among you who are known to be full of the Spirit and wisdom. We will turn this responsibility over to them and will give our attention to prayer and the ministry of the word" (Acts 6:3-4).

How Can a Social Concern Committee Assist You?

Are you hesitant to form yet another committee in your church? Do you think you already have too many? Here are a few final thoughts about how a social concern committee can make your job easier.

First: It can provide you with a group of people to run point for you on issues about which you might be uncertain.

Second: It can give you a point of reference or serve as a resource reservoir. Members can do research on your behalf, in order to provide information that is accurate and not skewed by the liberal press. They can go to the source and ask hard questions. They can stimulate interest within your congregation, which might be difficult for you to do.

Third: When you grow weary, they can hold your arms up, and when you are discouraged, they can be a Gideon's army—not many, but very dedicated. In addition they can prove to be a source of great prayer support.

Contrary to what many might say, I do not believe that everyone can be an activist. Not all in your church family have the gift of evangelism. But I do believe that everyone in your church can have a witness, just as I believe all in your church can have an opinion and a vote on social issues. You needn't stand alone when, in front of you every week, there can be a small remnant of people exercising their passion for the cause of Christ in the interest of righteousness and godliness.

"Righteousness exalts a nation, but sin is a disgrace to any people" (Proverbs 14:34).

Shepherding a Church

I began pastoral ministry in 1963. I was 23, fresh out of seminary, and assigned to a church on the wrong side of the street in a Southern California community. I was given practically no chance of pulling my little charge out of the doldrums. But I had learned from my heritage how important it was to love people. So I did.

I visited their homes, paid attention to their children, visited the sick in hospitals and nursing homes, prayed for the downtrodden and lonely. I made myself available and told them publicly that, next to my family, they were the most wonderful people in the world.

It is critical for your congregation and community to know that the shepherd of the flock is truly that—approachable, responsive, gentle, and genuinely filled with compassion. Those characteristics are more significant for the leader of the flock than academic degrees, church growth numbers, or status achieved.

The Pastor Shepherd (John 10:1-28):
- Lays down his life for his sheep.
- Knows his sheep.
- Protects his sheep.
- Feeds his sheep.
- Encounters his sheep.
- Can locate the sheep in his pasture.
- Searches for the lost sheep.
- Promises eternal life to those who believe in the Good Shepherd.

It is a ministry modeled after the Good Shepherd Himself.

"I am the Good Shepherd. The Good Shepherd puts the sheep before himself" (John 10:11, MSG).

Marriage Development

Cultivating a satisfying marriage is an important part of emotional and spiritual wholeness. A commitment to marriage development is pleasing to God, fulfilling to both partners, and healthy for the church.

Marriage offers joy, meaning, and pleasure. The intense demands of ministry, which many consider harmful to marriage, can be used to cultivate closeness that grows out of sharing thoughts and experiencing service together.

Here is a partial "to do" list to help you maximize the potential in your marriage:

1. Allow your marriage to add adventure to ministry.
2. Focus on the process of marriage.
3. Spot warning signals.
4. Live by spiritual principles.
5. Commit to wholeness.
6. Put your marriage on the calendar (private time).
7. Rekindle love.

Every marriage can be better, and happily married pastors are more effective pastors. The time has come to stand up and get serious about our own marriages. Let's pay the full price to make our marriages solid, satisfying, and spiritually sound. Let's move up on our list of priorities the commitment to emotional, spiritual, and physical intimacy. It's time in our own marriages to demonstrate all we preach to others about commitment, integrity, accountability, and virtue.

"Wives, submit to your husbands as to the Lord" (Ephesians 5:22). "Husbands, love your wives and do not be harsh with them" (Colossians 3:19).

Staff Decisions

I have generally had good success in staff relationships, but like so many leaders, I was once asked to inherit another man's staff. They were loyal to the former leader—as they should have been—and they found it very difficult to adjust to my way of doing things. It was tough on them and tough on me. My biggest mistake—and, I might add, an injustice to them—was to allow my emotions to get the best of me. They had homes, friends, and a network of support, and I didn't want to jeopardize any of that. Instead, I jeopardized my own effectiveness.

I recall one pastor who said to his staff, "These are my requirements. I am going to give several months for us to consider my expectations. If I feel, in time, that you will be happier and more effective somewhere else, I will tell you that." I didn't do that, but I should have.

I also feel that staff difficulties should be dealt with swiftly. It is not unlike a cancer, in that it will in a very short time affect the total body. One time, I needed to ask a very well-known, talented staff member to work somewhere else. Because of his national reputation and his connections with a segment of our community, I was reluctant to do so. Things began to deteriorate to a point where it was becoming obvious to our people. I was sitting at home late one evening when the telephone rang. It was a member of my church board, who said to me, "We have just done what you should have done—we have terminated the staff member who should have been terminated weeks ago." I can't tell you how relieved I was. The fallout was painful, but the peace that permeated our staff from that day forward was worth the pain.

There is so much more that can be shared about staff, but *trust and loyalty* are the two common threads that must run through the mix. Staff relations can bring about the best of times or the worst of times—let's go for the best.

"And the Lord's servant must not quarrel; instead, he must be kind to everyone, able to teach, not resentful" (2 Timothy 2:24).

Church Style

I have developed the following guidelines for pastors and churches as they consider the question of "church style."

1. Build on your own gifts and personality. Be yourself! Use your best gifts more often.
2. Know your community. Fit your church mission around the needs of the community in which you live.
3. Sell your vision to spiritual people. Please do not give a larger group of people the opportunity to dash your hopes before you have allowed spiritual people to pray honestly with you.
4. Count the cost of change. If you are going to alter the way you do things, please do it prayerfully and with your eyes wide open.
5. Take a risk. Assess your world and prepare for the battle Satan will wage against you, your ministry, and the people you serve.

Go for it! Find a style that fits you, your community, and the gifts of your people, and take a risk for Christ's sake! The church is not a "style" show; it is an expression of Christ's love to a searching world.

"Let us not give up meeting together, as some are in the habit of doing, but let us encourage one another" (Hebrews 10:25).

There Are No Small Assignments

I've heard many people say that in the twenty-first century, it will not be the size of the church but its health that will ensure its survival.

I doubt if most people realize that more than 100,000 churches in the United States have 50 attendees or fewer. That means that the average church will have fewer than 100 worshipers this Sunday. So, in spite of all the press the megachurches receive, we are still a nation of small- to medium-sized churches.

For some pastors, serving in a small church creates something of a self-image problem. We look at the big church on the hill, compare ourselves to that operation, and feel inadequate or insignificant. Not so, my friend!

In *The Heart of a Great Pastor*, Neil Wiseman and I wrote, "Every assignment is holy ground because Jesus gave Himself for the people who live there. Every place is important because God wants something incredibly important to be accomplished there through us. Every situation is special because ministry is needed in that place. Like Queen Esther, we have come to the Kingdom for a time like this." All of these factors give a pastor a much-needed sense of destiny about his assignment.

In other words, there are no small assignments, and none of you is insignificant in any way.

You are needed, important, and empowered by God. You serve in the middle of the action. God wants to enable you to transform your present assignment into holy ground—a place where He accomplishes supernatural achievements through ordinary people.

Eugene H. Peterson puts a new spin on Jesus' words in his paraphrase of the Scriptures, *The Message*. "When you're joined with me and I with you, the relation intimate and organic, the harvest is sure to be abundant" (John 15:5).

Church Health Checkup

May I suggest a few guidelines for assessing the health of a congregation of any size? Healthy churches are/have:

1. Biblically based. Do your congregation members have a clear understanding of what they believe and substantial information to assist them in defending their faith?

2. Mutually concerned. Do your people genuinely care for one another?

3. Socially connected. Church is fellowship as much as it is a formal worship service.

4. Community saturated. Are you aware of the day-to-day decisions that are made in your community that affect its school system, social programs, and overall moral climate?

5. Financially stable. The church that is fiscally responsible will be able to weather any situation.

6. A clearly understood vision. Every church needs to know who it is, what its calling is, and how it will be directed to meet the challenge of the future.

7. A positive outlook. See yourself as God sees you—full of potential and planted for a purpose.

I'm sure there are many other "good health indicators" for churches of any size, but I urge you to consider these, then add your own ideas to the mix. One thing I know: Christianity needs you to make your ministry meaningful and help change the way pastors and laypeople alike look at the church of Jesus Christ.

"The goal of this command is love, which comes from a pure heart and a good conscience and a sincere faith" (1 Timothy 1:5).

What Is a Healthy Congregation?

In his book titled *Excellent Protestant Congregations*, author Paul Wilkes identifies 311 excellent congregations—of every type and style—determined from research over a two-year period. He lists the factors that he feels describe "excellent" churches:

- Evidence of a "joyful spirit"
- Awareness of members' diversity
- Welcoming attitude toward all in the church community
- Emphasis on true spirituality and a deep relationship with God
- Innovative and thoughtful worship
- Collaborative decision making among pastor, leaders, and lay members
- Awareness of Christian tradition
- Scripture-based teaching and preaching
- Confrontation of real problems with members and the church's community

How does Mr. Wilkes's criteria match your church?

For several years now as I have written and traveled across the country, I have been preaching a message of "church health." I believe every body of believers can be healthy if they are willing to look honestly at themselves. These guidelines might be a start! My prayer for you is a healthy congregation.

"Every day they continued to meet together in the temple courts. They broke bread in their homes and ate together with glad and sincere hearts" (Acts 2:46).

How God Measures Success

This is an excerpt from the book *The Heart of a Great Pastor*, humbly penned by Neil Wiseman and me. In one section of the book, we take a fresh look at the misguided notions of "pastoral success." I'd like to share a few of our thoughts with you:

"Opportunity blindness always worsens when a pastor considers each assignment as a steppingstone to something better. Such a stance forces him to consider every pastorate as semi-temporary. In some unexplainable, self-fulfilling way, his thinking causes the assignment to actually become restrictive or even suffocating. Yet the opportunities he hopes to find in another place already exist where he resides.

"Francis Bacon's advice helps us bloom: 'A wise man makes more opportunities than he finds.' I would imagine that any long-term pastor has considered moving to another place only to be reminded by the Lord, 'I have not released you; I need you here; your work is not finished.' . . . The secret is to make our assignment ideal by blooming where God plants us."

God does not measure success by numbers. Neither should we. I believe that if you will determine to bloom where you are planted, opportunities will appear where before there were only walls.

"Let us not become weary in doing good, for at the proper time we will reap a harvest if we do not give up" (Galatians 6:9).

Where Do You Go When You're in Pain?

The phrase "I feel your pain" has been bandied around a great deal. Politicians say it, churches promote it, and well-meaning people use it to identify with those around them who struggle with life's harsh realities. The truth is that people do suffer pain from one source or another, and they need someone to understand.

Even we pastors know pain. But where do we go? What do we do when we hurt and no one seems to care? Let me make a few suggestions:

1. Turn to the Psalms. Read Psalm 103:2, 32:11, and 144:1-2, for starters.
2. Turn to music. Beautiful music has a way of reminding us that our situations are known to the Lord.
3. Turn to a friend. Find someone who "will not forsake you."
4. Turn to God. Find comfort in His words: "I will never leave you nor forsake you."

You're doing a wonderful thing for Christ and the church. We are proud of you. We salute you, and we stand beside you—and so does He! There's someone to turn to when you really hurt and no one seems to care.

"Surely I am with you always, to the very end of the age" (Matthew 28:20).

The Powerful Prayer
of the Intercessor

Do you remember when Jesus said to Simon Peter, "Simon, Simon, Satan has asked to sift you as wheat. But I have prayed for you, Simon, that your faith may not fail" (Luke 22:31-32)? Jesus became an intercessor on Simon's behalf.

Who intercedes for you? For whom do you intercede? Someone has said, "Praying for others is one of the best ways of loving people." I agree. When we pray for others, and others pray for us, several things happen:

- We become interdependent. We develop a sense of responsibility for one another that is awesome in its power. We take our relationships very seriously.
- We make God's resources available to others. The liberating, healing power of the Almighty God flows out to those about whom we care.
- We put the needs and hurts of the other individual into perspective. We understand more clearly the plight of another.
- We develop a spirit of hope and optimism. When we are lifted or lift another into the hands of God, we feel at peace because we are convinced God can conquer anything.
- We sense "belongingness" and significance. To say to another, "I am praying for you" is the sweetest sound imaginable—especially to a pastor when it comes from a member of his flock.
- We determine to do all we can to help be an answer to our own prayers. We do all in our power to become "labourers together with God" (1 Corinthians 3:9, KJV).
- We are obedient to the will of God, especially in the area of faithfulness. He desires to give good gifts to those who ask Him (Matthew 7:11).

"The prayer of a righteous man is powerful and effective" (James 5:16).

Struggles with Pornography

Sexual addiction is a major problem in the ministry. At Focus on the Family, we estimate that up to 20 percent of pastors have a problem with pornography. One day one of our assistants in the Pastoral Ministries Department said that she had received five calls that morning from pastors on the issue of pornography. Initially, I thought the callers were looking for counseling aids to help others, but I soon discovered that they themselves were hooked. One had been struggling for more than 20 years.

Dr. Archibald Hart's research concludes that sex has become dehumanized. In many circles, it is no longer regarded as an act between loving, responsible couples. Sex has become a sport. And, as in all sports, there is a strong desire to improve one's performance. Pornography is a sport too, and ministers are not excluded from the game.

How do men break the pattern of pornography? First, they must realize that they choose their behavior. The men I have counseled say they could never break the habit gradually. It had to be done cold turkey. *The Sexual Man*, Dr. Hart's book, makes the following suggestions for the man who is faced with a pornography habit or any other sexual addiction:

1. Be honest with yourself and acknowledge that you have a problem.
2. Be accountable to another person. Tell someone else you can trust about your addiction.

3. Dispose of all the pornographic material you own. Don't keep any of it. If you're tempted to rent DVDs, don't go near a video store of any kind.

4. Be patient, and resist feeling defeated each time you fail. Your addiction took time to develop; it will take time to overcome.

5. Pray about your problem. Rely on God for deliverance and strength. God promises to make a difference in our lives. Allow Him to give you the special strength you need to overcome this battle.

If you still struggle, seek professional help from a counselor who specializes in sexual addiction. To speak to a counselor, or for a referral to a counselor in your area, call 1-800-AFAMILY. For a list of resources and other help, go to www.parsonage.org.

One last thing. As difficult as it might be for some of us, our spouses must act as an enabler to healing. That means not only do we confess our challenges, but we give permission to our mates to ask us the difficult questions.

"It is God's will that you should be sanctified: that you should avoid sexual immorality; that each of you should learn to control his own body in a way that is holy and honorable, not in passionate lust like the heathen, who do not know God" (1 Thessalonians 4:3-5).

Leading in the Quest
for Spiritual Renewal

I think the one thing that I prayed for most often in my more than three decades of pastoral ministry was revival in my church. I remember praying at first for a return to something, although I wasn't exactly sure what—just something that was a happening, a spirit, a feeling. Eventually, I realized that what I was praying for was not really a revival or return but a new vitality and commitment to God and His will. Not something old—but something new.

As I prayed about ways to lead my people out of the past and into the newness of God's greater blessing, I was struck by the realization that what they experienced was secondary to what I needed to experience. My first priority for spiritual renewal needed to be with myself—a rebirth of my own vitality and commitment. It was a wonderful discovery.

Praying is only one part of the equation for renewal and a rebirth of spiritual vitality in the church. According to 2 Chronicles 7:14, humility and repentance must also be present.

As pastors and change agents in the church of Jesus Christ, shouldn't we begin with a look inside our own lives? It just might be that spiritual renewal in the church will begin when we, its leadership, freshly examine our own priorities, motivations, relationships, attitudes, ambitions, and call from God.

"Examine me, O LORD, and prove me; try my reins and my heart" (Psalm 26:2, KJV).

"Will you not revive us again, that your people may rejoice in you?" (Psalm 85:6).

Divine Calling

Let me ask you a very personal question. Have you ever awakened early on a Monday morning with the thought, "I wonder how long I can keep doing what I'm doing?" Have you ever scripted a resignation letter in your head . . . but never got around to writing it? How are you feeling about your assignment today?

In my work with pastors, I have found the following to be true: (1) We need to see progress. (2) We need to be allowed to dream new dreams. (3) We need to be around positive people rather than negative thinkers. (4) We need times of rest and restoration. (5) We must have the support of our families. (6) We need to be able to relate in a positive way to colleagues. (7) We need periods of personal revival to see us through the dark times. (8) We want to be seen as change agents. The list could go on.

When you think about what we do, it becomes obvious that ministry is not for cowards. Are you able to fulfill the mandate of your call, and, also, are you using your gifts effectively? I know it's a lot to think about, but it is really vital if you are to enjoy what God has called you to do.

"But you, keep your head in all situations, endure hardship, do the work of an evangelist, discharge all the duties of your ministry" (2 Timothy 4:5).

Resolving Conflict

So often, those we serve with are unwilling to face their responsibility to God to be compassionate and forgiving. When this happens, conflict results, and inevitably, walls are built.

Truth: Christ came to tear down all walls of hostility that separate one person from another. Scripture: "For he himself is our peace, who has made the two one and has destroyed the barrier, the dividing wall of hostility" (Ephesians 2:14).

The definition of reconciliation is: "The restoration of friendship and fellowship after estrangement." Reconciliation has to do with relationship. It does not mean agreement or understanding on every issue. Reconciliation and resolution of issues are two different things. The Bible teaches unity, but it does not demand uniformity.

Jeremiah 17:9 says, "The heart is deceitful above all things, and desperately wicked" (KJV). Are you blaming the other person? Are you willing to begin to resolve the conflict by asking God to examine you and change your heart?

Three lessons learned: Always accept personal responsibility. Make whatever effort necessary to move toward the person with whom you are in conflict. Take the risk of confronting the issue for the sake of the relationship. I urge you to be the peacemaker that God honors. Actively pursue peace, and be an instrument of peace yourself.

"And the peace of God, which transcends all understanding, will guard your hearts and your minds in Christ Jesus" (Philippians 4:7).

Just Pray

I remember a time in the early days of my pastoral ministry when I was facing a very difficult situation. I decided to share my burden with an older gentleman in the congregation whom I admired greatly for his spiritual insight. I poured out my heart to this wise man and then sat back awaiting his response. After several moments of silence, he looked over his eyeglasses at me and simply said, "Pray, brother, pray."

I'm not sure that was the answer I was looking for, but it was the answer I needed. As the prayers I prayed were answered, his advice proved to be invaluable. So, whatever you might be currently facing, I'd like to pass these words of wisdom on to you, my colleagues: "Pray, brother (sister), pray!"

I do not know all I would like to know about prayer and how it works, but I do know from my own experience that the prayer of the intercessor is powerful. It projects faith and love in the name of Jesus Christ.

"I urge, then, first of all, that requests, prayers, intercession and thanksgiving be made for everyone—for kings and all those in authority, that we may live peaceful and quiet lives in all godliness and holiness" (1 Timothy 2:1-2).

God's Love for Each Individual

Many years ago in my pastoral ministry, I began to use a phrase that I probably repeated in some way every Sunday in worship. It is: "God loves you as though you were the only one in all the world to love—that makes you a very special person."

Although St. Augustine had a similar phrase, I think the apostle John crystallized the thought when he said, "For God so loved the world that he gave his one and only Son." He was saying, "Jesus has come in person for you—as though there were only you!"

That is a truth your people should hear over and over again. They are loved in a unique way by Almighty God. What a great message! If people could, as little children, embrace that truth, the Christian walk would come so much easier for them. When they struggle with that truth, faith always seems difficult.

What about you? Do you understand that God loves you as though you were the only pastor-teacher-leader in all the world to love? He loves you to that degree. He really does.

So many influences in the world would like to discourage us by getting us to believe we are simply one in a billion. Don't ever believe that, my friend. You are one that God loves as though you were the only one. God's love for you is the greatest love story ever written. And it was written just for you.

"And so we know and rely on the love God has for us. God is love. Whoever lives in love lives in God, and God in him" (1 John 4:16).

Presenting the Call to Ministry

Evidently, there is a shortage of new clergypersons to take the positions being vacated by an aging ministry force.

In my years as a pastor to pastors, I have witnessed this deficiency. Fewer seminary students are seeking a career as senior or associate pastor. Many of those who graduate with advanced degrees do not plan to work in the local church. Bottom line: There is a shortage in many fellowships of newly assigned spiritual leaders.

I am sure you can see the faces of those you influenced who are now walking in your footsteps. Can there be a greater thrill than to see the hand of God directing the paths of those you have shepherded?

I recall the many times when, as a teenager or college student, I heard men of God preach messages imploring those present to "surrender" to God's call. They often quoted from Acts 16:9, "Come over to Macedonia and help us." Or from Matthew 4:19, "'Come, follow me,' Jesus said, 'and I will make you fishers of men.'"

I think that we would see more of our congregants entering into ministry if, one, we were more positive about the experience; two, we challenged them; and three, we recognized the value of God's unique call.

When was the last time you presented a message like that?

"So they pulled their boats up on shore, left everything and followed him" (Luke 5:11).

Paying Attention to Those Who Slip Away

How do you respond to those in your church family who slip out the back door unnoticed? Those who don't get involved? Those who stay away for one reason or another?

Suggestion: take a few minutes each week and look over your church rolls. If names of people you haven't seen for a while pop up, just pick up the phone and call them. Tell them they have been missed, that they came to your mind and you just wanted to see how they were doing. If you can't call, then drop them a note just to let them know they are important to you. Personal attention from the pastor or any staff member will be very instrumental in helping people know they are loved and valued.

While we're on the subject, what about the disaffected teens in your congregation? Kids who don't fit in, who may be troubled? There are thousands of them in the churches of our nation—young people who act out, stand back, live with uncontrolled anger, and hunger for someone to accept them, talk to them, value them. All too often it is the brightest, strongest, and prettiest who get the attention, while the others go home to emptiness.

I challenge you, my colleague, to listen to their cries. Be aware of the tell-tale signs. Risk being rejected, if you must, to befriend them. You, because of Christ, may be their only hope! Don't miss the opportunity to show His love to those who hurt—whether adults or teens—in your congregation.

"Then Jesus told them this parable: 'Suppose one of you has a hundred sheep and loses one of them. Does he not leave the ninety-nine in the open country and go after the lost sheep until he finds it? And when he finds it, he joyfully puts it on his shoulders and goes home. Then he calls his friends and neighbors together and says, "Rejoice with me; I have found my lost sheep"'" (Luke 15:3-6).

Life Passes Quickly—
Make the Most of It

I can't get over the fact that my life has passed so quickly. I think of that first little church that began 31 years of pastoral ministry and the fact that I have served Focus on the Family for nearly two decades as a pastor to pastors. Could that be possible?

I have often wondered what I would do differently if I had the opportunity. My personality is not to slow down, but I should have. My nature is to take life much too seriously, but I could have mellowed some. There were times when I allowed the work of the church to dominate my life, and there really was no need for that. I always wished I were smarter; I should have studied more. And I probably should have stayed home instead of traveling so much.

But what has been cannot be changed. I just know it all happened so quickly—so much so, I can't even remember some of it. Life can become a blur.

The truth is, today is all you have. Yesterday has passed. Tomorrow has not arrived. So make the most of what you have—and do it with no regrets! Make memories! Keep a short list of offenses. Enjoy the remainder of your journey. And walk 30 minutes every day.

"If the LORD delights in a man's way, he makes his steps firm" (Psalm 37:23).

The Church Is Becoming More Tolerant—and Not in a Good Way

A lot of us believe that a relationship with Jesus Christ is the road to eternal life, but a study by the Pew Forum on Religion and Public Life showed that 57 percent of evangelicals believe many religions can lead to eternal life. Amazing! That pretty well answers the question of why it is so difficult to preach absolutes, especially when the pulpit and the pew are not on the same page. It also points to the fact that a "feel good" message is much easier to preach than one based on a biblical foundation.

There was a time when evangelical church leaders, at least, were mostly on the same page but, sadly, that does not appear to be the case anymore. I wonder where all of this will eventually lead. I think I know. The church will become more tolerant and forgiving where basic absolutes of the Scripture are concerned. In time, the church will be in chaos—and it will become impotent. I pray I am mistaken, but I fear I am not.

"Do not be wise in your own eyes; fear the LORD and shun evil" (Proverbs 3:7).

Encouraging Pastors

The apostle Paul wrote to the church in Ephesus from a prison cell in Rome. He was writing to a church located in and around the temple of the Roman goddess Diana. Ephesus was a pagan city devoted to idolatry. It must have been a very difficult assignment for the elders of the fledgling church there—not so unlike what many of you have been called to.

Here is what we say on the www.parsonage.org to laypeople who inquire how they can best recognize your contribution to their lives and community: "God has entrusted to pastors and their families one of the most precious of assignments—the spiritual well-being of the flock. That's why God has instructed us to recognize His servants."

The Bible says, "Give a bonus to leaders who do a good job, especially the ones who work hard at preaching and teaching" (1 Timothy 5:17, MSG). Let me encourage you, my colleague. Let your people encourage you. Encourage one another.

Among Paul's last words to the church at Ephesus were, "I am sending him [Tychicus] to you for this very purpose, that you may know how we are, and that he may encourage you" (Ephesians 6:22).

Every Day Is an Opportunity

Do you begin each day with a purpose in mind? Do you have goals for each day, or do you just start your day with no specifics in mind? When we have a plan, it is God who completes that plan—but do you have a plan? "Why, you do not even know what will happen tomorrow. What is your life? You are a mist that appears for a little while and then vanishes" (James 4:14).

Each of us must surrender our plans to the Lord each day. He will orchestrate the day, but He needs to know we are workers who are diligent and productive. In fact, if we know what should be done and can be done to God's glory, and we fail to seize the opportunity, we have failed God. James calls it sin: "Anyone, then, who knows the good he ought to do and doesn't do it, sins" (James 4:17).

So, my colleague, today will pass by quickly. When the day is over, what will you have contributed to the greater good, and how will you have embraced God's plan? The ministry is one calling that can be easily short-changed. Please do not make that mistake. Your contribution is much too important.

"Serve wholeheartedly, as if you were serving the Lord, not men" (Ephesians 6:7).

Standing Firm

With the transaction of 30 pieces of silver, Judas gave it all away—his life, his ministry, his reputation, and his soul. He just gave it all away.

I deal with members of the clergy nearly every day who, for one reason or another, give their ministries away. Sometimes, it is for "30 pieces of silver." Other times, it is for a fleeting moment of pleasure. There are even those times when "power needs" overtake them and they feel they can operate by another set of guidelines. In other words, they do whatever they feel like doing. Most often, the result is a betrayal of the trust our Lord has placed in them.

Satan and the forces of evil stand before you with an offer you must refuse. "The wages of sin" can cast a shadow that covers your whole ministerial history. We must be willing to count the cost of our words and deeds. When we are tempted, our defense is always the whole armor of God so that we can "stand against the devil's schemes" (Ephesians 6:11). We cannot risk our ministries for "30 pieces of silver."

These days are challenging for our nation and the church. The battles we face are turbulent and demanding, but you who lead the church are standing in the gap for righteousness. Whatever you do, please do not give up. Pray more, study more, read more—gird yourself in the whole armor of God and stand firm.

"In everything set them an example by doing what is [right] good" (Titus 2:7).

The Power of the Cross

In the Middle East, East Asia, and other places around the globe, people are turning to Islam in record numbers.

I wonder why. Where is the hope? Where is the love? Where is the living Lord? Personally, I see all of that in the cross of Christ. I hear it in the words of songs like "When I Survey the Wondrous Cross" by Isaac Watts: "Did e'er such love and sorrow meet? . . . Love so amazing, so divine, demands my soul, my life, my all!" Or John Bowring's "In the Cross of Christ I Glory": "When the woes of life o'ertake me, hopes deceive, and fears annoy, never shall the cross forsake me. Lo! it glows with peace and joy." Or Elizabeth Clephane's "Beneath the Cross of Jesus." She wrote, "Upon that cross of Jesus mine eye at times can see the very dying form of One who suffered there for me."

I saw it at Ground Zero in New York City where a huge replica of a cross was raised out of the rubble and placed high so people could see. In that place of death, anger, frustration, and despair, the cross became a symbol of hope and stability. That is the power of the cross. It always has been and it always will be.

"So I'll cherish the old rugged cross, till my trophies at last I lay down; I will cling to the old rugged cross, and exchange it some day for a crown."—George Bennard

"Jesus . . . endured the cross, scorning its shame" (Hebrews 12:2).

Living in the Present

I think often about the fleeting of days, how time passes so quickly. Our children get older and form their own family traditions. Grandchildren seem to sprout up like flowers in the garden. Some things never change, but most things do.

The message of my book *The Heart of a Great Pastor* is essentially to "bloom where you are planted." In other words, make the most of your present situation. Don't look back and don't look ahead. Live in the moment and expect God's blessings upon the assignment He has given you.

You might be missing the present because you are bemoaning the past or, maybe, fixating on the future. Please don't. Bloom where you are planted. The present is where God is at work, and His plans are for you to prosper.

You miss so much when you live in the past. Enjoy the present. Soak up every special memory, and whatever you do, let those you love know how much you love them. It's easy to just leave those emotions to speak for themselves. That may not be enough. Words and actions speak volumes.

If you are in a struggle right now, consider the following: Thank Him for the present, confess the challenges you are facing, remember God's unmistakable love for you, see His majestic presence at work in your ministry, hold your head high, encourage your family, and today do something for someone who needs to know they matter. Make up your mind to bloom where you are planted.

"Jesus replied, 'No one who puts his hand to the plow and looks back is fit for service in the kingdom of God'" (Luke 9:62).

Peace in Turmoil

Not long before Jesus left His beloved disciples, He spoke straightforwardly to them. They were confused when He alluded to His departure. They just didn't understand.

He said things like, "You will grieve, but your grief will turn to joy." He used the illustration of the pain associated with childbirth. He minced no words when reminding the disciples of certain sorrow (John 16:20-22). Yet, He held out hope.

I am grieved today. The world is so much smaller now, and when you watch the evening news or read the daily newspaper, you can't help but be troubled by what you see and hear. There is so much hatred.

Jesus said, "Whoever believes in him [me] shall not perish but have eternal life" (John 3:16). But what if they have not believed? Does the fact that thousands of people every day are entering the gates of hell concern you?

Jesus was honest with His followers because He wanted them to have peace in the midst of turmoil. I know we can't save everyone, but we can be facilitators of peace—the peace that comes through knowing Jesus. Do you really believe that? If so, how is your passion expressed?

"In this world you will have trouble. But take heart! I have overcome the world" (John 16:33).

Perseverance

James wrote, "Blessed is the man who perseveres under trial, because when he has stood the test, he will receive the crown of life that God has promised to those who love him" (James 1:12). Now, you can relate to the writer. Why? Because you have persevered, you have been equal to the test, you have played even when hurt—and the trophy (crown) is yours.

I used to be a duffer. Many of you know how difficult a game golf is. One good shot—one close to the pin or one 250-yard drive—gives you the feeling you can make that same shot every time. But you know you can't, just like you can't solve everyone's problems, preach the perfect sermon, always live up to others' expectations, or even live up to your own. But there is one major difference—golf is a game. Your lot in life is determined by a calling. I can quit golf and look at my clubs in the garage without any guilt. But I cannot give up on my calling—nor can you! You, my colleague, are my hero because you "endure hardship" and just keep right on going.

So tee it up, give it your best effort, and let our Lord—the One who called you—keep the score.

"But you, keep your head in all situations, endure hardship, do the work of an evangelist, discharge all the duties of your ministry" (2 Timothy 4:5).

Those Who Stand
in the Gap

In my thoughts, I love to embrace the "great cloud of witnesses" who have passed through our sanctuary doors over the years of our church's existence.

As I reminisce, I vividly remember those in my congregation who have passed on to their heavenly reward, who were instrumental in both my success as a pastor and the life of our fellowship.

Through good times and bad, they persevered. Pastors would come and go, but they would remain faithful to the local church. They would pray, sacrificially give of their income, hold multiple jobs of service, take leadership assignments, and always remain hopeful.

I can picture that cloud of witnesses in my mind—names too numerous to mention.

Every one of you has in your ministry history the names of those who, like the one our Lord was searching for in Ezekiel, would "stand in the gap" (Ezekiel 22:30, KJV). Talk about them! Honor them! Validate them! Where would your congregation be today had it not have been for those faithful men and women who never gave up? By faith they lived, and in faith they died. And your church is richer for it.

"Therefore, since we are surrounded by such a great cloud of witnesses, let us throw off everything that hinders and the sin that so easily entangles, and let us run with perseverance the race marked out for us" (Hebrews 12:1).

Allowing Your People
to Use Their Gifts

At a prayer marathon held a while back, I was blown away by the ability of my co-workers to express themselves. Some sang; some cried; one even rang a bell. But most just prayed and, in a humble and sincere way, made their requests known unto the Lord.

As I sat, prayed, and listened, I thought about you and your congregation. How many in your flock sit and listen? They worship, but how many of them ever have a chance to use their gifts to bless your congregation? I wonder how many of your people are ever asked to pray, to sing, to read Scripture, to testify, to bless the Lord? There are so many diamonds in the rough. In my years in ministry, I made that discovery. Churches need to hear new voices. Are new voices being heard in your church?

"But in fact God has arranged the parts in the body, every one of them, just as he wanted them to be. If they were all one part, where would the body be? As it is, there are many parts, but one body. The eye cannot say to the hand, 'I don't need you!' And the head cannot say to the feet, 'I don't need you!' On the contrary, those parts of the body that seem to be weaker are indispensable. . . . But God has combined the members of the body and has given greater honor to the parts that lacked it, so that there should be no division in the body, but that its parts should have equal concern for each other" (1 Corinthians 12:18-22, 24-25).

Bitterness Has Consequences

You and I have been told we can either "be bitter or be better." The apostle Paul wrote, "Get rid of all bitterness" (Ephesians 4:31). In other words, bitterness can be, and often is, hazardous to your health and spiritual well-being.

I come in contact with a lot of our colleagues, and even their spouses, who are controlled by bitterness. Most of the time, that feeling of bitterness stems from being mistreated, disrespected, or betrayed. If I let myself, I can easily be convinced that they have a right to their opinion. But reality tells me that they should not entertain those feelings and, if they continue to do so, bitterness will define their ministry.

Paul tells us to "bear with each other and forgive whatever grievances you may have against one another. Forgive as the Lord forgave you" (Colossians 3:13).

Maybe you are paralyzed by bitterness. If so, I beg you to face your feelings and deal with them. Lifting the load is so liberating. One other thought: Deal with bitterness as soon as possible—Satan has a way of causing us to procrastinate!

"Do not seek revenge or bear a grudge against one of your people, but love your neighbor as yourself. I am the LORD" (Leviticus 19:18).

Everybody Needs a Vacation

What is your idea of the perfect vacation? You might like to pack up the car, load up the family, and head for a destination like Disneyland or Six Flags. Or you might live for the times when you head to a campsite, unpack the tent, and enjoy nature for a week. There are some who cruise and love it. Others like to spend vacation visiting relatives. You may fill your vacation so full that you have to come back home to rest up.

Regardless, everybody needs a vacation, even if it's just a day at a time. Do you have yours planned? You need it!

There was a time, when I served in the church, that I forfeited my vacations to go preach somewhere. Our summers were usually spent with me traveling around on preaching trips, showing up for a few days at the family vacation spot. I also had a weird philosophy that it would be a positive for our church if I were in the pulpit during the "low Sundays" of the summer months of July and August. It would appear that I was more interested in the attendance at our services than I was in being with my family. It was not fair to my family, my church, or me. I learned my lesson much too late. Please do not make the same mistake.

When are you taking your vacation?

"Come with me by yourselves to a quiet place and get some rest" (Mark 6:31).

Depression

When was the last time you read Psalm 88? I'm telling you—there was a man who was really going through some rough water.

The psalmist suffered from mood swings. From 5 to 12 percent of men suffer from clinical depression at some time in their lives, along with 10 to 25 percent of women. Those who do suffer depression will most likely not seek treatment, even though it is a treatable illness.

I have been, at one time or another, in that percentage of men who have suffered from depression. The sadness and darkness were miserable.

As a pastor you have probably counseled members of your congregation suffering from depression. But what about you? Are you foundering in the depths of depression?

If so, what should you do? The first steps to wellness are a physical examination by a physician, prayer with a colleague, and openness with your spouse. Don't be too proud to admit that you need help and the support of others.

One of the most painful expressions from Scripture is found in Psalm 88:18: "The darkness is my closest friend." I pray that never becomes your expression.

"We wait in hope for the LORD; he is our help and our shield" (Psalm 33:20).

The Gospel Is for Everyone

I often sit and ponder the reality that all people will not get into heaven, because not all will respond to the life-changing, eternal life-giving message of the gospel.

I walk through airports and sit in packed stadiums. I eat in crowded restaurants and travel busy highways. I have the opportunity to look deep into the eyes of others and wonder, if life ended for them this day, would they enter into the safety of our Lord's arms? They represent all men and women.

Embrace these words:

"For God so loved the world that he gave his one and only Son, that whoever [all people] believes in him shall not perish but have eternal life" (John 3:16).

"I write these things to you who believe [all people] in the name of the Son of God so that you may know that you have eternal life" (1 John 5:13).

"But because of his great love for us, God, who is rich in mercy, made us [all people] alive with Christ even when we were dead in transgressions—it is by grace you [all people] have been saved" (Ephesians 2:4-5).

There are so many more scriptures. Most of you, as you stand before your congregations, cannot do much about all people. But you can do something about those you encounter and those to whom you proclaim the "unsearchable riches of Christ" (Ephesians 3:8). Preach the truth—Jesus Christ alive and available to all men and women.

"Salvation is found in no one else, for there is no other name under heaven given to men [all men] by which we must be saved" (Acts 4:12).

We Are Called for Such a Time as This

Every day I deal with pastors who put themselves and their earthly passions above their call and their ministry. Nothing hurts the body of Christ more than a halfhearted dedication to the call of God to "tend the flock."

I have been called, and assigned, for such a time as this—and so have you. You, in so many ways, are the comfort and grace of Christ to those you serve. Please stay strong, stay focused, stay pure, stay connected to the One who called you in the first place. You are vital to the world you serve.

The battles you engage in are His battles. The circumstances you face are familiar to Him. The burdens you bear may be placed on His shoulders with His permission. The weapons formed against you are, in a real sense, formed against Him, and they will not prosper. Nothing will ever separate you from His love or care.

So often, under the pressure of our assignments, we feel we must "make it work" or else. Not so! Your church is God's church. Your call came not from man, but from God. He guides each step you take. Please do not ever forget that!

"May God himself, the God of peace, sanctify you through and through. May your whole spirit, soul and body be kept blameless at the coming of our Lord Jesus Christ. The one who calls you is faithful and he will do it" (1 Thessalonians 5:23-24).

Something Is Happening

I had a college professor who would often say, "When you think nothing is happening, be assured [with God] something is happening." He is not sitting idly by. Do you believe that?

Today you may be facing a challenge or opportunity that seems unmanageable. My words to you: Please do not despair, do not make a hasty decision, do not think you are all alone, do not let your situation diminish God's ability to bring a good result, and do not fret. Hear God's Word:

"Be still before the LORD and wait patiently for him" (Psalm 37:7).

"Refrain from anger and turn from wrath; do not fret—it leads only to evil" (Psalm 37:8).

"If the LORD delights in a man's way, he makes his steps firm" (Psalm 37:23).

These words may be written especially for you. Celebrate God's love and His knowledge of your situation. Be at peace!

"Commit your way to the LORD; trust in him and he will do this" (Psalm 37:5).

Treasure in Heaven

I travel often by plane and have learned that it is not much fun. When you get to where you are going, it's great, but the getting there? Not so much. Especially when the airline loses your luggage.

But you can always replace stuff. Just think of those things you can never replace.

You can never replace time. You cannot take back a harsh word. You will never be able to duplicate an opportunity. There will never be a second time to make a first impression. You can buy stuff with money, but just think of all the things money cannot buy—like healing for a broken heart.

We often concern ourselves with stuff that has no real eternal value. That is why, in times of emergency, people will risk their lives to rescue picture albums and gifts that could never be replaced. You can never recapture a "Kodak moment." Yet, we seem to put so much value on stuff—like possessions and position. I see so many of our colleagues who have disqualified themselves from ministry because of their desire to possess stuff.

What matters most to you? I would imagine if you are really honest, it will be something you cannot replace. Am I right?

"For where your treasure is, there your heart will be also" (Matthew 6:21).

Christic-Centered Integrity

A message I once gave was titled "There Is an 'I' in Integrity." The three points in the message were wrapped around three words: CHARACTER, INTEGRITY, and MOTIVATION. It is like a three-legged stool. You lose one leg, and the whole piece of furniture will collapse. For instance:

1. CHARACTER—"Who you are." We were created to be like God. Your character is composed of the attributes that determine who you are—in public and in private.

2. INTEGRITY—"How you live." There is a code of moral and ethical values that you accept and apply to your everyday life.

3. MOTIVATION—"What influences you." Why do you do what you do? Where do you find your value system? What are your priorities? Who do you attempt to please? Jesus made it very clear: We are to "love the Lord your God" with all of our being and also love His creation.

Psalm 15 is a marvelous reminder of who God honors: "He whose walk is blameless and who does what is righteous . . ." (Psalm 15:2).

Dream the
Impossible Dream

In *The Heart of a Great Pastor* Neil Wiseman and I wrote, "Dreams are the raw materials of adventure and achievement. They stir people's blood and make them believe that they can move mountains."

Martin Luther King Jr.'s stirring "I Have a Dream" speech impacted human rights around the world. Irish dramatist George Bernard Shaw's visionary words still inspire the masses whenever they are quoted: "Some men see things as they are and say, 'Why?' I dream things that never were and say, 'Why not?'" Senator Ted Kennedy used those words in his eulogy to his slain brother Bobby. I have never forgotten them.

Joe Darion's lyrics from "Man of La Mancha" move us deeply and have added vitality to many sermons:

> *To dream the impossible dream*
> *To fight the unbeatable foe*
> *To bear with unbearable sorrow*
> *To run where the brave dare not go . . .*

To stay in the fight, every pastor needs dreams for the congregation he serves. Sadly, it is not always the case. "My dream is dead; I can't go on. Our church services feel like we are tossing prayers into a wishing well. Worship is empty." Those despairing comments in a letter from a conscientious Midwest pastor are too common.

It's alarming how many dreamers are reducing kingdom commitments at a time when dreams and dreamers are needed most. The dreams Christ gives us for our lives and for our ministries can't be allowed to die. Something must be done to revive them quickly.

Think of the possibilities. Think of the needs. Dream on, my colleague! Dream on!

"In the last days, God says, I will pour out my Spirit on all people . . . your young men will see visions, your old men will dream dreams" (Acts 2:17).

Small Steps to Success

Most of us in ministry don't begin at the "mega" level. It takes time to learn your strengths and weaknesses—some of us take time to do that, others do not.

The New Testament tells the story of one who began to build a tower in the field and never finished. The unfinished portion was a reminder to everyone of his failed attempt (Luke 14:28-30).

I promise you, there is always a cost to success, and being sensible when you begin will give you the very best chance of succeeding. So, you don't need to read several chapters in the Bible each day—begin with one. You may not need to read a book a week—read one a month. You want to pray more—pace yourself, or you will give up much too soon. If you need to lose weight, you don't have to lose it all in one month—just cut back . . . exercise . . . and don't eat french fries.

The Lord promises us that, if we are faithful with the small things, He will in time trust us with greater things (Matthew 25:23). He knows human nature.

So, where do you begin? With small, determined, committed steps. Before long, you will be sprinting toward the finish line, and I will be there cheering you on.

"Commit to the LORD whatever you do, and your plans will succeed" (Proverbs 16:3).

The Gospel Can't Be Compromised

"Salvation is found in no one else, for there is no other name under heaven given to men by which we must be saved" (Acts 4:12). The scripture is pretty plain.

I know we must be tolerant of other faiths—even though, when I was a kid, I thought the only ones getting into heaven had to believe like me. But I wonder how healthy it is for the church to become so inclusive and accepting that, in our preaching and teaching, we fail to draw a very important line in the sand that cannot be compromised—namely, faith in Jesus Christ.

During our Sunday school days, we memorized a lovely verse: "For God [whose God?] so loved the world [what world?] that He gave His one and only Son, that whoever [anyone?] believes [accepts] in Him [God's only Son] shall not perish [be lost], but have eternal [forever!] life [live in heaven with God]."

The bottom line for all of us remains—"Is anyone being saved here?" How do we return to that passion? We do it by pointing people from survival to surrender, to the power and love of God. That is our answer. Thank you for all you do to point people to Jesus!

"This is good, and pleases God our Savior, who wants all men to be saved and to come to a knowledge of the truth. For there is one God and one mediator between God and men, the man Christ Jesus" (1 Timothy 2:3-5).

Freedom in Righteousness

We all know that "cheaters never prosper," but so often they try. The ministry is full of that kind of thing. Some of our colleagues cheat on their spouses. Some cheat on their income taxes. Some cheat on attendance figures. Others cheat when it comes to their walk with God. Why?

Normally, our actions will find us out, and we know when we have violated a sacred trust. The problem is when cheating becomes so common that we no longer feel the offense.

With the blessing of your call also comes the hard truth of accountability—to "set an example for the believers in speech, in life, in love, in faith and in purity" (1 Timothy 4:12). Are you doing that? Are you giving yourself to the most important aspects of your assignment?

We need to invest in one another and ask each other "big questions." We need to live transparent lives.

"An evil man is snared by his own sin, but a righteous one can sing and be glad" (Proverbs 29:6).

That is freedom! We need not cast stones at anyone—just be faithful to examine our own lives!

"As obedient children, do not conform to the evil desires you had when you lived in ignorance. But just as he who called you is holy, so be holy in all you do; for it is written: 'Be holy, because I am holy' " (1 Peter 1:14-16).

Working Together with Physicians

I used to be highly intimidated by physicians as I would make my hospital rounds. When one would enter a room while I was visiting a patient, I would move away quickly from that patient until the doctor had concluded his or her business.

One day it dawned on me that a combination of spiritual counsel and medical advice could be the perfect medicine. From that point on, I worked at getting to know as many physicians as I could. I soon found out how delighted they were to work with me. In short, we became a "healing team."

Question: Do you work with your parishioners' physicians? Do you seek to foster friendships with medical people? I learned a long time ago that, as much as I needed them, they also needed me. I encourage you to see yourself as part of the team whenever you visit the hospital. Your presence and care say so much to your parishioners—and to their physicians. Remember that it's not only about physical healing.

"When Jesus had called the Twelve together, he gave them power and authority to drive out all demons and to cure diseases, and he sent them out to preach the kingdom of God and to heal the sick" (Luke 9:1-2).

Make Your Day Count

"This is the day the LORD has made; let us rejoice and be glad in it" (Psalm 118:24).

We have quoted that scripture often, but I wonder if we have given it adequate thought. God has ordered and ordained the day. He has put us in His plans for the day, and that should make us feel really good. The psalmist does not say how the day will go or what it will look like. He simply says the Lord has made it. My advice: Surrender to the day with thanksgiving and live in awe that God has given us permission to join Him in its unfolding.

It always amazes me how some can get so much out of 24 hours, while others waste much of the day.

The psalmist says, "Show me, O LORD . . . the number of my days" (Psalm 39:4). He is frustrated. He is being assailed by the enemy. Like a lot of us, he wonders if he is making any difference. The days are just flying by. What is the use?

Suddenly it dawns on him that he does what he does because God has asked him to. Though men's opinions must be taken into account, it is how God sees things that matters. And, in Psalm 40, the psalmist rejoices, "He put a new song in my mouth, a hymn of praise to our God" (Psalm 40:3). The day may not look exactly like you want it to, but wait patiently for the Lord. Just make your day count.

"Then will I ever sing praise to your name and fulfill my vows day after day" (Psalm 61:8).

Walk Humbly
with the Lord

There are parallels between baseball great Barry Bonds and the many pastors I have dealt with who have tainted their reputations and minimized their ministries.

The first is that Barry Bonds was a great ballplayer before suspicion of his use of steroids arose. Most pastors I meet are gifted—without taking shortcuts or playing too close to the line.

The second parallel is a spirit of pride. Bonds is arrogant. I have never understood why some clergy I meet are prideful. Why would you be? Yet, I see it all the time. "Look what I have done. Look how big we are. Stop and serve me," their persona seems to say. Why? Is it not God who gives us our talent and places us in the area of ministry that will bring Him the greatest glory?

The parallel is a tendency to forget those who have helped us achieve and have stood by us. If you are like me, there are very few days that pass without your thinking about the many influencers in your life.

My point: Walk humbly with the Lord.

"So, if you think you are standing firm, be careful that you don't fall!" (1 Corinthians 10:12).

"When pride comes, then comes disgrace, but with humility comes wisdom" (Proverbs 11:2).

Four Things We Should All Say

A book titled *The Four Things That Matter Most* promotes four things that everyone needs to say. It caught my attention because it really makes sense. It's not a Christian book, but it is a practical one.

What four things would you guess the author had in mind? Well, let me tell you.

1. FORGIVE ME

The longer we let our list of personal offenses grow, the greater the bondage we find ourselves in. Sometimes we pastors say and do things that hurt others. If you have offended someone, be courageous enough to ask him or her to forgive you. Who do you need to talk with? It might be a member of your own family. "Be kind and compassionate to one another, forgiving each other, just as in Christ God forgave you" (Ephesians 4:32).

2. I FORGIVE YOU

There are those who live with a little black book of "wrongs" around their neck—especially in the ministry. I did for a long time. Though forgiveness is unnatural, it is essential. Some of you have held on to your hurts for so long they have become a part of your personality. People see you as damaged. Why not let a colleague help you find healing?

3. THANK YOU

Have an attitude of gratitude. A long time ago, a wise pastor/mentor told me to look for ways to thank people. I found one of the best ways to do that is to write a note—not an e-mail, but a mailed expression of thanks. Those who do not thank others soon begin to take for granted what people do for them. Who do you need to send a note of thanks to today? Do it while you're thinking about it.

4. I LOVE YOU

Because I didn't grow up with people close to me saying, "I love you," it has been difficult for me to comfortably say those three little words. I feel it and I want to, but I often struggle. I'm really trying to do better. I love deeply, but express poorly. I dislike that in myself. How well do you do?

There they are: four things everyone needs to say—probably every day.

"If it is possible, as far as it depends on you, live at peace with everyone" (Romans 12:18).

Writing Down Your Story

The last paragraph of the Gospel of John ends, "Jesus did many other things as well. If every one of them were written down, I suppose that even the whole world would not have room for the books that would be written" (John 21:25). This passage makes me think about you and your story. You have a story—an amazing story of God's grace and goodness. Have you ever written it down? Have you taken the time to start at the beginning and chronicle the events and miracle moments of your life?

Oh, I'm not saying you should do it for publication—but for your own sake. Yes, you face many challenges, but if you would make the time to "write your story," it would be filled with many more good times than bad. How do you begin? Just start writing things down. That's what I did.

For instance, talk about your childhood and those who influenced you. You will find angels in that chapter.

How did you enter into the ministry? What brought about that call? Did it happen suddenly in a service or at camp, or was it through a series of unmistakable divine interventions in your life?

How did you meet your spouse? Who you are and what you accomplish can often be traced to that moment.

What about the challenges? We have all faced both sorrow and happiness. Each one of us has known failure, but we have also experienced victory. What about the miracles of God's grace that have caused you to shake your head and say, "He does care about me." Write it down—let other people read it. Use it as a testimony but also as a point of reference when you are faced with reality.

"I will remember the deeds of the LORD; yes, I will remember your miracles of long ago" (Psalm 77:11).

Remembering Your Ministry

Not convinced that you need to write down your story? Consider this. You have probably gone through situations that caused you pain, but you made it, and now you are on the other side. How you handled those situations might be helpful to someone else, perhaps another pastor. I would also imagine you've learned hard lessons as a parent and spouse—and maybe we all could learn something from you.

Your diary would contain remembrances of good times and bad—successes and failures. You would be reminded of times when you were a good mom or dad and when you made some mistakes.

You would also come face to face again with ministry issues that changed your life. For instance: "Today, I made a decision to move on. I will assume the leadership of a new congregation. My wife and family are thrilled. I feel I should have had a better chance to turn things around here."

Or . . . "My son needed me today, but I had pastoral duties that would not allow me the time to be the dad I wanted to be. I hope he will understand."

Or . . . "I'm sad today. The baby we had been praying for died. I was there with the family, but I didn't have answers. I could only say, 'God loves you now more than ever.' They seemed to appreciate my concern and prayers."

Or . . . "I was at lunch today with a man in our community. As we talked, I could see he was hungry for a new life. I led him to Jesus Christ. It was awesome. What a day!"

Or . . . "Sunday came too quickly this week. I didn't have time to prepare well—but God helped me. Some said it was the best sermon I have ever delivered. I think it's because I had to trust Him more."

Our stories should be told if for no one else but our families. Please consider doing that. You, my colleague, have a story—tell it!

"Look to the LORD and his strength; seek his face always. Remember the wonders he has done, his miracles, and the judgments he pronounced" (Psalm 105:4-5).

Vetoing Anything Unbiblical

Wouldn't it be something if every pastor had the privilege of a veto in the local church? I know you will say that your congregational type of government does not allow for such a thing—but stay with me.

For example:

- A couple in your church decides they will divorce. They have not had adequate counseling and could be prematurely throwing their relationship onto the "ash heap." As a pastor you say, "No way! I veto that decision."

- A small group of "joy suckers" in your congregation begin to stir up contention and division. Stability in the body is at stake. You, as the pastor, know their behavior is not in keeping with our Lord's expectations. So you veto their activity.

- A staff member has allowed a spiritual weakness to develop into a moral dysfunction. Only a strong veto of that person's lifestyle can save him. You walk boldly into that life in the authority of Almighty God.

- Some church members begin to tell you how and what to preach. They want you to water down the truth and make everyone feel more comfortable. You exercise your veto right as a man of God.

I know this is just wishful thinking. But wouldn't it be great if, at those times when you see people acting from intentions more selfish than spiritual, you could step in with a veto? Proclaim, "No! I will not allow you to diminish the unity of Christ's church or misrepresent the truth of God's Word"? Sometimes I wish I could.

Jesus exercised His veto one day when He walked into the temple only to find it being defamed. He said that this was not a swap meet. "My house will be called a house of prayer" (Matthew 21:13).

And so today, anything less is unacceptable.

"Why do you call me, 'Lord, Lord,' and do not do what I say?" (Luke 6:46).

God Does Not Condemn Us

Who of us has not failed our Lord either in private or in public? Who of us has not cast the first stone? Who of us, while with a plank in our own eye, has not been guilty of trying to remove the speck from the eye of a brother or sister? We sometimes have the inclination to "hang" a fellow clergyman before we know the facts—or even when we do know the facts. I have often heard Dr. James Dobson say, "I don't mind being shot at from the enemy, but when it comes from my friends, that is when it really hurts."

The gospel message is one of hope and grace and second chances. Jesus' intent is not to condemn you, but to save you. When a fellow clergyman fails, I pray he makes it!

Mistakes—though sometimes innocent—for those of us who serve the church can determine our legacy. While we extend grace to those who fail, it is a reminder that all of us really need to be careful about how we relate to others. I deal with clergymen all the time who made one "little" mistake in behavior or judgment that disqualified them for further service as pastor to their church.

The solution? Constant safeguards—building a hedge of protection around your life and ministry. I don't mean to be simplistic, but this verse is a definite safeguard: "Submit yourselves, then, to God. Resist the devil, and he will flee from you. Come near to God and he will come near to you" (James 4:7-8).

Practicing Simple Prayer

The psalmist David wrote, "Teach me your way, O LORD, and I will walk in your truth" (Psalm 86:11). He was probably referring to the things he learned both through experience and meditation after he had prayed. He seemed to keep asking God to "Hear my prayer."

I learn a lot through my private prayer life, especially when I can just be quiet and talk to the Father as a son. It's after the prayer when I reflect on our conversation that I most often hear from God, or at least find direction.

When I pray, I find myself removed from the norm of my everyday activity. All formality aside, I just communicate my feelings and often my frustrations. In the end I don't ask for much. I just talk, and then when it's over (my part), I listen.

There were a lot of years I was guided by the "A-C-T-S" formula for praying (Affirmation, Confession, Thanksgiving, and Supplication). But as the years have passed, my time with the Lord has become less emotional, not as animated, and much more conversational. I still wonder why we make such a show of prayer in public and why we need to pray so predictably. God listens when His children humbly and faithfully seek His face.

Remember the Lord's instruction regarding simple prayer in Matthew 6:5-6, before He taught the disciples how to pray? "And when you come before God, don't turn that into a theatrical production either. . . . Here's what I want you to do: Find a quiet, secluded place so you won't be tempted to role-play before God. Just be there as simply and honestly as you can manage. The focus will shift from you to God, and you will begin to sense his grace" (MSG).

Strengthening the Family

A strong family requires more than a comfortable bank account, expensive house, respectable neighborhood, or top-notch schools. It exists only on a minister's wish list until it is a lived-out relationship, characterized by love and hard work among those who occupy the same household. The primary impediments to a strong ministerial family are not church politics or other environmental disadvantages. Instead, impediments arise from the lack of lived-out love in the couple for each other and for their children.

Strengthening clergy families demands an intentional commitment to the abiding values of the home. Whatever the minister's family has is contagious in the church, either good or bad. Society will be strengthened when the homes of spiritual leaders are improved. Here are some guidelines:

1. Consider the advantages of being a ministry family.
2. Strive to please the people who matter most.
3. Get your family in tune with God.
4. Feed faith to your children.
5. Refuse to blame common problems on the ministry.
6. View your family as a gift you give yourself.

"Now the overseer must be above reproach, the husband of but one wife, temperate, self-controlled, respectable, hospitable, able to teach, not given to drunkenness, not violent but gentle, not quarrelsome, not a lover of money. He must manage his own family well and see that his children obey him with proper respect." (If anyone does not know how to manage his own family, how can he take care of God's church?) (1 Timothy 3:2-5).

Why Do Bad Things Happen?

Why does God allow bad things to happen, you may be asking. In the Focus on the Family booklet *Why, God, Why?* Dr. Dobson points out, 'Why'—will have to remain unanswered for the time being. We have been given too few facts to explain all the heartache in an imperfect, fallen world."

Do we believe God is obligated to explain Himself to us? Trying to analyze His omnipotence is, as C. S. Lewis described, like attempting to teach physics to a four-year-old. Dr. Dobson adds, "Unless the Lord chooses to explain Himself to us, which He does not often do, His motivation and purposes are beyond the reach of mortal man."

Our role as clergy is not to construct answers to a complex question. Our role is to comfort people, to point them to life not death, to remind them of the brevity and uncertainty of life, and to encourage them to live each day with purpose and thanksgiving—to prepare them for eternity.

"The LORD himself goes before you and will be with you; he will never leave you nor forsake you. Do not be afraid; do not be discouraged" (Deuteronomy 31:8).

Being Involved in Men's Ministry

For the major part of my pastoral life, I invested huge amounts of time in men. Early on, I realized it was a ministry that would reap great dividends. When fathers and husbands become convinced that church and spiritual things have value, they become a pastor's greatest asset.

Statistics have shown that there is a decline of younger male leadership and involvement in church activity. That may not be the case in your congregation, but the facts underscore the truth that, when men are involved in the church and committed to living a consistent Christlike life, the congregation is healthier and families are more stable.

I further believe that the pastor cannot simply pass the responsibility of a relevant men's ministry on to someone else. You may not be required to head the endeavor, but you must be willing to participate. Further, keep in mind that a successful attempt to reach the men of your congregation cannot be limited to activity; it needs to reproduce leadership.

How are you going to reach men? One word: Invest! As a pastor, you must make time to connect with your men in a nonthreatening way. They need to be able to trust you, confide in you, believe in you, and learn from you without intimidation. Please trust me on this one. It will transform your ministry.

The words of Paul are essential: "And the things you have heard me say in the presence of many witnesses entrust to reliable men who will also be qualified to teach others" (2 Timothy 2:2).

Preaching Without Words

There is a famous quote attributed to St. Francis of Assisi: "Preach the gospel always and when necessary use words." In many of the sessions I conduct for pastors, I say, "The sermon you live will speak at a greater volume than the sermon you preach."

I am reminded of a story of a parish priest in rural England who announced in the morning that, at the evening vespers, he would deliver a sermon without using words.

At the appointed time, when all the congregants were seated, he walked toward the crucifix that was very prominent in the chapel. The place was void of light, so he took a lantern and stood beneath the suffering Jesus. He held the lantern to the feet of Jesus. The nail prints were obvious. Next, he raised the light to the part of Jesus' body that had been pierced with a sword, then to the hands—each side. He positioned the lantern to light the blood of Christ flowing freely from the vicious hammering of the nails. Then, he moved to the head of our Savior, illuminating the crown of thorns roughly placed, the blood coursing down the side of His face and into His matted hair. The priest lingered there for a while then slowly moved his lantern into place to show the agony on our Lord's countenance. It was almost too vivid to see.

Then the parish priest blew out his light, leaving the people in darkness as he quietly exited the little church. A sermon without words—unforgettable!

"My message and my preaching were not with wise and persuasive words, but with a demonstration of the Spirit's power, so that your faith might not rest on men's wisdom, but on God's power" (1 Corinthians 2:4-5).

Lessons from a Christian Coach

Coach Tony Dungy of the Indianapolis Colts gave a clear testimony and Christian witness after winning the Super Bowl in 2007. It brings to mind the words of the apostle Paul: "I am not ashamed of the gospel, because it is the power of God for the salvation of everyone who believes: first for the Jew, then for the Gentile" (Romans 1:16). Would that all of us were so bold.

Coach Dungy is a realist. The Associated Press quoted him as saying, "You're not going to win every game. Every season is not going to end the way you like. But that's the real test of a champion. Can you continue to fight when things don't go your way?" A good reminder for those of us in the ministry. We can't control all the people or circumstances we encounter.

The message Dungy gave to the Colts before they took the field for the Super Bowl was a simple one: "There will be some storms out there and we've got to get through those and hang together." Some more good advice for those of us who might be facing adversity today.

Bill Pugh, president of Athletes in Action said of Dungy, "You can be a Christian coach who really does live out Christian values and be very successful in terms of wins and losses." Another great lesson for all of us: We do not have to compromise to succeed.

"The path of the righteous is level; O upright One, you make the way of the righteous smooth" (Isaiah 26:7).

The Importance of the Altar

A recent report from the Southern Baptists indicates that most of their pastors still give an altar call or extend an invitation at the end of their sermons. The purpose: for people to accept Christ or renew their commitment to Him. Do you use the altar area for such purposes?

I grew up in an environment where the altar area was used much like the "mourner's bench" in Methodism. As a pastor, I used that area for evangelism, but also for times of emotional and physical healing. I don't see that as much in today's churches as I used to. I wonder why.

If we do not give people an opportunity to seek God in a quiet, safe place, at what point in their lives will they? Do you make an attempt to "close the deal," so to speak, or just leave it up to chance? More people would turn to Christ if someone would just ask them to.

Personally, I think many people are frightened by the altar area. One way to overcome that is by using it as a place of prayer during the service—not only for those who are seeking, but for those who just need to feel closer to God and receive the support of a church family, as long as it is a safe place.

"God looks down from heaven on the sons of men to see if there are any who understand, any who seek God" (Psalm 53:2).

Providing for the Poor

When I visited Kenya some years ago, I returned with story after story of what HIV/AIDS can do to a country. I visited orphanages and talked with many who had adopted AIDS babies or taken children whose parents had died from the terrible disease.

In a world where compassion is so necessary, the church needs to step up and fill the gap. I believe the church in the United States could do much more in our own communities to "offer a cup of cold water" in the name of Jesus. What I am learning is that it is not the first cup that makes the difference, but cup after cup after cup. I know Jesus said we will always have the poor with us, but those of us who have so much and spend so lavishly on ourselves must be on the lookout for legitimate ways to be a part of the healing process.

Many years ago my grandfather wrote a book titled *Love Is the Key*. In the preface, he wrote, "Love touched the unclean leper and made him well again. It flashed light into the eyes of the blind, and caused them to see. Love said to the 'scarlet woman'—'go in peace.' Love had compassion on the fainting multitudes and fed them in the wilderness." Do we have that kind of love for those outside our congregations? Reaching a dying world means getting out of our comfort zones once in a while, ministering to people who may be different from us. Encourage your people to do that.

"Give to the poor, and you will have treasure in heaven" (Matthew 19:21).

Addressing Your People
with Clean Hands

Many of us agree that if the gospel is weakened from the pulpit, it will also be weakened in the lives of those who preach it.

We are called to motivate, but we are also called to correct and rebuke. We are called to encourage and show great grace, but we are also called to address sin and provide an escape. It is my opinion (for what it's worth) that if we abandon hard truth, "easy believism" is the result. A full sanctuary is the dream of every pastor. I want that for you, but I am much more concerned about the fullness of your relationship with Christ.

I remember sitting in an airport with one of the godliest men I have ever met, Dr. Jerry Bridges. We were talking about our respective concern for moral purity within the clergy. He said, "If every pastor, before they took their text or began their message, would look their congregation in the eye and say sincerely, 'It is well with my soul,' it would result in greater credibility for all of us." That would speak volumes, wouldn't it? It would say, "I have been with my God, and as I stand before you, my heart is pure and my hands are clean."

"Let us draw near to God with a sincere heart in full assurance of faith, having our hearts sprinkled to cleanse us from a guilty conscience and having our bodies washed with pure water" (Hebrews 10:22).

Having a Heart for Peace

In our Lord's discourse on the end times, He indicates that "nation will rise against nation, and kingdom against kingdom" (Matthew 24:7). In other words, there will be war everywhere you look. That seems to be the case today. Not only do we have wars raging; we also have rumors of more wars to come.

I hate the thought of war. I am well aware of the concept and why we engage in war, but it is difficult to think of so many people hating so many other people enough to want to kill them. I am not being overly naïve—I just hate war.

Paul explained part of the reason for mortal conflict when he said, "The acts of the sinful nature are . . . hatred, discord . . . [and] dissensions" (Galatians 5:19-20). In Jeremiah, it states, "The heart is deceitful above all things, and desperately wicked" (Jeremiah 17:9, KJV). The NIV says, "And beyond cure." In other words, the motivation that causes war between nations is the same one that causes a father to almost kill a Little League coach because his son is not playing more. Or neighbors to do bodily harm to one another because the snow is not removed from the sidewalk. Or a church member to have such hatred for his pastor that he would do nearly anything to see the pastor lose his or her job. Or someone to assassinate Martin Luther King Jr. Or kill a president. Or murder a spouse. The heart—that which tempers our reactions and causes us to love or hate—is basically evil. And unless there is radical surgery on the heart, there will never be peace. That is why Jesus said, "Peace I leave with you; my peace I give you. I do not give to you as the world gives" (John 14:27). His peace is a transformation of the mind brought about by a changed heart.

Hearts must be changed. That is why you need to preach it: "Change my heart, O God."

"He will judge between the nations and will settle disputes for many peoples" (Isaiah 2:4).

How Our Choices Hurt Others

Once when I was in an airport, the wife of a disgraced clergyman recognized me and began to talk about her husband's indiscretion—an indiscretion that has cost him his ministry and possibly his family. I myself am the son of a father who, because of moral failure, caused our family great pain. Nearly every day in my work, I hear from a pastor or spouse who is heartbroken over the choices made by someone they love. Why?

There are no easy answers. One could just blame it on sin and let it go at that, but there is always more to the story.

For one thing, men especially have the ability to compartmentalize their actions. For some reason, they can live one lifestyle in sin and another related to the church. Another reason is unresolved conflict at home. Rather than address issues that arise with their spouse, they let them fester. Soon the couple is married in name only. One other reason I hear colleagues talk about is a kind of rationalization. We set our own rules, live by a different standard, and resist any kind of accountability.

Among other ministers, the reason for moral failure is emptiness. So many do not see a lot of progress in their day, and there is a need to fill it with counterfeits like pornography or other addictions. But the explanation that scares me the most is what I call a lack of godly intimacy—one day we find ourselves separated from God and morally unprotected. Brother, sister, guard you heart!

"But your iniquities have separated you from your God; your sins have hidden his face from you, so that he will not hear" (Isaiah 59:2).

The Process of Restoration

For many years I have been involved with clergy who have "fallen" and need help regaining their footing. I am sure you have had those opportunities as well. Or perhaps you are one who has been helped back into the ministry. If you have had the assignment of helping to guide someone through the restoration process, you know it is painful. The process, though necessary, is often brutal. God's grace is the enabler. The Bible says, "Do it gently."

When and if you have either helped a brother or been helped yourself, what were the most pivotal aspects of the restoration process for both family and ministry? How long was the restoration process? What percentage of the time did you find restoration successful? Does your denomination or association have guidelines for restoration? Do you believe a colleague who has failed morally can be restored to the preaching pulpit?

The men I know who have come through the hard work of restoration were men who, after confessing their sin, accepted the consequences of their actions. They submitted themselves to the rigors of personal introspection and willingly accepted the direction of godly men who held, first, the church of Jesus Christ and, second, the family and pastor in question at ultimate value.

Each of us must continually examine our hearts. If you have an area of concern—please, deal with it!

Paul writes, "Put to death, therefore, whatever belongs to your earthly nature" (Colossians 3:5).

Steps to Restoration

I have learned a lot about restoration/renewal over the years as I have worked with clergy families facing severe challenges. Here are some steps I've found helpful in the restoration process:

1. Don't deny your feelings. Express them and seek both to forgive and be forgiven.
2. You don't need to keep kicking yourself around. God forgives you! There will be consequences, and people will draw their own conclusions. But it does not do any good to wallow in self-punishment.
3. The next day always comes. How you enter and surrender that day determines its conclusions. Stay humble.
4. Those who have stumbled need people around them—not just to affirm, but to listen. We must not push people away, especially those who love us most.
5. No matter what, hold on to your faith. Remember, God knows the future, and His second best is usually pretty good.
6. You can't fool God. No one ever has. "But the thing David had done displeased the LORD" (2 Samuel 11:27). If you are struggling with an issue, He knows about it. Deal with it. If you do not, everyone loses.

"Would not God have discovered it, since he knows the secrets of the heart?" (Psalm 44:21).

Opportunities for Evangelism

Nearly half of Americans are not sure God exists, according to a 2006 Harris Poll. To be exact, 42 percent of U.S. adults are not "absolutely certain" there is a God, compared to 34 percent who felt that way three years before.

Now before you panic, 93 percent of Christians who describe themselves as "born again" feel certain God exists. Makes you wonder about the other 7 percent, doesn't it? The increasing number of "those who wonder" creates a fertile opportunity for evangelism. But I wonder if the church as a whole is really responding passionately to those who may be searching for the answer.

It is the undecided and unconvinced that Satan entices. In 1 Peter 5:8, we read, "Be . . . alert. Your enemy the devil prowls around like a roaring lion looking for someone to devour." Are we awake to the reality of a nation that increasingly feels (44 percent) that "God observes, but does not control what happens on earth"?

We had better wake up—we had better face reality. And, by the way, could the alarm get any louder?

A revived church is not so much trendy as it is obedient. There are alarms going off everywhere you look. Are we alarmed by the alarms? Can you hear them? I pray so.

"Be merciful to those who doubt; snatch others from the fire and save them" (Jude 1:22-23).

Intentional Evangelism

The film *The Passion of the Christ* made an indelible impression on me. I walked away from it not wanting to talk to anyone. I wanted to be alone to reflect upon God's love for me and the suffering our Lord endured to show that love. When Jesus died, He died with my name—your name, all names—on His lips. That's the "whoever" in John 3:16.

I sometimes wonder if there is the urgency in our preaching anymore. This Sunday could very well be a time of intentional evangelism. Please, my colleague, give your people the opportunity to receive Christ. Sins must be forgiven. "Yet to all who received him, to those who believed in his name, he gave the right to become children of God" (John 1:12).

The fields are ripe for harvest—and the harvest is plentiful (John 4:35; Matthew 9:37). The time for evangelism is now. I cannot help but recall the account of Jesus as He went from village to village: "When he saw the crowds, he had compassion on them, because they were harassed and helpless, like sheep without a shepherd" (Matthew 9:36). We must not settle for anything less than a renewed interest in, and an intense burden for, the millions who are lost.

The danger: There is complacency among those who do believe. In 2004, less than one-half of all born-again Christians shared their faith with a non-believer. Do you consider that acceptable? We need to change some hearts!

Jesus said, "As you go, preach this message: 'The kingdom of heaven is near'" (Matthew 10:7). Paul said, "By all means save some" (1 Corinthians 9:22, KJV).

Standing Firm When Basic Beliefs Are at Stake

We need to hear the urgent call today to a once-and-for-all loyalty to the mission of Christ, a never-say-die commitment to His person and message. Yet, we live in a day of fickle followers, fair-weather worshipers, and slumbering saints. It is, therefore, vital that we pause to reflect, to be reminded that it is not easy to be a Christian, that it never has been, and it never will be. We need a renewed commitment on the part of those who call Jesus "Lord" to stand up and be counted—regardless of the cost.

You have probably preached from the 26th chapter of Acts where Paul went before King Agrippa. Paul's argument, aimed to change the king's life forever, was powerful but not enough to convince the man. "Almost" was his response. Our society is in jeopardy of losing its moral compass, and we, as Christian leaders, cannot quit when we face a loss here and there. You cannot win every fight, but you can be engaged in the battle.

Three words move all of us forward:

- Perseverance (We are in the fight to save our children and grandchildren.)
- Resolve (There is no turning back.)
- Determination (We are convinced of our position.)

In every community, basic beliefs are at stake. There are threats to the moral fiber of those you serve. Like Paul, we may not win every argument or succeed in every endeavor, but we must engage the opposition. *Will you?*

"Consider him who endured such opposition from sinful men, so that you will not grow weary and lose heart" (Hebrews 12:3).

Why We Need Pastors

Let me tell you why we need you now—at your best—more than ever.

First: We need stability. The nation is spinning out of control. We need you steadfast and sure. We need you to point us to God.

Second: There are so many questions. Why war? Why killings of the innocent in schools? Why so much corruption in our government? Why the lack of moral outrage? Why is the church so hesitant to get involved? Where do you find answers? We need to know what you think.

Third: Christianity is under attack. Everywhere I turn, I see the liberal media taking shots at Christ and those who follow Him. We need you to encourage us, to guide us.

Fourth: We see truth undermined at every turn. In Bible days, it was said that people did what was right in their own eyes. It is not so much what man says—we need to know what God is saying. We need you to tell us, "Thus says the Lord."

Fifth: We need consistency. We need to be able to look at you and know that you practice what you preach. We need to see a renewal of faith in you and what you represent. We need to be able to trust your morals, your commitment, and your determination. We want to do that with confidence. We need you now more than ever . . . at your best!

In a little-quoted scripture, the writer of Hebrews proclaims, "Obey your leaders and submit to their authority. They keep watch over you as men who must give an account. Obey them so that their work will be a joy, not a burden, for that would be of no advantage to you" (Hebrews 13:17).

Keep Your Marriage Strong

Think for a moment about the topics you cover in your counseling sessions with potential brides and grooms—issues like open communication, personal finances, spiritual oneness, common interests, time alone, emotional support, marital fidelity, and expressions of love for one another. Successful marriages demand time, dedication, and work. And that's true even in the parsonage.

Do you routinely take time to work on your marriage? Do you practice the principles you recommend to the couples you counsel? Make a concentrated, deliberate choice to strengthen your marriage by just talking to one another about ways each of you could improve the union. Take some time to get out the wedding pictures and reminisce. Play the video of your wedding. Renew your vows. Have a date night for the specific purpose of talking about your marriage and family. Gifts would not be inappropriate either. But, for sure, take a moment away from the hectic pace you're keeping just to say to the one God has given you, "I love you!"

If your problems are more serious, find a Christian counselor who can help you work on your relationship. As the pastor, you must keep your marriage strong.

"In everything set them an example by doing what is good" (Titus 2:7).

Staying in the Battle

I realize that when it comes to the role you play in the pastorate, some of you are "underdogs and undersized." Some people do not give you much of a chance, and you don't play in the same league as the "big boys," but every day you lace 'em up, get out on the playing field, and give it your all. That is why you are a winner. You do not sit around and whine about your situation, but you see every day as an opportunity to give God the glory and to be more than a conqueror (Romans 8:37). I salute you!

Yet, there are others of you who, for some reason, have underestimated your value. You have diminished the significance of your assignment. Let me tell you—where you are is where your game is. The battle is before you.

A lot of pastors I talk to have given up on the church, the culture, their goals, and even their effectiveness as leaders in the church. Not me! We may go down to defeat in some battles, but if we do, those who defeat us will bleed before they win. And the Bible tells us that we will eventually win the war. That is why we are called "more than conquerors." So, hold your head up, my colleague. Balance the good and the bad, and never forget who your leader is—and "what a mighty God we serve!"

"No, in all these things we are more than conquerors through him who loved us. For I am convinced that neither death nor life, neither angels nor demons, neither the present nor the future, nor any powers, neither height nor depth, nor anything else in all creation, will be able to separate us from the love of God that is in Christ Jesus our Lord" (Romans 8:37-39).

Expect the Unexpected

If there is any profession that must deal with the unexpected, it is that of serving the church. As a church leader, you must respond to those who face sudden, unexpected, life-changing events.

I don't want to appear too simplistic, but the one thing we can expect in this life is the unexpected. How we deal with the unexpected becomes the issue, because the next day always arrives—no matter what. The psalmist noted that "Each man's life is but a breath" (Psalm 39:5). His response: "Lord . . . my hope is in you" (v. 7).

So, as we go forward, I am reminded that: (1) Every day is a gift. Please do not take that for granted. (2) Do not let the sun set on anger or contention. Keep a very short record of offenses. (3) Walk close to your Lord. Do not depend on your own skills or position. (4) Give thanks in all things. God knows what He is doing. (5) Don't get bitter. Live each day with joy. (6) And remember—no matter what—God loves you as one loves an only child. Please, pastor, be there for your people. Don't stand in the shadows. They need you when the unexpected happens. And you need a colleague.

"Since no man knows the future, who can tell him what is to come?" (Ecclesiastes 8:7).

"Do not boast about tomorrow, for you do not know what a day may bring forth" (Proverbs 27:1).

Guidelines for Finances

Some pastors I see do nothing but talk about their financial holdings or businesses they have on the side. They do not talk much about the church or their ministry. When I leave them, I feel empty.

Oh, I'm not saying you can't receive gifts from your church family or even individuals in the church—but you must keep it in perspective. What will it cost you in the long run? Will you be indebted forever, or will the lure of money take priority over the call of God in your life?

I remember once, many years ago, when members of my church came to me with a "can't lose" business deal. "Don't worry," they said. "We will handle all of this for you." Well, the deal went bad, and I had to go to my dad for help with the $10,000 I lost. I was duped but had no recourse because these men were in my church. So I just had to eat it.

Since that time, I have followed several guidelines:

- If it seems too good to be true, it probably is.
- If the search for financial gain becomes so strong it detracts from your ministry—it is wrong.
- Under no circumstances should you sign church checks or have access to church funds without dual signers.
- If you have a church credit card, it should have a limit and be paid off each month.
- Do not fall for get-rich schemes.
- The line between what's legal and what's ethical is thin. Be careful.
- If you pay taxes quarterly, save up! Don't be hit with a tax bill at the last minute.

These are common sense suggestions you've heard before. But we can let go of common sense when money is involved. Don't be fooled.

"For the love of money is a root of all kinds of evil. Some people, eager for money, have wandered from the faith and pierced themselves with many griefs" (1 Timothy 6:10).

Vindication and Forgiveness

Vindicate: "to free from allegation or blame"

Have you ever been falsely accused of something? I know—silly question.

I remember back a bunch of years when I was being considered for a pastoral position at a fairly substantial church. I was one of the finalists, and at the meeting when the ultimate decision was to be made, my name was placed in front of the board for a vote. Just before the ballots were distributed, the organizational leader said, "Now you understand H. B. has had an emotional breakdown." Well, as you might imagine, that was the end of my consideration. Another man was chosen.

Time and circumstances have a way of vindicating a person who has been falsely accused of something, but it does not remove the scars left behind or the negative impression created in the minds of many. Those days are behind me now, but I'll never forget the feeling.

You may have gone through a similar experience. Most of us will. I learned big lessons through it all:

1. In time the truth usually surfaces.
2. In your heart, you know what's right.
3. We most often are stronger after the dust has settled.
4. Revenge or retaliation is never the solution—nor is self-defense. All of that is God's business.
5. Forgiveness is a must. If you don't forgive, it will eat at you like a cancer.

"Do not take revenge, my friends, but leave room for God's wrath, for it is written: 'It is mine to avenge; I will repay,' says the Lord" (Romans 12:19).

How Do You Measure Your Church?

I once read the results of a survey taken to determine the 50 most influential churches in the United States. I smiled to myself as I looked at the list.

All of the churches had multimillion-dollar budgets, huge staffs, a megaprofile, and charismatic leadership.

Then I thought about the next rung of churches. What separates #51 from #50? And then I thought about you. What separates you from #50? Is it reach or size or who speaks at the most conferences? Is it a personality or a last name? I mean, if you came out #69 on the list, does that make you any less influential than #47? Would you think, "Maybe I should be in the top 50"? What if you were #152,687 on the list?

If the work of the church can be measured simply by the visible, then there is a problem. The most influential pastors and churches I know operate with a hands-down faith and mind-set. "It all belongs to You, Lord," they say, and, "Thank you for the privilege of serving You in whatever capacity."

In the words of Moses: "You may say to yourself, 'My power and the strength of my hands have produced this wealth for me.' But remember the LORD your God, for it is he who gives you the ability to produce wealth" (Deuteronomy 8:17-18).

"Wouldn't You Know It?" Moments

Every one of us has had those "wouldn't you know it" experiences. They are those things that happen in spite of all you do to stop them. For instance:

You are the next speaker at a conference, and the presenter before you uses your favorite illustration. Wouldn't you know it?

You are attempting to enlist a family to attend your church. The husband is in the hospital. When you arrive for your visit, the pastor down the street has already been there. Wouldn't you know it?

You're playing golf. You have skipped your monthly board meeting so you can get in 18 holes. Your church leaders do not know that, and you get a hole in one on the 10th hole. Now, who can you tell? Wouldn't you know it?

You are rushing to get a sermon ready for Sunday. You throw something together, knowing it is below your standard. When you have finished, your people say it's the best you've ever done. Wouldn't you know it?

So what do you do when those "wouldn't you know it?" moments present themselves? Most of the time, you just tip your hat and go on. Like the old saying, "There is no use in crying over spilled milk." Sometimes, things just happen.

Yet, I know a lot of folks who spend far too much time agonizing over things they can't change. They even grow calloused and bitter. Please don't let that happen to you. Accept the fact that some things will happen and you can't do a thing about it.

Like the writer of Proverbs says, "Many are the plans in a man's heart, but it is the Lord's purpose that prevails" (Proverbs 19:21). In other words, the Lord knows, and He also has a sense of humor.

Continuing to
Fight the Battle

To many of you, it seems like you're fighting a losing battle. Statistics related to the church are dismal. When you see the limited number of Christians out there in the world, it appears hopeless. But, just remember, the game is not over. The final buzzer has not sounded. The last shot has not been taken.

I am constantly reminded of the great admiration I have for all of you who are asked to go out day by day and make a difference in your world. You have accepted a difficult calling, but you do it so well. In many ways you make it look easy, but you and I know better. Even when it's tough I urge you to never give up. Keep keeping on! As Paul said, "I can do everything through him who gives me strength" (Philippians 4:13). You can as well!

The church of Jesus Christ has fought from behind for a long time now, and it continues to do so. Paul may have had you in mind when he wrote, "Let us not become weary in doing good, for at the proper time we will reap a harvest if we do not give up" (Galatians 6:9).

Three Steps to Clergy Failure

More days than not we hear the sad news of another clergy failure.

I will tell you how it can happen to a leader such as you. Become isolated from accountability, live with unresolved issues in your home, and neglect your intimacy with God. Violate these three guidelines and you will open yourself up to temptation that could destroy your ability to continue to serve the church in your present capacity.

If you do not have someone to whom you are accountable, you are vulnerable. If you do not give your spouse permission to ask you big questions regarding your Internet use, you are vulnerable. If you do not have someone outside your door, or the door ajar, when you counsel a member of the opposite sex, you are vulnerable. If you do not address difficult issues at home, you are vulnerable. But most of all, if you do not have a quiet, intimate time each day with the Lord—to speak and listen and contemplate—you are vulnerable. I challenge you to be vigilant.

"Nevertheless, God's solid foundation stands firm, sealed with this inscription: 'The Lord knows those who are his' and, 'Everyone who confesses the name of the Lord must turn away from wickedness'" (2 Timothy 2:19).

Guarding the Tongue

Our speech is powerful: (a) Words do matter. (b) They have a way of following you. (c) When you get away from the truth, it is easy to preach heresy.

"The tongue that brings healing is a tree of life, but a deceitful tongue crushes the spirit" (Proverbs 15:4).

Here's a great passage for all of us: "Do not let any unwholesome talk come out of your mouths, but only what is helpful for building others up according to their needs, that it may benefit those who listen" (Ephesians 4:29).

I have said a lot of things in my ministerial career that were damaging and uncalled for. Perhaps you have as well—but you need to know that the higher the profile, the greater the damage done. Paul said we are called to be an example "in speech" (1 Timothy 4:12).

Weigh your words very carefully, my colleague.

"The tongue of the wise commends knowledge, but the mouth of the fool gushes folly" (Proverbs 15:2).

An Audience of One

So much of what I do, and what you do, is filtered through the judgment of our peers and the perceptions of others. There are times when we in the ministry feel like we have to do a lot of "spin" to keep everyone happy. But do we really? If we are honest, faithful, diligent, prepared, and in close contact with the One who matters most, then the audience that really counts is that audience of ONE!

I wish we could be more secure in that knowledge. Several times every week, you are called upon to step up to the plate and knock the ball out of the park—to produce, to win, to satisfy the crowds—just as a professional athlete would do. To most who observe you, it looks easier than it really is. Folks seldom consider how you're feeling, what's going on at home, or your own personal battles. They just expect you to produce, and most of the time you do.

But it's not about producing *or* pleasing others. We do what we do because we love our Lord and are grateful for the confidence He has placed in us. In fact, without Him we can do nothing (John 15:5). Ultimately, only one voter matters—the One for whom we do all we do. It is a foreign concept to a lot of us because conventional wisdom says the reverse. When you do what you do, why do you do it, and for whom do you do it? Remember, in the end, only One voter counts!

"For every house is built by someone, but God is the builder of everything" (Hebrews 3:4).

Your Legacy

When one of our colleagues leaves the ministry and is immediately replaced, I wonder about my/our/your legacy. We work so diligently only to be so easily replaced. The conclusion I have drawn from all of this is that we need to make the most of each day God allows us because no one really knows what tomorrow will bring.

Oh, your name will appear on the long list of pastors who have served your church. Your picture might be placed in the foyer or your name given to a room, but you will best be remembered for what you do today.

That is why it bothers me to hear those in the clergy, especially local pastors, lament about their present situations. They live in the world of "if only" and "what if" and "why me?" They really need to be careful because those words may become their legacy. You build your legacy one day at a time. If you were gone tomorrow, there would be another filling your pulpit on Sunday. None of us is indispensable. We can all be replaced.

So, what do you say? Let's do the best we can today! Let's determine not to coast or simply go through the motions. Have a plan for each day. Do things that matter and give you satisfaction. Value people just as the Lord does, and help them feel good about themselves. Be thankful for your family. And when the day is done, give God the glory. We will all be remembered for something, so let's give folks something beautiful to remember today!

"He has made everything beautiful in its time" (Ecclesiastes 3:11).

Tee It Up Again

I know we do not believe in luck, but do you remember the song from the television show *Hee Haw*? It went, "If it weren't for bad luck, I'd have no luck at all."

Probably you have felt that way from time to time. It's the old feeling you get when your team loses. So what do you do when that happens?

Well, I'll tell you what you do. You tee it up again. You take a deep breath, and you do it all over again. Why? Because losing every once in a while doesn't mean you are a loser.

In my ministry I have lost a lot. A sermon I thought was surefire fell with a thud. A couple I had worked with to reconcile didn't. A program I had worked on failed. And a dream I had hoped for vanished. Did that make me a loser? Of course not. I preached another sermon, prayed with one more person, tried something new, and dared to dream again. And a lot of those things worked out just fine.

So, my friend, if you are facing difficulties and it looks pretty bleak, you have not lost—you're getting ready for a special blessing. But remember, you must get up and do it over again, only better the next time. And look who is rooting for you! Those who love you and the God who called you! You can't lose!

So take a deep breath, say a faithful prayer, and tee it up again. Hey, nice shot!

"Consider him who endured such opposition . . . so that you will not grow weary and lose heart" (Hebrews 12:3).

Defending Traditional Marriage

Marriage, as we know it, and the wedding ceremony, as you perform it, are in jeopardy. The question I ask is, "What are you as a clergyperson doing to properly inform your congregation of the value of marriage and the danger it would pose to our nation if we just opened the door to same-sex unions or, for that matter, any combination of men and women—even polygamy?"

I am sure you have read the text of the often-used marriage ceremony. If you have not, you should review it. For instance:

". . . gathered in the sight of God"—He is a witness.

". . . to join this man and this woman in holy matrimony"—The union is sacred, not careless or immoral.

". . . instituted of God." Marriage was not an idea of man or the media or any political party. It was God's idea. We must respect this honorable estate, not tamper with it.

We should never tolerate unelected judges changing our societal values or politicians, for the sake of reelection, undermining God's intent. You can make a difference. Stay abreast of what's going on in our nation and your community, and encourage your people to get involved. You, as God's anointed, have the authority to take a bold stand on the marriage issue.

"But at the beginning of creation God 'made them male and female.' 'For this reason a man will leave his father and mother and be united to his wife, and the two will become one flesh'" (Mark 10:6-8).

How to Pray for Your Church

How do you pray for your church? Consider the following:

Pray . . .

For the hearts of your people to blaze with love and loyalty to Christ our King and Lord of all.

For church members to recognize their sin and openly confess the many ways they have grieved God.

That God would draw near to His people, revealing His presence with times of refreshing like water on a parched desert.

For reconciliation, the removal of divisions and hostilities—for the church to work in unity.

For a renewed passion for those who represent the least, the lost, and the lonely. That the church might be the initiating agent to eradicate loneliness around the world through Jesus Christ.

When you pray, how do you pray for your church family? How do they pray for themselves? The early church "joined together constantly in prayer" (Acts 1:14). I believe the local church—your church—is the catalyst for real transformation in our nation. But it can happen only as we are willing to pray urgently, humbly, and often.

Pray, brother, pray! Pray, sister, pray!

"Do not be anxious about anything, but in everything, by prayer and petition, with thanksgiving, present your requests to God" (Philippians 4:6).

Easing Conflict

How do you handle conflict in your congregation and in your relationships with others? What do you do when you have a challenge that seems so much bigger than your ability to solve it? Let me pose a few questions.

First, what is your responsibility in this matter? Are you guilty? Did you violate God's moral values?

Second, have you taken steps to solve the issue by moving toward the person or persons with whom you are in conflict? Are you determined to win at any cost, or could you shoulder blame to ease the tension? A simple "I'm sorry" would speak volumes.

Third, are you acting in obedience to what you know God says?

Fourth, would you be willing to step back from ministry to begin the healing process? The key to any kind of reconciliation is not the absence of conflict but exhibiting a Christlike spirit. A reconciler is one who seeks an unselfish solution.

Jesus was a reconciler. He attempted to bring men to a place of discussion where they could—in an open and honest manner—look at the issue. This will not always result in unity. But it will, at least, establish peace as the goal.

"For he himself is our peace, who has made the two one and has destroyed the barrier, the dividing wall of hostility" (Ephesians 2:14). In every way!

The Undivided Body of Christ

Does not the Bible—God's Holy Word—make the point that it takes a combination of gifts and efforts for the church to be strong? "We have different gifts [mandates], according to the grace given us" (Romans 12:6). The question: Are we using our variety of gifts and making the most of our opportunities? We, in the body of Christ, do not need everyone to be on the same page or concentrating on the same issues. There is so much to be done, and so few to take a stand.

There was a characteristic that clearly accompanied the early church: UNITY! Acts 2:41-47 makes the point that, even though the original believers were outnumbered by the new believers, there was still harmony in the church family. They worshiped every day, and they were out in the marketplace daily as witnesses. The result: The Lord added to His church every day.

I have a passion for a revival of UNITY in the church. I know there can be a variety of opinions when it comes to music and methods, but we must never lose sight of the purpose of the church: to lead people to accept Jesus as Lord and Savior and then to guide them to become more Christlike. When obstacles arise that complicate our achieving that goal, we come very close to quenching the Holy Spirit's work among us. So, my colleague, is yours a unified church? Perhaps the Spirit of Pentecost can be revived in your fellowship. I pray so.

"All the believers were together and had everything in common" (Acts 2:44).

Unity Among Denominations

I enjoy visiting ministers from other denominations. A few years ago, I was with a circuit of Lutheran-Missouri Synod pastors. I will not tell you where because they might get in trouble for inviting an "outsider" to share with them. My time with these men, and a few of their wives, was very enlightening. I could not take communion with them, but I could relate to their challenges.

As I travel the country and have opportunity to interact with so many ministers from various perspectives, I often wish and pray that we might be able to focus on the things that unite us rather than the things that divide us. The early church might not be the perfect example I am looking for, but that one phrase—"All the believers were together" (Acts 2:44)—intrigues me. The more pastors I meet, the more I am convinced that the hope for the church is to build on commonality without surrendering our uniqueness.

Each ministry and local church must find an avenue that leads to the greater good outside the four walls of its buildings—to honor God, not look for credit. Satan would like to see the evangelical church divided, as would some in-house critics. We can't let that happen! The more we in the Christian world learn about one another, the more we will find in common. We really do not need to be cookie-cutter clones. We need to emphasize our common ground to win the world for Christ.

"Make every effort to keep the unity of the Spirit through the bond of peace. There is one body and one Spirit—just as you were called to one hope when you were called—one Lord, one faith, one baptism; one God and Father of all, who is over all and through all and in all" (Ephesians 4:3-6).

Assessing Your Church's Demographics

Have you ever stopped to consider the demographics (statistical characteristics such as age or income) of your congregation? Knowing the demographics of an audience can help an organization understand how best to reach it. For instance, television marketers seek out consumers between 18 and 45 years of age because they are the ones who buy products. Demographics tell a lot about the people your church seeks to influence.

My point is this: If you ignore your congregation's demographics, you will borrow trouble. That is why music is such a divider in the church. Some attempt to force-feed music to an age group that neither enjoys nor relates to modern worship tunes. If your church is filled with older adults, change and growth will be more difficult. Why? Because many of them are satisfied with the way things are and they refuse the burden of change. A reason why many churches fall into contention can be traced to a pastor/leader who did not prepare his people for change. "Shock change" always divides.

A place of worship can become a battleground when all things, including demographics, are not considered. Consider the makeup of your congregation before making big changes. And when you make these changes give your people ample time to make a peaceful transition.

"May the God who gives endurance and encouragement give you a spirit of unity among yourselves" (Romans 15:5).

The Challenges of a Pastor's Spouse

I realize that not all clergy spouses struggle with the challenge of sharing their mate and family with a congregation. But I haven't met many who have not had their moments.

This is what I hear: "Our family needs more balance. It seems we are owned by the church." "Sometimes, when I see how my husband is treated by the church leaders, I wonder if it's all worth it." "I'm concerned about my husband's health. He does not sleep well, eat well, or find time for himself."

When spouses talk about themselves, often it is in the area of their own identity or relationship. "I'm not sure who I can trust." "So many of the expectations for me are unrealistic." "If we didn't work here, I'm not sure we would even attend this church." "Sundays are my roughest day of the week." "I feel a heaviness in my heart that I can't describe."

Well, you know the rest. As couples in ministry, you must keep talking, keep observing the one you love. Don't be afraid to ask how the other is doing, and take time to be together. Ministry should be a joy—full of love and respect for one another.

"When anxiety was great within me, your consolation brought joy to my soul" (Psalm 94:19).

The Fundamentally Sound Church

I wonder how fundamentally sound we are in the North American church? How about those of us (you) who are leaders in the North American church? Are we fundamentally sound?

Paul advised Timothy to "preach the Word; be prepared in season and out of season; correct, rebuke and encourage—with great patience and careful instruction" (2 Timothy 4:2). In an earlier letter, he told Timothy to "set an example for the believers in speech, in life, in love, in faith and in purity . . . devote yourself to the public reading of Scripture, to preaching and to teaching" (1 Timothy 4:12-13).

He also admonished him to "pursue righteousness, faith, love and peace" (2 Timothy 2:22). Paul gives a lot more advice about unity and consistency. Fundamentals! You can't maintain a high level of ministry without good fundamentals.

What do you think? What do you perceive to be a fundamentally sound church and/or Christian leader? Yes, prayer—above all, prayer! What else? Please take some time to consider the fundamental principles and whether your church needs a course correction.

"They must keep hold of the deep truths of the faith with a clear conscience" (1 Timothy 3:9).

Living Up to God's Expectations

When it comes to members of the clergy, I sometimes wonder if our problem could be that we have lower, rather than higher, expectations.

I believe God's expectations for me—and, yes, even you—are much more than we can imagine. You and I might differ on how we interpret 1 Corinthians 2:9: "No eye has seen, no ear has heard, no mind has conceived what God has prepared for those who love him." But the one thing I see when I read Bible stories of great men and women is that they all found courage when they realized God's expectations for them were greater than their own. We may think we lack what we need to accomplish all God has in mind for us. But God can turn that weakness, that caution, into strength. In other words, I believe we need to begin to see our ministries through the eyes of the One who called us and promised to empower us.

Don't live with the regrets of "if only" or "what might have been." Seek God's direction and go for it! I talk to so many who operate in the world of excuse after excuse, who never know the thrill of exceeding their expectations to find the applause of God cheering them on.

Bring glory to the Father—reach beyond your grasp. Live up to His expectations! So, buckle up. You're in for quite a ride. As the saying goes, "Better to run the risk of running out than rusting out."

"Be strong and courageous. Do not be terrified; do not be discouraged, for the LORD your God will be with you wherever you go" (Joshua 1:9).

Salvation—One Soul
at a Time

It's a really big world, isn't it? I mean, when you think of the more than seven billion people who populate our planet and all the issues they deal with on a daily basis, it really gives you pause.

Like you, I can do only so much. But I am often reminded of the fact that probably two-thirds of the world's population do not know Jesus, and the effort to change that figure is a real step of faith. How do we make a difference? One soul at a time.

I can't say for sure, but I've heard that in North America, in a given year, one-half of our churches do not receive even one new member into their fellowship by a "profession of faith." Could that be true? What is it like in your fellowship? Is anyone getting saved? Do we still ask that question? Do we preach for conversion? Do we give people an opportunity to accept Jesus Christ as their Savior? Have we become so contemporary that the altar is too much of a threat to people? Does it make our church crowd uncomfortable?

Oh, I know times have changed, but have words like *conviction, repentance, surrender,* and *confession* lost their significance? It is at the foot of the cross that salvation is granted. Is anybody being saved in your world? I pray so!

Jesus said, "I tell you the truth, no one can see the kingdom of God unless he is born again" (John 3:3).

When We Shoot Each Other

When my cousin, James Dobson, and I were kids, I almost shot him twice. The first time, we were squirrel hunting, and I didn't know if the safety on my gun was on or off. It was off, and I whistled a shot close to his ear. I will not soon forget that day—neither will he. The second time, I was bird hunting with him, and as I was walking across a gully on a log, I lost my footing, fell from the log, and the shotgun went off. It was another close call.

I have often thought to myself, "I could have altered the course of history." I did get a tongue-lashing from my cousin and his dad. What do you do when you almost shoot someone? You apologize like crazy!

Now to the point: So often in our worlds, we shoot one another. We do not use guns, but we do use a weapon. Words become our firearm. We can do irreparable damage to another by accusations, innuendos, gossip, and idle conversation.

All of us have been "shot at" by a colleague or parishioner. It always hurts and can result in permanent injury. I bear the scars, as do you.

Proverbs 21:23 says, "He who guards his mouth and his tongue keeps himself from calamity." In other words, whatever you do—don't shoot anyone. If you do, you lessen yourself in the eyes and ears of those who watch and listen.

Paul suggested to the church at Ephesus, "Do not let any unwholesome talk come out of your mouths, but only what is helpful for building others up according to their needs, that it may benefit those who listen" (Ephesians 4:29).

Don't Let Status Take the Upper Hand

Although we don't talk about it in clergy meetings, we struggle with status in the ranks of our colleagues all the time. A larger church, a bigger budget, the "in" conference, the seminary you attended, who you know in the world of clergy superstars, the length of your sabbatical, your retirement benefits, who provides your automobile, the number of weeks you are allowed away from your pulpit each year, the latest book you have written . . . and the list goes on.

I am aware that, in any profession, there are symbols that say to the watching world and to others who share the same vocation, "I am successful." It seems that, in the last couple of decades, we have worked overtime to elevate our personal status among our brothers and sisters. Yet, I am reminded of the words from Deuteronomy 8: "Be careful that you do not forget the LORD your God. . . . You may say to yourself, 'My power and the strength of my hands have produced this wealth for me.' But remember the LORD your God, for it is he who gives you the ability to produce wealth, and so confirms his covenant" (8:11, 17-18).

My words may be a bit unsettling for you, but just think how much of your time and conversation are given to "status" things. Remember the words of the prophet Micah: "Walk humbly with your God" (6:8).

God's Love

Let me remind you of a very meaningful love note:

"Love is patient, love is kind. It does not envy, it does not boast, it is not proud. It is not rude, it is not self-seeking, it is not easily angered, it keeps no record of wrongs. Love does not delight in evil but rejoices with the truth. It always protects, always trusts, always hopes, always perseveres. Love never fails."

I LOVE YOU!—God

My attempt here is not to be trite, but to remind you how genuinely loved you are. The passage from 1 Corinthians 13:4-8 is a love letter from God and a partial description of how He chooses to love you.

Genuine love is found in word and deed. You don't just say the words—you live them. And people are always better for that love.

Genuine love validates your verbal expressions. It is one thing to tell someone how much you love them, but true love is when those words are backed up with patience, kindness, and selfless support.

Romans 5:8 says, "But God demonstrates his own love for us in this: While we were still sinners, Christ died for us." That's how valuable each of us is to God. Oh, how He loves you and me!

"The LORD appeared to us in the past, saying: 'I have loved you with an everlasting love; I have drawn you with loving-kindness' " (Jeremiah 31:3).

When Stuff Happens

Stuff happens.

The real question is not so much why stuff happens as how you deal with stuff when it happens. The Bible makes it very clear that we will face tribulation and trials. We will have accidents, get sick, fail from time to time, contend with rebellious children, struggle in our marriages, and even be asked to live among the "joy suckers" every now and again. And that's just for starters . . . it can get a lot worse. I'm sure you know that.

In John 16:33, Jesus wishes peace for us in the midst of tribulation. Hand wringing and hair pulling do not accomplish much, leading only to the distress of others. But when we view the dilemma in the light of eternity—or even a few days later—it can result in a much brighter conclusion.

When Isaiah wrote in chapter 43 about the waters, rivers, and fire, it was not a matter of *if* you would face them, but *when* . . . always with the Lord's presence to sustain you. Stuff happens. That's for sure. That God is with you is even *more* sure.

"I have told you these things, so that in me you may have peace. In this world you will have trouble. But take heart! I have overcome the world" (John 16:33).

"I have summoned you by name; you are mine" (Isaiah 43:1).

Surveying Your Church

What if, at least once a month, you put a survey into the hands of your church attendees and asked them to express their honest opinion about your church, the services, and even the content of your sermons? I don't know about you, but I'm pretty sure I'm not that secure.

Let's consider a few simple questions to include in your survey: Were you greeted and made to feel welcome when you arrived? Did the music point you to the preached Word, or was it simply one song after another? Did the message have relevance? Did it apply? Were your children well cared for? Was the Lord's house honored with neatness and order? Did you feel the church service was performance-oriented or Christ-centered? And the big questions: Will you return? Would you invite someone else to attend with you?

I know churches are not airplanes, but sometimes it is good to know how your people are feeling. Don't you agree? If you're not brave enough to survey your church, please consider more informal ways to find out how people—both congregants and visitors—feel about how things are going.

"Plans fail for lack of counsel, but with many advisers they succeed" (Proverbs 15:22).

Your Calendar

"What's on your calendar?" The more I pondered that question, the more profound the thought became—"What's on your calendar?"

The psalmist wrote in the beautiful 139th Psalm, "All the days ordained for me were written in your book before one of them came to be" (v. 16). A divine calendar whose entries were penned by God Himself. He has things in mind for us. I often wonder how my calendar compares with His.

I travel a lot. Some of my trips are "calendared" several years in advance. There are times when I forget them until they are upon me. I live my days by a calendar, some days hour by hour. But the question remains: "What's on your calendar?"

For instance, does each day include adequate time for you to spend with your Lord? I hope those times are early in the morning. I trust your calendar provides you sufficient time to honor your family members. Does each month have a notation that reads "date with spouse" and/or "quality time with my daughter"? Perhaps, "basketball game Friday at 7:00 P.M." What we hear so often from pastors is a cry from their families just to be included.

How about clearing an afternoon or two each week to "walk in the village," to rub shoulders with those in your community who need to see you from a perspective outside the pulpit? You shepherd best one-on-one. Oh, and what about your day off? Do you guard it, or do you allow other things to take away your sabbath? Is your vacation scheduled for the coming year? If you don't schedule it, soon your calendar will be filled with other things.

I don't mean to belabor the point, but your calendar tells more about you than anything. It speaks of spiritual discipline, priorities, and most of all, your intimacy with the God who called you and blessed you with your special gift called "family."

What's on your calendar?

"Many are the plans in a man's heart, but it is the LORD's purpose that prevails" (Proverbs 19:21).

Pastors' Kids

People in our congregations have a fascination with our children's lifestyles and behavior. Most of our children do really well, but from time to time, we are faced with a prodigal living in the spotlight—and the judgment of a church family. What do you do? How do you "train up a child" (Proverbs 22:6, KJV)? Here are a few general guidelines:

- Support your children. Convince them that your concern is for them, not what people say.
- Get them help, especially if their behavior could be addictive. Don't be afraid to reach out.
- Talk to them. Don't avoid them. Stop what you are doing and make your children a priority.
- Evaluate their peers. Who are their influencers?
- Choose carefully the individuals in your congregation with whom you talk. Your problems don't need to become public knowledge.
- Be in agreement as parents. Make decisions together.
- Pray for your child and love him or her, but do not minimize the seriousness of your child's unacceptable ways and behavior.

"Fathers, do not exasperate your children; instead, bring them up in the training and instruction of the Lord" (Ephesians 6:4).

Hope Even in Defeat

Remember the old introduction to ABC's *Wide World of Sports* in which a skier goes head over heels off the edge of the platform? The announcer coined the phrase "the thrill of victory and the agony of defeat."

Skiing is one thing—real-life experiences are quite another. When you deal, as you do, with life-and-death issues, you know firsthand what it is like to win and how painful it is to lose.

In ministry, however, there is the hope that comes even in defeat. Romans 8:28 gives us a reason to be optimistic even when things look bleak: "And we know that in all things God works for the good of those who love him, who have been called according to his purpose."

Some clergy have known the great joy that comes with victory, while others have known the pain of loss. But regardless, you are a winner because you love and serve the God who called you. Be humble in victory and brave in defeat. Hold your head high. You serve an awesome God who enables all of us to be more than conquerors.

"Therefore, since we have such a hope, we are very bold" (2 Corinthians 3:12).

Experiencing Peace

Jesus said to his disciples, "Peace I leave with you; my peace I give you. I do not give to you as the world gives. Do not let your hearts be troubled and do not be afraid" (John 14:27). What was Jesus saying? We experience His peace as we commune with the Father and the Son in love.

How many times have you prayed for peace with a hospital patient or someone who has lost a loved one? What were you praying? That the situation might be surrendered to the One who loved them and had the answers to their suffering and sorrow. That as you prayed and they surrendered, there would be a lifting of heaviness, a realization that someone had entered their personal world with a divine presence.

In all our suffering there is the assurance echoed in Hebrews 13:5, originally from Deuteronomy 31:6: "Never will I leave you; never will I forsake you." That is the atmosphere of peace I am talking about. The assurance of His love, His presence, His direction, His understanding of your situation, and His willingness to become involved in your life as though you were the only one He had to care for. The challenge is in the surrendering, isn't it? In the letting go.

As you preach and teach about peace, may you experience that same peace in your own life.

"Grace and peace be yours in abundance through the knowledge of God and of Jesus our Lord" (2 Peter 1:2).

Who Will Replace You?

As I watched a television tribute to a friend in ministry, the thought crossed my mind—"Who replaces a man like that?" When Moses died, the Lord said to Joshua, "As I was with Moses, so I will be with you" (Joshua 1:5). I was sure someone would come along, but who? And then I thought about all of the other church leaders who are in their "fourth quarter." When the time comes, who will replace them?

When I say "replace," I am not talking about another body. I refer to the character of the person whose resolve is not simply to better their own life and image, but one whose focus is on Jesus even more than their ministry. The Lord gave us a hint of the qualifications in Micah 6:8—men who act justly, love mercy, and walk humbly with God.

Ever think about who will replace you? What kind of person would you choose to follow your legacy? Would you want someone like yourself? The body of Christ faces leadership transition in the next decade. Who will accept the baton? I think about such things, and I hope you do too.

"The company of the prophets from Jericho . . . said, 'The spirit of Elijah is resting on Elisha'" (2 Kings 2:15).

Recognizing Divine Moments

Our lives are filled with divine opportunities. What I mean is, there are times when you and I confront moments that only God could arrange. Think about it! Those are the times when you cross paths with a person or a situation that, as you reflect on it, could have happened only by divine appointment.

Once I was on a flight from Cincinnati to Chicago. It was scheduled to take 56 minutes. It took nearly five hours! It was one of the most frustrating days I have had in a long time. But during those five hours, I was seated next to a lady from the East Coast who was going through marital problems. During the long delay, she shared some heartbreaking information about her family. I mostly listened. She needed someone to hear her out. To be honest, I feel God had me on that plane for that lady. Maybe it was for more hours than I had wanted, but nevertheless, it was a divinely directed moment.

With so much pain in our world, and so many people needing to be helped to their feet, you as a Christian leader need to be even more aware of such divine moments. Those are the moments when God places you in the right place at the right time to represent Christ to someone who needs "a cup of cold water" in His name.

Many of my most meaningful ministry moments have occurred outside the pulpit and in the marketplace, where people live who may never enter the doors of a church. How about you?

So—be alert! Be available! Be sensitive! Be prepared! God has some divine appointments set for you. They may appear subtle at first but, in eternal terms, are life-changing.

"Be very careful, then, how you live—not as unwise but as wise, making the most of every opportunity" (Ephesians 5:15-16).

Watching Your Words

The news today is full of stories about "who said what and who they said it to and did they really mean it?"

I remember one time an old pastor said to me, "Young man, every word you speak may have consequences that could follow you for a lifetime." I'm still paying for some of my thoughtless words. We all need to heed that old pastor's advice.

Satan loves to trip us up. I'm sure he delights in our stumbles. We all need—I need—to be really careful. We need to consider what we say, how we say it, and who we say it to. Weigh your words and deeds carefully, my colleague. What you say or do can and will follow you for a lifetime. Your words can haunt you and be used by others any way they choose. There are times when it's best to just say nothing!

The psalmist wrote, "Keep your tongue from evil and your lips from speaking lies" (Psalm 34:13).

"A gentle answer turns away wrath, but a harsh word stirs up anger" (Proverbs 15:1).

Further, "A man who lacks judgment derides his neighbor, but a man of understanding holds his tongue" (Proverbs 11:12).

Well, I think you know where I'm going with all of this. Watch what you say and when and how you say it. I have had to eat my words too many times. Instead, speak the truth in love (Ephesians 4:15).

"If anyone considers himself religious and yet does not keep a tight rein on his tongue, he deceives himself and his religion is worthless" (James 1:26).

Persistence

Persistence is one of the most important characteristics of pastors, those who just keep showing up for work with one goal in mind—winning the prize for God's glory. The writer of Proverbs penned, "In his heart a man plans his course, but the LORD determines his steps" (16:9). Paul said, "I press on toward the goal to win the prize for which God has called me heavenward in Christ Jesus" (Philippians 3:14). Jesus said, "For everyone who asks receives; he who seeks finds; and to him who knocks, the door will be opened" (Matthew 7:8). In other words, be persistent!

Unfortunately, I run across a lot of our colleagues who are just going through the motions. They have given up on ever winning the prize. I am concerned for them because these men and women are in danger of growing calloused, even angry.

Paul advised young Timothy, "Fight the good fight of the faith" (1 Timothy 6:12). I say that to you, my friend—don't ever give up. The game, the fight, the battle, the call is never over until the lights have been turned off. You matter, and, regardless of the circumstances, there is a prize awaiting you! A crown of righteousness. I'm never sure who will win the Super Bowl or the World Series, but I do know that "We will reap a harvest if we do not give up" (Galatians 6:9).

Filling a Vacant Position

Almost all of us have memories of "our call" to fill a vacancy as a pastor or staff member in a local church.

You know the feeling. You get a call asking if you are interested in the position. You wonder if this is something you should consider. You talk to your spouse, pray about it, and then take inventory of your present position. *Have I completed my assignment here? Do I still have a passion for the church I serve? How will my family be affected by this move? Will I be able to use my gifts in the new assignment? How did the leadership treat the pastor or staff member just leaving? Am I considering this call because I need to move, want to move, or just feel restless? What is the average life span of a pastor at that church? Is the fellowship contentious? Does it have a "church boss"? Is it God's will?* The questions are endless.

And then you go and meet the leadership. Remember how you felt? It's kind of like a "fishbowl" experience. You answer questions. You meet many people. You feel a bit dazed by all the encounters you have. Then you go back home and attempt to digest all you have seen and heard. Finally, you say, "Okay, put my name before the church." They do. They vote. You pray. You go. The honeymoon begins, or maybe never does, and then people evaluate you.

Some do not even give you time to unpack before they evaluate you. The sad thing is that so many of you stay only a short time, not even four years. And the process goes on. But those who commit to the long haul find—even with the challenges—a sense of completion.

The process is often unnerving and cumbersome, but I guess necessary. My advice: Stay where you are for as long as you can. Of course, God will have something to say about that.

"They chose Stephen, a man full of faith and of the Holy Spirit" (Acts 6:5).

Dealing with Criticism

How do you as a pastor handle criticism? How do you react when people falsely accuse you of something or misinterpret your motives? We know conflict is inevitable—how we handle it will either make or break us as a servant-shepherd. You may not agree with my following advice, but I hope you will at least consider it.

1. Accept personal responsibility for the situation. It may not be your fault, but you must take the initiative for reconciliation.

2. Make every effort to move toward the person or persons in the conflict. (They may not be receptive.) Playing the blame game only leads to more torment. Try the following approach: "I understand this was said. Do you have some time when we can sit down and discuss our differences? Perhaps we can find common ground."

3. Confront the issue for the sake of the relationship. In the end, it will make little difference who wins or who is right. What really matters is how you walk away from one another.

I know most of us are people pleasers and we want folks to accept us and follow our lead. But reality is reality. If you can look beyond those who are critical of you, fine. For most of us, if we fail to address the issue, there will always be unrest, maybe even anger.

"Get rid of all bitterness, rage and anger . . . along with every form of malice. Be kind and compassionate to one another, forgiving each other, just as in Christ God forgave you" (Ephesians 4:31-32). Amen!

Go Forward in Times of Trouble

I regularly receive letters and e-mails from pastors with "here we go again" messages. By that I mean a troubled church, followed by a rebellious teen, followed by a negative health report on the heels of emotional and physical distress.

Job lived in that "here we go again" world. He endured test after test after test. In chapter 3, verse 25, he uttered these words: "What I feared has come upon me; what I dreaded has happened to me." He even began to doubt himself: "If I have sinned, what have I done to you?" (7:20). When trouble upon trouble heaps itself on us, we tend to feel the same way. I don't have a lot of answers. There are some things we face that appear too broken to mend unless God intervenes.

When the children of Israel were in a state of disarray and Moses was downtrodden, God stepped in and commanded him to "move on." Moses said to the people, "Do not be afraid. Stand firm and you will see the deliverance the LORD will bring you today. . . . The LORD will fight for you" (Exodus 14:13-14). What great news!

I urge you to go forward. When it's dark, look for the light. When it's daytime, look for the cloud of promise. The Lord God is with you, and He offers all the power of His command.

"The LORD is compassionate and gracious, slow to anger, abounding in love" (Psalm 103:8).

Having Compassion

Sometimes I get compassion fatigue. Do you?

At times, it all just boils up within you, and you wonder what will happen next. That is "compassion fatigue"—when you come to the place where there is so much to care about that you just can't care anymore.

As clergy, we deal with heartbreak all the time, and we must guard against growing calloused or cynical. We can never lose our empathy or take other people's suffering for granted. Our hearts must remain sensitive—even as our Lord's heart—although sometimes we just want to stick our fingers in our ears and say, "No more!"

How? Well, for one thing, we should pray for a heart like Jesus'. For another, we can never come to a place in our ministry when we can walk away from those who are suffering without letting them know of God's love. We must attempt to be an answer to our prayers and do what we can to help.

We cannot do what we do for people with selfish motives, but as unto the Lord. We should place a high priority on getting enough rest and spiritual food, or we will wear down very quickly. We are reminded to "cast all your anxiety [care] on him because he cares for you" (1 Peter 5:7). He promises to restore and make us strong.

There are times when I feel so helpless. Then I remember it is not about me, but those whom our Lord called me to serve, to be His compassion in a world that hungers for solutions. And I feel His power again to do whatever I need to do—because of Him.

"Restore to me the joy of your salvation and grant me a willing spirit, to sustain me" (Psalm 51:12).

Trusting God

How do you explain sadness? How do you make sense out of suffering? Why are we so surprised when evil triumphs? Why do bad things happen to good people? So many questions—so few answers.

I don't begin to understand how God works, but I do know He is always love. Kenneth Samples wrote, "While God's universe is majestic and eloquently designed to provide humankind with a fine habitat on Earth, it can also be a powerfully dangerous place at times."

So often in trials, we have a tendency to say, "Where is God?" The answer is not a simple one, but from His Word there is comfort amidst the suffering: "When you pass through the waters, I will be with you" (Isaiah 43:2). The psalmist writes, "God is our refuge and strength, an ever-present help in trouble. Therefore we will not fear, though the earth give way and the mountains fall into the heart of the sea, though its waters roar and foam. . . . The LORD Almighty is with us" (Psalm 46:1-3, 7). Where there is no answer, there comes this word from our loving Lord: "Trust me."

I don't understand God's ways, but I trust Him. I remember reading once where C. S. Lewis, in deep despair over the loss of his wife, cried out to God, "Why?" The answer he received was, "Son, even if I could explain it to you, you would not understand. It would be like attempting to teach physics to a four-year-old." We just trust Him—even when the answers don't always emerge!

"But I trust in you, O LORD; I say, 'You are my God'" (Psalm 31:14).

Partnership with Sister Churches

If you put the populations of North America and Africa together, the total would not equal India's population of 1.1 billion people. Of that number, less than 7 percent of Indians are Christians. How do we relate to numbers like that? Disease and paganism—like a mighty army—are marching across our world. We must fight back with the love of God, human compassion, and positive partnership with those in needy places around the world.

I believe every American congregation should have a sister congregation somewhere outside of North America. Does your church have one?

How do you go about finding a sister congregation? Check with a mission organization or your denominational mission board. Communicate with a local pastor in that area of the world to learn what his church's challenges are. Provide that pastor with books and CDs. Send items that we in America take for granted but most pastors elsewhere would consider luxuries. Exchange family pictures, and enlist your spouse and children to be pen pals. But most of all, commit to pray for one another.

Any church, large or small, can engage in a sister church relationship. Will you investigate the possibility? I pray so. Every time I step across our nation's borders, I am captivated by the desire to assist those who labor in vineyards so much different from our own.

"Praise the LORD, all you nations; extol him, all you peoples. For great is his love toward us, and the faithfulness of the LORD endures forever. Praise the LORD" (Psalm 117:1-2).

God's Constancy

Sometimes I can't help but marvel at the contrast from one day to the next. Proverbs 27:1 says, "Do not boast about tomorrow, for you do not know what a day may bring forth." We really don't, do we? We think we do. We act like we do, but in truth, each and every day is a gift, often filled with life-changing surprises.

Just think how many of your people each week awaken to an unforeseen occurrence. How do we prepare our flocks for such events? How do we prepare ourselves?

The psalmist cried, "But now, Lord, what do I look for? My hope is in you" (Psalm 39:7).

I don't want to be too simplistic, but I am comforted by the words of the 23rd Psalm: "Even though I walk through the valley of the shadow of death, I will fear no evil, for you are with me; your rod and your staff, they comfort me" (v. 4).

Uncertain times call for stability. The one constant is our God's never-failing presence and His unconditional love for His people.

"God is our refuge and strength, an ever-present help in trouble" (Psalm 46:1).

Why We Feel Insignificant

We in the clergy can find ourselves in a struggle for significance. A thread runs through Rick Warren's book *The Purpose Driven Life*, that says, once a person finds his or her place in society, there will be eternal impact. In other words, we will make a difference for God's glory. It seems that ministry can at times diminish one's effectiveness . . . at least in our own eyes.

I have attempted to analyze—from the notes I have received from pastors and from my own perspective—why we sometimes feel insignificant. As a result, I share the following unscientific conclusions:

- We unfairly compare ourselves to others whose ministries seem more effective.
- We are battling against the power base in our organizations, which doesn't accept our dreams.
- We are worn out from stressful ministry. When we find ourselves in that condition, everything looks dim.
- We may have forgotten that the church we serve is God's church and our people are His people.
- It might just be that we are finding our source of encouragement in the praise of people rather than in the Lord through His Word and private worship.
- There could be conflict in our families that complicates our lives. Unless we resolve those issues, we will always be in the negative.

Self-pity is a lousy prison, and if we ever think God doesn't care, doesn't know our situation, or may have mistaken our assignment, we will be less than content! Give yourself a few minutes to pout, and then move on!

As I've said before, just make up your mind to bloom where God has planted you. Greet each day with a smile, and end each day with a feeling that you have done your best.

"I can do everything through him who gives me strength" (Philippians 4:13).

The Ten Commandments

Warren Wiersbe writes, "God's people have three responsibilities when it comes to His commandments: hear them, learn them, and do them. God's laws are clear and simple; man's laws are complex. Beware of a mere outward obedience to the laws of God. We must have true fear of God in our hearts as well as love for him."

Hear the Word of the Lord: "Oh, that their hearts would be inclined to fear me and keep all my commands always, so that it might go well with them and their children forever!" (Deuteronomy 5:29).

I wish the laws of God, which have been the model for man's behavior for centuries, could be displayed everywhere. And my greatest concern is that, in this day of "grace," some, even within the church, see God's commandments as mere suggestions. That could be one of the reasons for so much chaos in the body of Christ.

In the past, you have probably preached a series of sermons on the commandments. This is a good time to pull them off the shelf, dust them off, and once again emphasize the Word of our Lord. "Learn them and be sure to follow them" (Deuteronomy 5:1). God's plan for us is not restrictive, but liberating.

"We know that we have come to know him if we obey his commands" (1 John 2:3).

Being Yourself

I have a suggestion for you that might appear controversial. "Be yourself!" I see so many colleagues who have pretty much given up on their uniqueness. They have become like clones—almost afraid to venture out and be unique in their own assignment. That may be an overstatement, but I talk to many who live so much in the fear of failure that they never reach their potential.

Suggestion: Dare to dream an impossible dream for your ministry. Go beyond your reach. Invest in an original thought each day. Ask God for a challenge. Be around people who stimulate you to newness rather than people who drag you down. Don't have heroes—be a hero. Live a life that others will view as anointed.

Remember the scripture often used in "life-issue" sermons: "I am fearfully and wonderfully made" (Psalm 139:14). That refers to you, my colleague. God had you in mind before you even took a breath, and His intention was that, because you were created uniquely, you would live uniquely—different from any other human being—especially any other pastor. It's fine to admire another's uniqueness, but please do not neglect your own. You are wonderful! You are an original.

"Now the body is not made up of one part but of many. . . . But in fact God has arranged the parts in the body, every one of them, just as he wanted them to be" (1 Corinthians 12:14, 18).

Giving Control to God

A while back, I lost my voice completely. And even though it was a blessing to many, it was a very disturbing and humbling experience for me. I was forced to cancel several engagements and realized just how little control I had over something that you and I take for granted—our voices. Through the ordeal, I was forced to accept the fact that "things happen," even to God's "anointed." I felt helpless, frustrated, and at times, angry. Yet my problems were minimal compared to so many others.

You may be facing events, people, and circumstances you cannot control. But everything is under the control of a loving, caring, understanding God. There are times when we must accept His ways and surrender to His care. We can wear ourselves out attempting to change the unchangeable.

I am reminded of the words of the psalmist: "Be still before the LORD and wait patiently for him" (Psalm 37:7).

A Change of Perspective

Long ago I learned an important lesson about standing for what's right. I'll share it with you with the hope that you can avoid my mistake.

One Sunday, as parishioners exited the service, they stroked my ego with comments such as, "God used you today. Thanks for your courageous stand against abortion."

I felt good about myself because I had been an enthusiastic spokesman for God on a controversial subject. The reactions were so positive that I made a mental note to preach on abortion again.

Then, as I did following every service, I went to my study to unwind. A young woman knocked on the door. I could tell she was troubled.

"Pastor, I know you're tired, and I don't want to keep you. But could you spare a few minutes?"

"Sure," I said. To be perfectly candid, I expected more affirmation, anticipating that she would also comment positively about the sermon on abortion. But she surprised me by asking, "Pastor, do you know how many women like me were sitting in the congregation today?" I thought maybe she was talking about the number of women who came to church alone.

"No, I really don't. I don't think I know what you mean."

Then like water from a broken dam, the pain from her own abortion gushed out. She graphically shared her sense of loss. She explained the agony she felt every anniversary of her unborn child's death. She described how far from God she felt. Then she shocked me even more by saying that perhaps 1 in 10 women in her age group had had an abortion—and some were probably sitting in church during that morning's sermon.

"You seemed so determined to communicate your pro-life message that you forgot about women like me who have lived through an abortion. You failed to realize that many men also feel guilty because they insisted on, or at least consented to, an abortion by their girlfriends or wives."

That woman changed my life. She opened my eyes. She brought me back to the reality of what it means to be a pastor—learning to hate sin more and love sinners to Christ's forgiveness.

"Therefore, I tell you, her many sins have been forgiven—for she loved much. But he who has been forgiven little loves little" (Luke 7:47).

Husband-Wife Communication

I am a huge fan of my wife, Beverley, and I want her to know it. But sometimes there is a language barrier. Do you know what I mean? Consider the following (just having some fun). When a wife says:

"FINE"—This is a word women use to end an argument when they are right, and a husband should not say anything more.

"NOTHING"—This is the calm before the storm. This means "something," and a husband should be on his toes. Discussions that begin with "nothing" usually end in "fine."

"WE NEED TO TALK"—What that means is that a husband probably will not be saying anything for a long time.

"OH, GO AHEAD"—This one is tricky. It may be a dare, not really permission.

"JUST FIVE MINUTES MORE"—If she's getting dressed, this could mean "I'll be down in 30 minutes."

"THANKS"—If you are thanked, do not question or faint. Just say "You're welcome."

Express your love genuinely. "Beloved, let us love one another: for love is of God; and every one that loveth is born of God, and knoweth God" (1 John 4:7, KJV).

Living with Passion

If I were to ask you what your greatest passion is, what would you say? Oh, I know you are passionate about your God, your family, and your church. But beyond the expected, what motivates you? What drives you? What occupies your attention?

The pastor without a dream, without a cause, without an unquenchable passion will eventually grow tired in "well doing." The excitement once so crucial to his or her ministry will become status quo. And then it will be just a job—a worthy job, but one lacking enthusiasm.

I meet pastors all the time who are worn out. The passion for what they do is gone. And in its place is secondary activity or unrelated fulfillment. I understand how this can happen. It's tough bumping our heads against stone walls or coming up empty for effort given. But the answer is not in striving; it is in believing. It's not in success; it is in attempting. It is never found in the words "I can't do it anymore," but in determining to get up and give it another try.

"And let us not be weary in well doing: for in due season we shall reap, if we faint not" (Galatians 6:9, KJV).

Living by the Truth

As pastors, our role is to help people to find the truth—to help them sift out the lies and find the real story.

I am campaigning for "truth telling" in this painful world environment, and for "truth living" by all of us who serve the body of Christ. Those seem so basic to our faith.

There is a passage in Titus that, though difficult, has great wisdom: "In everything set them an example by doing what is good. In your teaching show integrity, seriousness and soundness of speech that cannot be condemned, so that those who oppose you may be ashamed because they have nothing bad to say about us" (Titus 2:7-8).

As a speaker of truth and leader in living the truth, don't you feel it is your responsibility to lead your people to the truth? Please give this question some thought. May our Lord give you boldness as you stand for righteousness and renewal.

"Then you will know the truth, and the truth will set you free" (John 8:32).

Who Will Tell Them?

Central Park is a great place. Suddenly you are out of the hustle and bustle of New York City, and you are experiencing trees and water, people enjoying times with their children, a ride on the Ferris wheel, an ice cream cone, or a moment to sit on a park bench, feed the birds, or read a newspaper. The park is, for many, an oasis.

But here are the thoughts that kept coming to my mind as I recently shouldered my way through the crowds and sat and watched parents with their kids in Central Park: Who of them know Jesus as their Lord and Savior? How many of them really know how much God loves them? And, if they don't know, who will tell them? Of course, there were street preachers— but no one stopped to listen. I'm sure many of the people I saw are believers, but likely, the majority have never been born again.

The next question is, what do we do with John 3:18: "But whoever does not believe stands condemned"? My answer: Work harder. Double our passion. Never give up on anyone. Reach and preach for a decision.

Do you recall the incident in Acts 26 when Paul was in a discussion with King Agrippa? Paul had been called insane by the king, but the apostle would not be silenced. The king asked Paul if he, in such a short time, could persuade him to be a Christian. Remember Paul's response? "Short time or long—I pray God that not only you but all who are listening to me today may become what I am" (v. 29). That was a debate Paul won—but in the world's view, lost.

Still today, this is the great challenge. How can we as pastors and Christian leaders make such a compelling case for salvation in Christ that people will be persuaded to accept it? The most important decision people will ever make is not who will be president, but where they will spend eternity. This is one debate we dare not lose. But you knew that!

"Jesus answered, 'I am the way and the truth and the life. No one comes to the Father except through me'" (John 14:6).

Investing in Your Children

I read somewhere the following words: "A son will forgive his father for almost anything if the son can hear—in whatever way, at whatever age—his dad's genuine affirmation."

I have two sons who do two things much better than I did as their father. They spend a lot of quality time with their children, and they talk often to them. Next in importance to one's walk with the Lord is the effort we fathers make to become part of the life of our families. I know how difficult it is to find balance, but the investment you make in the "first family" of your congregation will have eternal ramifications.

Do you have any unresolved issues you need to address with your family? Have you told your kids lately that you love them, that you're proud of them? Have you affirmed them? And one last thing, have you shown your children in word and deed just how much you love their mother?

A couple of thoughts to consider: "Listen, my son, to your father's instruction" (Proverbs 1:8) and "Fathers, do not embitter your children, or they will become discouraged" (Colossians 3:21).

Your Spouse's Relationship with the Church

Unfortunately and unfairly, the impression your spouse makes on the congregation can greatly impact your effectiveness. That is a lot of pressure. So, I ask you two questions:

One: What do you do as a pastor to take the pressure off your spouse?

Two: How have you encouraged your spouse to find an emotional outlet beyond the church?

Forty percent of the calls on Focus on the Family's Pastoral Care Line come from spouses. Many of those calls reflect anger, frustration, concern, and despair.

Pastor, have you taken time lately to thank your partner in ministry for his or her support? Have you attempted to help them find fulfillment by using their best gifts rather than simply handling chores pressed upon them by others?

There is a great deal of pain in the lives of many spouses. We must take the initiative and show genuine concern. Where would we be without them?

"The LORD God said, 'It is not good for the man to be alone. I will make a helper suitable for him'" (Genesis 2:18).

Representing the One
Who Called You

As I was settling in on a plane for a flight from Colorado Springs to Denver, I looked out my window and saw the massive form of Air Force One waiting to take President George W. Bush to his next appointment. He had just addressed the graduating class at the Air Force Academy. As we waited past the scheduled time of our departure, the pilot announced that we would be held at the gate for an undetermined amount of time because we were waiting for the president to depart. I was waiting on the president. Wow!

You and I will never reach the lofty position of president, and it is unlikely that an entire flight will ever be asked to wait just because of us. But we have been called to the honorable office of pastor. It is an office that deserves the respect of the people we serve, not because of who we are, but because of the One we represent, the One who called us. However, as we represent our Lord in this special way, we are held to a higher standard.

"Do not neglect your gift, which was given you through a prophetic message when the body of elders laid their hands on you" (1 Timothy 4:14).

What Makes a Good Sermon?

I remember hearing someone say, "If all speakers were laid end to end they would be much more comfortable." The point is that the world is full of people who want to make a speech. But do all those who want to speak have anything of consequence to say? Good question.

You're a speaker. What makes a speech or sermon interesting to you? So often, content is lost in rhetoric, and style is substituted for substance. What makes a good sermon? Thanks for asking.

Here it is:

Connection with the audience

Straight-line content (few rabbit trails)

Supporting Scripture

Meaningful illustrations

Believable emotion and gestures

Humor that is appropriate

Humility that is both vulnerable and transparent

Grasp of the subject matter

An obvious anointing from God that began in prayer and study

Eye contact with limited pacing (a distraction)

Ability to end the sermon effectively and on time

A concluding action assignment (invitation, direction, application, correction, etc.)

There are many more ingredients I could list, but the ones I have shared came instantly to mind. My dad, who was a master pulpiteer, counseled me this way. He would say, "Junior, if you want to connect with your congregation, don't use notes, speak 25 minutes or less, and use humor." He did all of those things very effectively. Who of your colleagues most influences you in sermon delivery? And why is that?

"When they heard him [Paul] speak to them in Aramaic, they became very quiet" (Acts 22:2).

Let's Be Positive!

In a world where it is much easier to be negative than positive, to be critical rather than uplifting, I have a suggestion: Let's be positive!

For instance:

- How can we call the most people to a renewed prayer life?
- How can we help our people respond when they hear that nearly 40 percent of our country's population is unchurched?
- How can we convince our people to forgive and start over with a new slate of love and acceptance?
- Is there a weakness in your own life or character that you could begin right now to assess and adjust for the better?
- Have you dared to pursue your dreams?
- Are you living boldly and recklessly for the cause of Christ? Or do you play it safe? Go for it!
- And finally, have you positioned yourself for the long haul?

"So then, let us not be like others, who are asleep, but let us be alert and self-controlled" (1 Thessalonians 5:6).

The Unexpected

I have been witness to many events that suddenly and forever changed the lives of those involved. One moment, life was normal—the next, it was not.

Suddenly! The world is complicated and, at times, laced with fear. Suddenly, a baby dies. Suddenly, a marriage is over. Suddenly, a job is lost. Suddenly, a diagnosis is made. Suddenly, a ministry ends.

Yet, on the other hand, "suddenly," can be positive and liberating. Suddenly, a baby is born. Suddenly, a marriage is reconciled. Suddenly, there is good news. Suddenly, a ministry is given new hope.

How do we as clergy react to those moments in our personal and professional lives when we are confronted with the unexpected? Are we ever really prepared for such times?

I would suggest that one can better cope with "sudden moments" when one is living consistently close to the Lord. I would further suggest that the rain and the sunshine touch all of us. I am reminded that this world is fallen, and we are admonished to be thankful regardless of the situation. I believe we can be assured that the circumstances of our lives—difficult or pleasant—in no way change how God feels about us. I also know life is tough, and often the greater witness for our Lord is in times of adversity.

So we say with confidence, "The Lord is my helper; I will not be afraid. What can man [suddenly] do to me?" (Hebrews 13:6).

Advice from Reverend Billy Graham

In October 1959, Rev. Billy Graham visited Christian Theological Seminary in Indianapolis. A report said he spent time with the students and faculty and shared the following:

- Be sure you maintain a personal encounter with Christ. (The blind can't lead the blind.)
- Be sure you've had a call from God.
- Have systematic daily devotions. (You need at least a half hour alone with God daily, said Rev. Graham. At the time of the report, he was reading five psalms a day to learn how to get along with God and one proverb on how to get along with people.)
- Have a consuming love for others. Show compassion by entering into their emotions.
- Be sure you have a message to preach. With authority, simplicity, and urgency, preach to a decision.
- Be an example. Back up your spoken witness with your life.

There are some principles of ministry and pastoral discipline that never change, nor should they.

The call to full-time Christian service is not a sprint; it is a marathon. We just cannot allow ourselves the luxury of complacency. We must endure to the end. Don't ever give up!

"But you, keep your head in all situations, endure hardship, do the work of an evangelist, discharge all the duties of your ministry" (2 Timothy 4:5).

A "State of Our Church" Summary

Do you deliver a "state of our church" summary each year? If so, what does your message entail?

The Bible presents a template for us to consider. How does your congregation or organization measure up to the following?

Acts 2:43—"Many wonders and miraculous signs were done by the apostles."

Acts 2:44—"All the believers were together and had everything in common."

Acts 2:47—"The Lord added to their number daily those who were being saved."

1 Thessalonians 5:12-13—"Respect those who work hard among you, who are over you in the Lord and who admonish you. Hold them in the highest regard in love because of their work."

1 Thessalonians 5:19, 22—"Do not put out the Spirit's fire. . . . Avoid every kind of evil."

Ephesians 5:27—"Present [to Him] . . . a radiant church, without stain or wrinkle or any other blemish, but holy and blameless."

Perhaps it borders on the ideal in our fickle world, but the goal is worthy, don't you agree? May the state of your church and home be blessed!

Jesus Christ said, "I will build my church" (Matthew 16:18).

Facing Contention

I hear more and more reports of conflict in the local church. It is painful for me to see eager colleagues literally fighting for their ministerial lives while Satan sits back and smiles at the limited progress most churches are making.

I also know that type-A personalities like me feel the need to win most of the time. The truth is, we really need to learn how to choose our battles better. I made some big mistakes by thinking I would lose face in my assignment if I did not get my way.

There are three questions we need to ask ourselves when we are facing an issue or a project that we care about: (1) What does God want? (2) How does He want to accomplish it? (3) What will He use to fulfill His desire?

So many conflicts could be avoided if we would first assure ourselves, and then our people, that the issue at hand is critical to the kingdom. Does it really matter, or is it just something I want? Is it a hill I am willing to die on?

So, what battles are you fighting that are of little consequence? What is causing you grief and anxiety? What would you be willing to let go of? Do you have someone in your life whom you would trust to help you choose your battles?

In his end-of-the-age message, Jesus said, "I will give you words and wisdom" (Luke 21:15).

"When pride comes, then comes disgrace, but with humility comes wisdom" (Proverbs 11:2).

Providing Stability
in the Church

For a lot of years now, I have attempted to point the laypeople of our churches to 1 Thessalonians 5:12-13, "Now we ask you, brothers, to respect those who work hard among you, who are over you in the Lord and who admonish you. Hold them in the highest regard in love because of their work. Live in peace with each other."

These words make a great deal of sense to me, but unfortunately, I am afraid the admonition from Paul has not been widely heeded. In fact, near the top of the list of calls that come in to the Focus on the Family Pastoral Care Line are ones concerning division in the local church. It has been proved that constant contention leads to decreased productivity, and that is a bad thing.

Paul wrote to Titus, "Warn a divisive person once, and then warn him a second time. After that, have nothing to do with him. You may be sure that such a man is warped and sinful" (Titus 3:10-11). I realize that is strong language, but some way, somehow, the local church must put division aside and concentrate on the mission our Lord has for us.

"Warn them before God against quarreling about words; it is of no value, and only ruins those who listen. Do your best to present yourself to God as one approved, a workman who does not need to be ashamed and who correctly handles the word of truth" (2 Timothy 2:14-15).

Let Not Your Walk
Be Lonely

Loneliness is, as Merriam-Webster defines it, "the quality or state of being without company."

You or I might define it as "the feeling of isolation and emptiness when faced with a task or situation."

Believe me, I know that feeling—and so do you. I am sure, for example, that you have felt loneliness when, for some reason, a parishioner rejected your love and decided to walk away. As pastors, most of us have stood beside the bed of a terminally ill child or young adult and felt the burden of their mortality. We wanted to do something—anything—to change the outcome. But we could only stand by helplessly, watching and praying.

Then there are the times when loneliness occurs because of personal failure. We say the wrong thing. We do not fully count the cost of our decisions or actions. We attempt to mend a wound, but find out too late we can't.

And, of course, we often experience loneliness as we make our own spiritual pilgrimages, frequently feeling estranged from the God we love so much. Our prayers seem hollow, the Word does not radiate, and our message to those around us is tepid at best.

There will be times of loneliness and isolation in your life, guaranteed. But God is always ready to fill the empty spaces in your heart. As the psalmist has written, "My eyes are ever on the LORD, for only he will release my feet from the snare. Turn to me and be gracious to me, for I am lonely and afflicted. The troubles of my heart have multiplied; free me from my anguish" (Psalm 25:15-17).

Practical Advice for When You're Lonely

So what do you do when you're lonely? Here are some questions to contemplate:

- Have you considered all aspects of your circumstances, your motives, and your attitudes? Is there any selfishness on your part?

- Is this something you can share with a spiritual mentor or friend? There are times when we find solace in our own pain. We take an odd comfort in believing things are more difficult than we can handle. Often, by sharing our need with a trusted friend, a whole new perspective emerges.

- Do you need to get away? Perhaps you need to put everything aside and take a walk, hit a golf ball, or go for a ride—anything that will take your mind off yourself and the issue at hand.

- Do you need some downtime? We all know fatigue can cause us to see life through windows that are cloudy and frightening. Are you getting enough rest? What if you could just sleep for one whole day? I know it's not very easy, but an occasional sick day works wonders.

- Are you seeking the Lord's comfort? Use devotional readings or inspirational music to facilitate His soothing ministry to your soul. In some of my darkest times, a song or a beautiful chorus has proven to be just the tonic I needed to keep on keeping on.

- Have you neglected your time alone with the Lord? One of the great fears I have as a pastor to pastors is that I or one of my colleagues will walk into spiritual warfare without the necessary protection to stand firm against the enemy.

"In my distress I called to the LORD; I called out to my God. From his temple he heard my voice; my cry came to his ears" (2 Samuel 22:7).

May God Have Mercy on the Church

I took a moment to look up the word *mercy* and found, among the many definitions, "compassion or forbearance shown to an offender or to one subject to one's power." Another reads, "implies compassion that forbears punishing even when justice demands it" (*Merriam-Webster's Dictionary*).

Have you, in one of your quiet moments, prayed this prayer of the distraught Episcopalian bishop: "May God have mercy on His church"? As one of my colleagues says, we are sometimes guilty of "shaking our fist in the face of God."

A pastor friend once prayed, "Purge the church, O God, from blandness, blindness, burliness, and bleakness. Deliver her leaders from casualness, timidity, mediocrity, hypocrisy, hesitation, and indecision. Let the church catch the vision of the gospel's power, a changed world . . . and miracles performed." Amen!

"All the paths of the LORD are mercy and truth unto such as keep his covenant and his testimonies" (Psalm 25:10, KJV). May God have mercy.

A Perspective on Suffering

Years ago I received a letter from Vonette Bright, the wife of Bill Bright—founder of Campus Crusade for Christ International. She wrote of Dr. Bright's declining physical condition.

In the letter, she related a conversation she had with Bill and a question she asked him: "Why do you think you're suffering? Why would God put you through this?" Bill's immediate reply was, "I'm not suffering! It depends on the definition of suffering. Even grasping for breath for extended periods of time does not compare with what Christ went through during his trial and crucifixion. He had six hours suffocating on the cross. Think about Peter being crucified head downward, Paul's persecution and finally being beheaded. All the disciples were persecuted and martyred, except John who was exiled." Dr. Bright continued, "What I am going through is very minor. Suffering is a matter of perspective. It is not pleasant . . . but God allows only so much."

Later, when Dr. Bright's blood oxygen level dropped to a dangerously low level, he asked his wife to read from 1 Peter: "These trials are only to test your faith, to show that it is strong and pure. It is being tested as fire tests and purifies gold—and your faith is far more precious to God than mere gold" (1 Peter 1:7, NLT). Hold on to your faith, my colleague—hold on! It's a matter of perspective.

"And the God of all grace, who called you to his eternal glory in Christ, after you have suffered a little while, will himself restore you and make you strong, firm and steadfast" (1 Peter 5:10).

Never Settle for Things as They Are

The "I Have a Dream" speech by Dr. Martin Luther King Jr. stirs me every time I hear it. Why? Because of the simple concept that all of us need a dream. We need to reach beyond our grasp and trust God for that which seems impossible. Stop dreaming and settle for things as they are, and soon your ministry will become mundane and ordinary. We must never allow challenges, pressures, and failures to destroy our ability to dream.

What is your dream? Can you articulate it? Have you written it down? Have you shared it with those you trust? Dreams many times parallel our faith.

In Genesis 37:19-20, there are simple but profound words related to Joseph and the brothers who hated him. " 'Here comes that dreamer!' they said to each other. 'Come now, let's kill him and throw him into one of these cisterns and say that a ferocious animal devoured him. Then we'll see what comes of his dreams.' " Much of the world, and especially the evil one, would be delighted if you gave up on your dream. Don't do it! Embrace it and live it.

"He gives strength to the weary and increases the power of the weak" (Isaiah 40:29).

Expressing Gratitude

Dr. Gene Getz, pastor of Fellowship Bible Church in the Dallas area, made the point that we all need to express gratitude to those who have helped mold our lives as clergypersons. It really resonated with me.

Many of the men and women I have known through the years who have invested in me and my education are church leaders who gave me a chance. How about you? Who are the people in your life who impressed you, guided you, mentored you, advised you? There could be many. Or maybe just one or two. Regardless, all of us are the recipients of someone's attention.

When was the last time you thanked those people? Where would you be without them? Have you corresponded with them lately? Maintaining right relationships is so important. I urge you to make a telephone call, send an e-mail or fax, or write a letter to that special person. Be specific—walk down the trail of remembrance and point out just how much that special person has meant to you.

One of the things I am most thankful for is my influencers. How about you? Now, go make that call or write that note . . . please!

"I always thank my God as I remember you" (Philemon 1:4).

A Godly Legacy

Some years ago, I was invited to Shreveport, Louisiana, to participate in the 65th anniversary of a church Dr. Dobson's and my grandparents planted. It was a marvelous experience.

Through good times and bad this church's faith has remained strong. Time and time again references were made to our grandparents—the Dillinghams—and their legacy that has carried on through more than six decades.

I stood at my grandparents' grave site and thanked God for my heritage and the godly influence they displayed. They were never famous people. I don't believe they wrote books or experienced fame beyond the churches they pastored. But they had a passion for the lost souls in their town, and a heart for people that was contagious.

In reality, that is where most of our legacy, what we do for God, will be played out—where we have been placed. I beg you not to downplay your value by attempting to estimate your own success. Just remain faithful. I promise you that your contribution will not go unnoticed by the One who matters most.

"Know therefore that the LORD your God is God; he is the faithful God, keeping his covenant of love to a thousand generations of those who love him and keep his commands" (Deuteronomy 7:9).

The Importance
of a Quiet Place

I think everyone—especially you, my colleague—needs a quiet place. Where is yours?

A quiet place? Yes, a spot where you can withdraw from the busyness of your assignment and recoup. A place where you can listen to music or read and study. Somewhere—a place of your own—where the noises of the world are drowned out by the quiet of the Lord's presence. A stopping place.

Where is your quiet place? It need not be a destination point. It could be in a park near your home, or the city library, or a spot you have chosen on the coast, or at a lake. Somewhere free of distractions and interruptions where you just walk and talk with the Lord.

The psalmist talked of "still waters." Jesus called his disciples to the other side of the lake. Peter went fishing.

I have not had many quiet places in my ministry. But this week, for a few hours, I was reminded how much I needed one. Where is your quiet place?

"But Jesus often withdrew to lonely places and prayed" (Luke 5:16).

"When Jesus heard what had happened, he withdrew by boat privately to a solitary place" (Matthew 14:13).

Welcoming Newcomers

I have learned that without fellowship (*koinonia*) or a place to belong—where people know your name and are glad to see you—church attendance can be bland and impersonal.

I once visited a well-established church in our community for the first time. I put myself in the place of a new attendee. I was a stranger, and it was scary. There was the perfunctory greeter who shook my hand while talking to someone else. An usher, protective of his aisle, handed me a bulletin. I took another aisle and sat in the middle of a pew near one more lonely soul. I was inundated with announcements I had already read while waiting for the service to begin. At the appropriate time, we were encouraged to greet those in our vicinity (the other lonely person)—limp handshakes all around. Then we sang, the pastor preached, and we sang again. After the benediction, I waited my turn for the aisle to clear, then I walked to my car wondering what had just happened. No one had said a word to me.

Lonely in a crowd is how I felt. On the drive home, I was haunted by the thought of how many people had gone in and out of my church—your church—without sincere notice, and never returned.

How do you welcome newcomers? Do you have folks on the lookout for first timers? Without *koinonia*, going to church can prove pretty empty.

"Do not forget to entertain strangers, for by so doing some people have entertained angels without knowing it" (Hebrews 13:2).

Ten Commandments for Preachers

These are Martin Luther's "10 Commandments for Preachers." They sound familiar:

(1) Teach so people can follow you.

(2) Have a good sense of humor.

(3) Be able to speak well.

(4) Have a good voice.

(5) Have a good memory.

(6) Know when to stop.

(7) Be sure of your doctrine.

(8) Be ready to sacrifice all to the Word of God.

(9) Suffer oneself to be mocked and jeered at by all.

(10) Be ready to accept patiently the fact that nothing is seen more quickly in preachers than their faults.

Sounds like great advice for all of us regardless of our denomination. Don't you agree?

"Preach the Word; be prepared in season and out of season; correct, rebuke and encourage—with great patience and careful instruction" (2 Timothy 4:2).

Respecting Ethical Sexual Boundaries

Dr. Roy Woodruff, former head of the Association of Pastoral Counselors, says, "A majority of sexual scandals in the Protestant church involve male pastors and female parishioners." He estimates that about 15 percent of Protestant pastors have either violated or are currently violating sexual ethical boundaries. On our Pastoral Care Line at Focus on the Family, we hear of these violations all the time. The result is normally devastating for all parties—especially the victim. Woodruff suggests that all pastors should take steps to avoid temptation by: (1) having accountability partners and (2) setting limits on counseling females. (I would add males, too.) Great advice! A ChristianityToday.com article states, "Evangelicals cannot afford to pretend that we are immune to sexual sin by clergy." In my opinion, youth leaders and workers are especially at risk. My advice: take every precaution. Do not find all of your validation in counseling. Do not counsel in private. Do not expose your weaknesses to your client. Do not think for a moment that you can change anyone. Do not forget the consequences of your actions. Do not forget you are an expression of Christ. That should save you a great deal of pain. *Be very careful!*

"Flee from sexual immorality. All other sins a man commits are outside his body, but he who sins sexually sins against his own body. Do you not know that your body is a temple of the Holy Spirit, who is in you, whom you have received from God? You are not your own; you were bought at a price. Therefore honor God with your body" (1 Corinthians 6:18-20).

A Passion for the Lost

What impressed me most about a discussion I once had with Franklin Graham was his great passion for the lost and his sincere belief that we are not giving our people enough opportunity to seek and meet the Savior. What he said made good sense to me.

If my math is correct, approximately 7,200 people die each day in the United States. How many of them are ready to die? How many have been given the opportunity to accept Christ and prepare for eternity?

According to figures we have shared before on Parsonage.org, nearly 50 percent of those who sit in your church service do not have a personal relationship with Jesus. Do you see this fact as an opportunity to give them that chance? Is there something you could do at the conclusion of your message this week that would challenge your attendees to seek the Lord? Would you consider an altar call—even in this seeker-sensitive world? I urge you to give some kind of invitation to attendees to embrace Jesus. Give them a chance!

I still believe that the bottom line for every individual fellowship and church organization should be, "Is anybody being saved here?" Every 12 seconds, another person enters into eternity. That is sobering!

Romans 10:13 says, "Everyone who calls on the name of the Lord [Jesus Christ] will be saved."

Taking Time to Slow Down

Do you remember the slogan "Kodak moment"? It's an attempt to capture an important event in one's life, to freeze-frame it in such a way that it will last forever. If we in ministry are not more careful, even the most significant moments in our lives will move so quickly across our horizons that we will soon forget them.

We need more "Kodak moments"—when life stops for a while and we enjoy, laugh, and encourage one another. When we look through the windows of God's blessings and rejoice, letting time stand still.

I'm making an office call today to see how you're doing physically. Are you getting enough sleep? Are you taking a day off each week? Are you using your vacation time? Are you spending time with your family? Are you getting some exercise?

Come on, guys and ladies. Make necessary changes as soon as possible. Why? Because the Lord has made a huge investment in you for the kingdom's sake.

My plea to you is please do not let your schedule or your circumstances rob you of your most precious possessions—your faith, your family, and your health. Let's slow it down a bit.

The psalmist said, "You have made my days a mere handbreadth" (Psalm 39:5).

Clergy Culture

I have, for some time, been concerned about the culture of the clergy in the United States. When I see a list of the 25 most prominent evangelicals or the 100 most influential pastors, it concerns me. That's because it creates pride in some and a desire on the part of others to qualify for such a list.

Who is to judge who should occupy these lists? The words of Micah the prophet resound loudly to me: "What does the LORD require of you? To act justly and to love mercy and to walk humbly with your God" (6:8). Somehow I doubt that God keeps a top 100 list.

We in the ministry must keep everything in perspective. Too much power and the lack of genuine accountability are two things that can bring down a gifted clergyperson. Hear the words of Moses: "Be careful that you do not forget the LORD your God, failing to observe his commands, his laws and his decrees" (Deuteronomy 8:11). He says that when you have success, there is the danger of becoming "proud" (v. 14) and forgetting to whom you are accountable. Then you might be tempted to say, "My power and the strength of my hands have produced this wealth [success]" (v. 17).

Big mistake!

We really need a colleague to keep us honest, and we need a trusted family member who has permission to speak the truth in love to us. Do you have people in your life like that? I pray so! Why? Because pride is deadly and very lonely.

Walk humbly, my brothers and sisters.

"The fear of the LORD teaches a man wisdom, and humility comes before honor" (Proverbs 15:33).

It Is God Who Calls Us

One year I attended a conference with officers from the Massachusetts Division of the Salvation Army. What a great group they are! On the front of their conference schedule was a simple verse titled "God Made Pastors." I don't know who the author is, but here's how it goes:

"God gave them tender hearts, to hold the hurts of others. He gave them gentle hands, to reach out with compassion and love. God gave them eyes to see the beauty and worth of a single soul. He gave them feet to move swiftly, to pursue justice, restoration and peace.

"God had His hand upon them—and breathed hope into their spirits.

"He filled them with His strength, and placed a message of urgency around their lives. God challenged them to greater works than He had ever done. Then, with His own hand of blessing, He wrapped them up in His mantle of love . . . and called them pastors."

Kind of nice, huh? God called you. He asked you to fill a spot, to carry a cross, to respond to an assignment that was exclusively yours. Thank you for your response.

Paul wrote to the church in Ephesus, "It was he who gave some to be . . . evangelists, and some to be pastors and teachers, to prepare God's people for works of service, so that the body of Christ may be built up" (Ephesians 4:11-12). That verse has your name all over it. Please don't overlook the fact that what you are doing for Christ and the church is no accident. I challenge you to live like the called-out one God created you to be. Blessings, my colleague!

"As a prisoner for the Lord, then, I urge you to live a life worthy of the calling you have received" (Ephesians 4:1).

Dance, Love, Sing, and Live!

William Purkey wrote, "Dance like no one is watching, love like you'll never be hurt, sing like no one is listening, live like it's heaven on earth." I'm a bit unsure of the theology, but challenged by the words.

So many of us as clergypersons are filled with worry and anxiety. Much of the way we live is on the defensive, and at times we forget that this world is not the end, only a short stop along our eternal journey.

Our Lord told us there would be tribulation, but that we should not despair. He is in charge. Trust God! In spite of the chaos around us, we must face each day with hope and promise. Be positive! Job cried, "Why have you made me your target?" (Job 7:20), but later exclaimed, "Though he slay me, yet will I hope in him" (Job 13:15). Do not despair! In Jeremiah, the Lord says, "For I know the plans I have for you . . . plans to give you hope and a future" (Jeremiah 29:11).

He has it all figured out. So, my colleague, in the Spirit of Christ—dance, love, sing, and live.

"Do not worry about your life. . . . Who of you by worrying can add a single hour to his life? . . . Therefore do not worry about tomorrow, for tomorrow will worry about itself" (Matthew 6:25, 27, 34).

Dealing with Grief

What do you tell your people when they have lost a loved one or suffered some major reversal? You tell them to manage their grief—never to become bitter. You urge them to remember the past—to take from it the beautiful pictures and apply them to their hearts. You tell them to trust in God—that when the unexplainable happens, He is never caught by surprise. You tell them to walk by faith, not by sight, into the unknown. You tell them that the world can destroy the flowers, but not the power that gave them life—they will grow again. You tell them, as Paul writes, to "examine yourselves" in times of distress. You urge them to hold their head up and live life in the sunshine rather than the gloom of disappointment.

How do we best help our parishioners handle grief? Here are some further suggestions from the Focus on the Family booklet *Good Grief: A Healthy, Courageous Response to Loss.*

1. Identify what you have lost—How has the loss affected your life?
2. Touch your pain—Attend a memorial service. Send a note. Call someone who is directly affected.
3. Tell your story—Conveying your feelings to others can bring a deeper healing.
4. Deal with regrets—Sometimes we have false guilt when others die or are injured. Clear up any differences you might have with someone else.
5. Don't bury your resentments—Talk about your anger. Recognize evil.
6. Take a break—Don't think about your grief all the time. Do other things.
7. Look forward—We can grieve, but not forever.

" 'Though the mountains be shaken and the hills be removed, yet my unfailing love for you will not be shaken nor my covenant of peace be removed,' says the LORD, who has compassion on you" (Isaiah 54:10).

Encouraging Other Pastors

I was walking through the airport in Denver and I heard my name paged. At first, I didn't respond, but when I heard it again, I dialed the operator. I was instructed to go to the information desk in Concourse B for a message. The attendant there handed me an envelope with my name on it. When I opened the enclosed card, the words "I prayed for you today" were in bold type at the top. The handwritten message that followed the printed one also blessed me: "Thank you for your ministry to pastors all over the nation. May God bless you richly this day! Thank you for letting God work through you." It was not signed.

I was on my way to a very challenging ministry assignment and believe the Lord knew I needed someone to say to me, "It's going to be okay . . . Just be yourself."

As I reflected on that situation, I thought, "How creative of someone to take the time to encourage me and to do it anonymously." And then I thought, "When was the last time I walked into someone's life unannounced . . . just to say thanks?"

There are so many of your colleagues who could use a note or a call this very day—something that lets them know they are not alone. How about taking a few moments to encourage someone.

"But we ought always to thank God for you" (2 Thessalonians 2:13).

I Can Do Everything
Through Christ

One of the most dramatic moments of the 2000 Olympics occurred when American Laura Wilkinson came from far behind to win the gold medal in the 10m platform dive. No one had given her a chance. When Andrea Joyce of NBC asked her to put into words the emotion she was feeling, Laura said, "I can do all things through Christ who strengthens me." Then the reporter asked her, "How much beyond your expectations was this?" The young lady responded, "At first, I thought it was impossible. But I just wanted to go out there and dive for God, for everybody, for everybody who ever dreamed." Wow!

Remember when the apostle Paul penned those words? He was in prison, cold, sick, and lonely. He was writing about his circumstances. In the mind of most, he was in an impossible situation. Most would have looked at the overwhelming odds against him and given up—but not Paul, and not Laura Wilkinson. Paul would exclaim, "I can do everything through him who gives me strength" (Philippians 4:13).

You may be in an impossible situation today. You're tempted to say, "What's the use? It's hopeless." Not so, my colleague. Please never forget you serve an awesome God who loves you and knows your needs. You, too, can be a come-from-behind winner. You can because He can!

"For nothing is impossible with God" (Luke 1:37).

Don't Look Back with Regret

Years ago, when I was a guest on the Focus on the Family radio program, Dr. Dobson and I shared some family memories (we are cousins; our dads were pastors), but most of the broadcast was about an interview I'd had a year earlier with my oldest son, Brad. We were taping a Pastor to Pastor segment on pastors' kids, and, as our conversation unfolded, Brad shared some of his honest feelings about our relationship when he was a young boy. It was an awesome moment for both of us. The revealed truth is that, as a young pastor and father, I was driven to succeed at the expense of my family. To this day, those memories haunt me.

Why these words? Because I care about you. Because it's easy to let the years slip by and the relationships grow stale or distant. Because you may have children who are uncomfortable in their roles living under a pastor's roof. Because there is no greater ministry than the one to your spouse and children. Because it may have been some time since you stopped to affirm and express love and appreciation to those who matter most to you. Because I want you to be able to look back a few years from now with joy rather than regret.

After the broadcast, one of my colleagues at Focus on the Family said, "I'm going home early today and spend some extra time with my kids." Not a bad idea.

"Fathers, do not exasperate your children; instead, bring them up in the training and instruction of the Lord" (Ephesians 6:4).

Just Do It!

A few years ago, a colleague in our division at Focus on the Family walked into my office and said, "H. B., I just talked to my physician, and I have made an appointment with him for you to get a physical." I had not had a proper physical examination for years, and I panicked at the thought. But I did it, and am I glad I did! I was given a clean bill of health, but even more important than that, I now had a doctor with my records—and a benchmark for future examinations. If my friend had not cared enough for me to insist, I would still be guessing.

Now, I care enough about you to ask, "When was your last physical?" Do you know your blood pressure? Have you had a stress test recently? Have you been screened for cancer? What is your cholesterol count? Have you had a body scan for any precancerous skin problems that need to be cared for? Have you talked to your parents or grandparents about any physical challenges in your family that you should be aware of? Do you have a personal physician who understands the stresses of your assignment?

I know I sound like I'm nagging, and I'm sure not one to talk. My results could have been so different. My biggest problems were the fear of the unknown and just not taking time.

P.S. Recently in a routine stress test, doctors discovered a blockage in the main artery of my heart and placed a stent in that artery to relieve the blockage. I'm glad I saw my doctor, and I hope you'll see yours soon. Please consider my request and make an appointment!

"I pray that you may enjoy good health and that all may go well with you, even as your soul is getting along well" (3 John 1:2).

Take a Vacation—Really

Since I'm on the subject of health, I want to remind you to take some uninterrupted time off to be with your family. As a pastor for three decades, I didn't do much vacationing. I would kind of pop in and out of those occasions, often interrupting our family times to go marry or bury someone. Or I would use my allotted vacation days to preach at a youth camp or a revival somewhere. When the summer ended, I was often more weary than when it began. In short, I robbed everyone in my family (including me) of valuable time together. What was I thinking?

I still find it difficult to totally "let down." I call the office a lot, bug the staff too often, and am very restless during my first few days away. It's only when the vacation comes to an end that I am finally ready to do some serious relaxing. One day I'll get it right.

My heartfelt warning to you is, don't do as I did. Treat yourself and your family fairly. Make the most of those opportunities to really get away, to refresh and retool. You will be a better servant-shepherd if you do. If you don't, you will pay a price . . . guaranteed!

"He gives strength to the weary and increases the power of the weak" (Isaiah 40:29).

Appreciating God's Small Wonders

As a pastor to pastors, I see a lot of pain and discouragement. One pastor said to me a while back, "If it were just a jungle out there, I could handle that, but it's worse than a jungle!" He was probably having a pretty rough day, but the truth is, there are many things in the ministry that take a toll on us—so much so that, if we are not careful, we can miss the blessings and overlook the joy.

Henri Nouwen writes in his book *The Return of the Prodigal Son*, "I am not accustomed to rejoicing in things that are small, hidden, and scarcely noticed by the people around me. . . . I have become accustomed to living with sadness and so have lost the eyes to see the joy."

Life will do that to us if we are not careful, and when it does, we will become calloused and cynical. If that ever happens, we need to step back, take a look at our motivation, and ask God to forgive us.

The roads I travel take me to places where my brothers are struggling with the "what ifs" more than the "why nots." They have permitted the naysayers and the joy suckers to influence their emotions and responses. They have overlooked their blessings.

My colleague, please be aware of God's small wonders. Look around you with eyes open and heart ready to receive even the simplest pleasures. When you do, you will be a vessel of happiness to those you encounter.

"Rejoice in the Lord always. I will say it again: Rejoice!" (Philippians 4:4).

Declare the Message
with Clarity and Passion

The American church has money. She has talent and exposure. She has massive buildings and gifted leadership. She knows how to get her message out better than ever before. She has variety and acceptance. She speaks nearly every language, and her story is in print virtually around the world. Men and women attend to her every need. It would seem that the church would say, "Oh, don't bother. I have everything I need." But not so.

The church needs a cleansing. She is not as radiant as she should be. She is stained, wrinkled, and blemished. She desires to be holy and blameless (Ephesians 5:27). She calls for her pastors to be faithful and bold, and to proclaim her message with clarity and passion. She cries for her members to love one another and cast aside those things that divide. She weeps over the multitudes around the world who know about her, but don't really know her. She longs for a revival of the apathetic, and a stirring of the comfortable. Why? Because she is aware the time is short, and whether they know it or not, the people of the world desperately need her.

What can you give the church? Yourself—in a renewed commitment to her cause and her message. For God so loved the world . . .

"Be diligent in these matters; give yourself wholly to them, so that everyone may see your progress. Watch your life and doctrine closely. Persevere in them, because if you do, you will save both yourself and your hearers" (1 Timothy 4:15-16).

Hearing the Concerns
of Your People

I believe that the people in your church—those under your care—want to know you. And they want you to know and hear them. So many congregations are wrapped in a black cloak of contention because they have few opportunities to ask questions of their leaders. More and more of America's clergy are retreating behind closed doors rather than walking in the village and hearing the concerns of their people.

I know we can use up a lot of energy dealing with troublesome members, but I also know your people have a right within reason to access you, your staff, and your other church leaders. In my dealings with church boards, I've often felt they could overcome many congregational struggles if they would just make themselves available to those who want to know how the budget is being spent, why the music style has been changed, or why a staff associate has been released.

I know this will add a few hours to your week, but I also know good communication can add years to your ministry. Do your people feel listened to? Do they have access to you and your staff? Do the leaders of your congregation clearly communicate what's being done and why? Maybe it's time for a town hall meeting!

"And all the believers lived in a wonderful harmony, holding everything in common. . . . They followed a daily discipline of worship in the Temple followed by meals at home, every meal a celebration, exuberant and joyful, as they praised God. People in general liked what they saw. Every day their number grew as God added those who were saved" (Acts 2:44, 46–47, MSG).

The Joy Meter

In the book of Hebrews are words written to a group of people about their pastors: "Obey them so that their work will be a joy, not a burden" (Hebrews 13:17).

I thought a bit about what that phrase really means, "joy, not a burden." I'm sure it does not mean people are just to be robot yes-men to their pastors. Rather, they are to honor the calling of their pastors and conduct themselves in a way that brings joy to pastoring.

What would make ministry joyful for you?
- People who continue to show growth in their walk with the Lord.
- People who have a genuine concern for their brothers and sisters in the faith.
- People who do not turn a deaf ear to the lost.
- People who walk by faith and not by sight.
- People who pray rather than faint.
- People who are drawn to peace rather than contention.
- People whose self-image is based on who they are in Christ rather than what they accomplish by themselves.
- People who pass the torch of righteousness to the next generation.
- People who love the church and give themselves to it.

I think each of us has a "joy meter." Please don't let yours be based on what happens around you more than on your contentment in Christ and the job He has given you to do. *Rejoice!*

"Be joyful in hope, patient in affliction, faithful in prayer" (Romans 12:12).

Making It Relevant

I am sincere when I admonish you to stay positive—stay pure.

So much negative talk has been directed lately at the church in North America. I, myself, have been guilty of that, but I am convinced it serves no real purpose. Whether the glass is half full or 10 percent full, we need to build on what we have to offer rather than on what we are missing.

There will always be a remnant who would lay down their lives for the church and its values. Many, like Dr. Phillip Hammond from the University of California in Santa Barbara, say, "Traditional Christianity will dwindle . . . but it will never die out." In other words, the world will turn to sources of spiritual guidance outside the realm of mainstream religion, dabbling in Eastern philosophy and New Age belief systems. But many will remain faithful. The challenge we face as clergy is to make our message relevant. Look closely at what you do and how you do it. Love your people. Be a shepherd to them. Get out in the village and refuse to be desk-bound. Watch your life and your doctrine closely. Don't be easily swayed by every new concept. Play to your strength. Preach the Word. And, at any cost, stay pure!

I love you, my colleague. Let's keep our heads up. Remember . . . it is His church.

"Finally, brothers, whatever is true, whatever is noble, whatever is right, whatever is pure, whatever is lovely, whatever is admirable—if anything is excellent or praiseworthy—think about such things" (Philippians 4:8).

Advice for Board Meetings

During my years as a pastor, at least every month I sat in a board meeting. Some meetings were very exciting, others somewhat depressing. But you know all about that.

From all those years of leading boards, I have learned a few things that I want to pass along to you:

- Never enter a meeting without first praying.
- Be in constant communication with your board to sell your vision in less official settings.
- Be willing to compromise on some things. It is not important for you to win on every issue.
- Stay on topic. So many meetings disintegrate when they are allowed to stray off the issue.
- When controversy exists in a meeting, be free to ask, "Is this discussion God-honoring; are our attitudes Christlike?" Don't hesitate to stop in the middle of an issue to pray.
- Treat every member and his or her contribution with respect.
- Make sure each member has ample information to make intelligent decisions.
- Remember it's God's church, not yours; His battle, not yours; His victory, not yours. Go forward!

"For lack of guidance a nation falls, but many advisers make victory sure" (Proverbs 11:14).

Doing the Mundane
with Excellence

Have you ever had a case of the "mundanes"? I woke up the other morning with a feeling of "Oh no . . . here we go again." I faced sameness . . . a day of doing things that would not make much difference even if I didn't do them. But I did them because it was a small part of a larger plan that would make a difference.

We have all used the illustration of Saint Brother Andrew, who centuries ago wrote that he performed his job of washing dishes to the best of his ability to the glory of God.

I know you must have times when you don't seem to accomplish much, when what you do does not get much notice, and when it would appear you are getting nowhere. I want to challenge you to do all you do with excellence. Don't take shortcuts; see very few things as insignificant. So much of what we do is discipline for the soul—even as monotonous physical exercise is discipline for the body.

Most of one's ministry is not meant to be in the glare of the spotlight—and, to be honest, it should not be. Our growth comes from doing the small things, the mundane things, well.

The Word says, "Well done, good and faithful servant! You have been faithful with a few things; I will put you in charge of many things" (Matthew 25:21).

Having Compassion Rather Than Holding Grudges

After the April 1999 shootings at Columbine High School in Littleton, Colorado, I watched with wide-eyed interest as Larry King interviewed, first, the parents of Cassie Bernall, the young lady who died with a testimony on her lips, then, evangelist Billy Graham. The subject was forgiveness. Mr. and Mrs. Bernall had a beautiful spirit that spoke of heartbreak but also empathy for the parents of the boys who murdered their daughter. The peace they modeled was amazing.

Then Billy Graham spoke of the joy one experiences when the decision is made to forgive another. Larry King treated him with such respect.

As I watched the program, I could not help but think of some of you who carry a grudge and live angry lives because someone has mistreated or betrayed you. I could not help but be reminded of the hundreds of churches throughout our nation wracked with contention just because one parishioner will not forgive another. Why do we Christians tolerate that in one another? Why do we let Satan establish such a needless foothold?

Please talk about these things. Tell your people to put down their right to strike back. Let the Bernalls' testimony be a message to all. Please!

"Make a clean break with all cutting, backbiting, profane talk. Be gentle with one another, sensitive. Forgive one another as quickly and thoroughly as God in Christ forgave you" (Ephesians 4:31-32, MSG).

Do You Love Him More Than Your Ministry?

I often preach a sermon based on the conversation between Simon Peter and the resurrected Lord as they walked along the rocky shore of the Sea of Galilee (John 21). It was a reinstatement of the apostle who, in so many ways and on so many occasions, failed Jesus. One portion of John Killinger's book *Christ in the Seasons of Ministry* touched me deeply, for I have failed—and so have you—to measure up to our Savior's expectations. Killinger writes:

"After the stormy night at sea . . . with no fish taken, we come in to the Christ of the open fire, with the fish quietly simmering in a pan, and feel again the excitement that has grabbed at our hearts all of these years. We walk with him along the shore, skipping rocks and thinking of far away places, and hear him ask, probing gently, 'Do you love me?' 'Yes, Lord, you know I do!' 'Feed my sheep.' You can resist a scene like that? I can't . . . 'I turn with disgust from everything to Christ.' Maybe not quite with disgust. But I know what he means. There isn't any comparison."

The Lord often appears in my life, uttering quietly those very same words—"Do you love me? Even more than your own ministry?" At times, I hesitate before I answer, but not for long.

What about you? How would you answer that question?

"Love the Lord your God with all your heart and with all your soul and with all your strength and with all your mind" (Luke 10:27).

Living with Hope

Louisa Tarkington wrote, "I wish that there were some wonderful place called the Land of Beginning Again, where all our mistakes and all our heartaches and all of our poor, selfish grief could be dropped, like a shabby old coat, at the door, and never put on again."

Probably, Ms. Tarkington was having a very bad day when she penned those now famous words. I have also been led to believe that she lived the remainder of her life with a sense of hopelessness. A lot of the people you pastor live like that. They have never really understood that surrender of their mistakes and heartaches to a gracious, merciful Lord is, in reality, the land of beginning again. That according to Isaiah, "he blots out your transgressions . . . and remembers your sins no more" (Isaiah 43:25). Or as David said, "You are God my Savior, and my hope is in you all day long" (Psalm 25:5).

It is so important that you not only preach the message of hope to your congregation, but that you also live in hope before them. Just think what your life would be like if you had not experienced God's grace and mercy—the land of new beginnings. Each Lord's Day presents a prime opportunity to encourage your people to forget and press on (Philippians 3:13-14). I pray that you will do the same.

"May the God of hope fill you with all joy and peace as you trust in him, so that you may overflow with hope by the power of the Holy Spirit" (Romans 15:13).

Hating Hate

In 1998, a confessed gay college student, Matthew Shepard, was savagely beaten, then tied to a ranch fence. He died shortly thereafter. His death sparked hate crime discussions all around the world.

I looked up the word *hate* and found it defined as *detest, abhor, loathe,* and *despise*. All of these words are terrible when focused on another individual. They speak of feelings so strong toward another person that one's actions, words, and attitudes are controlled by them.

Yet the Bible uses the word *hate* to describe both positive and negative reactions. For instance, Jesus said, "All men will hate you because of me" (Luke 21:17). That's a good thing. Paul wrote, "Hate what is evil; cling to what is good" (Romans 12:9). That is a positive emotion. John reminds us that if anyone claims to love God but hates his brother (1 John 4:20), it is unacceptable.

It's the last verse that confuses me. How can any of us who call ourselves by the name of Christ justify feelings so intense that we find ourselves—in mind and body—out of control?

Road rage, spousal abuse, racism, and intolerance are all a part of the human condition. That's a bad thing. Yet, it also exists in the church. I'm afraid as clergy we have tolerated these things in our own congregations. Where sin abides . . . the Spirit will not. Let's "hate hate" in Jesus' name and speak boldly against it!

"If anyone boasts, 'I love God,' and goes right on hating his brother or sister, thinking nothing of it, he is a liar. If he won't love the person he can see, how can he love the God he can't see? The command we have from Christ is blunt: Loving God includes loving people. You've got to love both" (1 John 4:20-21, MSG).

Everlasting Peace

I ponder the words of Jeremiah, who cried out, "'Peace, peace' . . . when there is no peace" (Jeremiah 6:14). Why is peace so elusive? Why do we struggle so for it in our homes, churches, and among people who are determined to destroy one another?

May I offer a simple but heartfelt opinion? Peace, wherever it is sought, will never be the result of negotiations or pressure. It will happen because of men and women who actively seek peace and in whose hearts rage, anger, resentment, and revenge are forbidden. Outside the influence and motivation of the Prince of Peace, we will never find it. The Bible says, "Let your light shine before men, that they may see your good deeds and praise your Father in heaven" (Matthew 5:16).

In so many ways, our hope for any kind of lasting peace begins with you and your relationship with your God. "You're blessed when you can show people how to cooperate instead of compete or fight" (Matthew 5:9, MSG).

Having Someone Pray for You

Why not share with our Lord the things that challenge us? My method of praying is pretty simplistic. I basically talk with God—not trying to barge in—knowing that He loves me and knows the best for me. I believe He hears me and understands the motivation of my heart. He wants me to confide in Him as I do my own children. By faith, I trust Him for the answer. He always has an answer for me. The right answer.

But we also need others to pray for us. Remember the words from the apostle Paul to the overseers in Philippi? "I thank my God every time I remember you. In all my prayers for all of you, I always pray with joy because of your partnership in the gospel . . . being confident of this, that he who began a good work in you will carry it on to completion until the day of Christ Jesus" (Philippians 1:3-6).

And again, to the brothers in Christ at Colosse: "We always thank God, the Father of our Lord Jesus Christ, when we pray for you. . . . We pray this in order that you may live a life worthy of the Lord and may please him in every way: bearing fruit in every good work, growing in the knowledge of God" (Colossians 1:3, 10).

Every one of us needs someone we can count on to pray for us, even as Jesus prayed for Simon, "I have prayed for you . . . that your faith may not fail" (Luke 22:32).

"Ask and it will be given to you; seek and you will find; knock and the door will be opened to you" (Matthew 7:7).

Golf Lessons: Following Through

My thought, as I watched and walked the course of the 2008 USGA Senior Open, was that you just keep swinging as long as you can. If you are faithful to your assignment, even when your active playing days are over, you will be remembered for your consistency and dedication.

While there was a lull in the action at the tournament, I even developed a three-point sermon with a golf theme:

WHILE PLAYING THE COURSE:

1. Keep your head down—Do not be distracted by all the stuff going on around you (Philippians 3:12-14).
2. Keep your eye on the ball—Make the main thing the main thing (1 Corinthians 2:1-5).
3. Keep your swing smooth and follow through—In the end, it will not be how far you hit the ball, but how you finished the course that people will remember (2 Timothy 4:2-5).

Okay, so I'm not Billy Graham, but it's a start. Hit 'em all straight.

"Forgetting what is behind [the bad shots] and straining toward what is ahead [the good shots], I press on toward the goal to win the prize for which God has called me heavenward in Christ Jesus" (Philippians 3:13-14).

Living Above Reproach

There has been some talk of late that certain professional athletes should have an asterisk by their names in the record books. Perhaps, they say, Barry Bonds or Mark McGwire or even Sammy Sosa. The reason: If they used banned substances, as alleged, their records would be tainted.

Have you ever preached from the passage in Titus that says, "In everything set them an example by doing what is good. In your teaching show integrity, seriousness and soundness of speech that cannot be condemned, so that those who oppose you may be ashamed because they have nothing bad to say about us" (Titus 2:7-8). My interpretation might be a bit faulty, but it reminds me to live our lives so that, at the end of our ministries, there will be no asterisks. *The Message* says, "We don't want anyone looking down on God's Message because of their behavior" (Titus 2:5).

It does make a difference how you live before others. But at the end, His opinion will be the one that matters most.

"Judge me, O LORD, according to my righteousness, according to my integrity, O Most High" (Psalm 7:8).

Called to a Higher Standard

I know divorce is a personal thing, and it is impossible to know the details of any marital failure. But it seems to me that in every case, there are character challenges that must be dealt with. This is especially true when a spouse has an affair and walks away from the marriage vow, which is as significant as the vow to uphold the Constitution of the United States.

In our ministry to pastors, we deal with marital issues all the time. We do what we can through counselors, resources, and events to help members of the clergy mend their marriages and find a reason for recommitment to one another. You, my colleague, are called to a higher standard. There are evil forces at work to separate you from your families and your divine call. *Resist it, my colleague. Resist it!*

"Now the overseer must be above reproach, the husband of but one wife, temperate, self-controlled, respectable, hospitable, able to teach, not given to drunkenness, not violent but gentle, not quarrelsome, not a lover of money. He must manage his own family well and see that his children obey him with proper respect. (If anyone does not know how to manage his own family, how can he take care of God's church?) He must not be a recent convert, or he may become conceited and fall under the same judgment as the devil. He must also have a good reputation with outsiders, so that he will not fall into disgrace and into the devil's trap" (1 Timothy 3:2-7).

Shepherding with G-R-A-C-E

It is easy for clergy to slip in and out of both good and bad behaviors. The Shepherd's Covenant, from Focus on the Family, is a simple concept that calls spiritual leaders to a new level of accountability and commitment to the call of God on their lives. Using the acronym G-R-A-C-E, it highlights five important things we should all keep in mind:

G—Genuine Accountability: Do you have someone in your life who asks you the big questions. I'm not so concerned about hyperaccountability, but I pray you have someone you can trust to keep you honest and vice versa.

R—Right Relationships: Is there anyone in your world you are at odds with? A family member? A parishioner? A colleague? You should take the initiative as peacemaker. Will you?

A—A Shepherd's Heart: Do you go out of your way to walk in the village and engage people? Do you look for ways to express God's love in deeds—not just words? People need to see you in their world.

C—Constant Safeguards: Do you have in place a "hedge of protection" around your ministry and family? Remember, like a predator in the bush, the evil one has his eyes on you. He is patient and will wait until your guard is down. Don't become vulnerable.

E—Embrace God Intimately: Do you feel comfortable in God's presence? Are you spending quality time with your best friend, Jesus? Do you study His Word? Do you confess your sins or misdeeds? Is it well with your soul? I pray so.

"Let us then approach the throne of grace with confidence, so that we may receive mercy and find grace to help us in our time of need" (Hebrews 4:16).

The Little Things Do Matter

Little things have a way of speaking volumes about who you are and what you value. What do you have on your desk? When people walk into your "private sanctuary," what will they see?

My office is filled with all kinds of things. Beverley is always saying, "What are you going to do with all that stuff? Our kids sure won't want it." But, as I look around and as I write this thought, I know that nearly everything in my office means something to me—especially on my credenza. That's where I look to see my family.

Little things like a positive testimony mean so much to so many. A smile. A thank-you. A prayer. A word of encouragement. A positive attitude. A cup of cold water in Jesus' name.

In the parable of the talents, our Lord recognized the investment—though small—of a servant when he said, "You have been faithful with a few things [small things]; I will put you in charge of many things. Come and share your master's happiness!" (Matthew 25:23).

In other words, the little things really do matter and, in the end, make a big difference. A thought: Too often we underestimate the power of a touch, a smile, a kind word, a listening ear, an honest compliment, or the smallest act of caring—all of which have the potential to turn a life around.

"Now it is required that those who have been given a trust must prove faithful" (1 Corinthians 4:2).

Relating Sports to Faith

There are many faith lessons to be learned from sports. Here is some advice from basketball coach John Wooden.

1. Get in Shape: A team must be conditioned to perform at its peak.

POINT: This lesson speaks to you and those you serve. Have you put on the whole armor of God (Ephesians 6)? Have you prepared yourself to fight the good fight?

2. Learn the Fundamentals: Teams do not win because they can dunk the basketball. They win because they play defense, pass the ball, rebound the ball, and play their positions.

POINT: The fundamentals of the faith, such as prayer, Bible reading, stewardship, and a heart for the lost are essential if we are to mature as a body of believers.

3. Play as a Team: The game of basketball is a team sport. We hear repeatedly that there is no "I" in team.

POINT: This is especially true in the church. Pastors will come and go. The look of a congregation will change over the years. The one constant in a successful church is unity. The second chapter of Acts becomes our playbook.

"May the God who gives endurance and encouragement give you a spirit of unity among yourselves as you follow Christ Jesus, so that with one heart and mouth you may glorify the God and Father of our Lord Jesus Christ" (Romans 15:5-6).

How to Get Things Moving Again

One thing I know for sure: There is an ebb and flow to ministry. We all have highs and lows. There are some days when things could not be going any better, and there are other days when we must pinch ourselves to make sure we are still in the same assignment.

Momentum is the answer to surviving the ebb and flow of ministry. If you get things moving and help people see there is something going on, they will move with you. Status quo and the "same old-same old" will stop momentum. The message must stay the same—but the methods can change.

Here is how you can get things moving in a positive way:

1. Ask God for a unique and meaningful idea or cause. He has a dream for you.
2. Be a believer. Sell your passion. People respond to optimism.
3. Surround yourself with positive people.
4. Keep your idea or cause constantly before your congregation.
5. Do not forsake your dream because of negative people. Live like a winner!

"May Jesus himself and God our Father, who reached out in love and surprised you with gifts of unending help and confidence, put a fresh heart in you, invigorate your work, enliven your speech" (2 Thessalonians 2:16-17, MSG).

Standing Firm

The church really needs to wake up and realize that our effectiveness and credibility come from "the church being the church" and not a finely tuned image campaign that creates a mirage. In many ways, the church is a mile wide and an inch deep. There are lots of folks who have been so deluded by our feel-good approach to the gospel that they are missing the born-again experience.

I will continue to be respectful of my critics, but I will not allow their watchdog mentality to stifle a message that I believe is from the Lord.

I often agonize for you and the power players you must deal with on a weekly (or daily) basis. But you cannot allow yourself to be emasculated or let the message God has placed in your heart to be weakened, even if it makes some people uncomfortable.

Paul wrote, "To the weak I became weak, to win the weak. I have become all things to all men so that by all possible means I might save some" (1 Corinthians 9:22).

"I want you to put your foot down. Take a firm stand on these matters so that those who have put their trust in God will concentrate on the essentials that are good for everyone" (Titus 3:8, MSG).

Offering Hope and Encouragement

You have often stood beside brokenhearted church members and friends. You have done your best to console them and challenge them to look forward. What if you had not been there? What if, as the apostle Paul wrote, we had to live without hope? How empty! How futile life would be. But you have offered them hope. Thank you!

I think of you and the constant encounters you have with folks who just need to talk and share an honest need with someone who really cares about them. Your response should not be trite, but one that shows a sincere interest in assisting that person to emotional wholeness.

As I sat down to write this note to you, this thought came to me: Who needs you today? Who in your circumference needs a phone call, an e-mail, a cup of coffee, an encouraging note, or a listening ear? Perhaps you need someone.

"When he saw [them], he had compassion on them, because they were . . . helpless, like sheep without a shepherd" (Matthew 9:36).

"And Jesus, moved with compassion, put forth his hand" (Mark 1:41, KJV).

Internet Rules

The Internet, as helpful as it might be, must be approached with caution, accountability, and a realization of your weakness (1 Corinthians 10:12). Limit your time on the Internet, especially on the weekend and before and after your office hours. Also, ask yourself a simple question: "If my family and my deacon/elder board were watching over my shoulder, would I be ashamed for them to see what I am accessing? What if Jesus Himself were here?" It is in the lonely moments that you are most vulnerable.

When I got a laptop, one of the first things I did was to have as many of the porn sites blocked as I possibly could. In our Pastoral Ministries office, we are receiving more and more calls from clergy and their spouses who have experienced addiction to the seamy side of the computer world. We see it as one of the major challenges to Christian leaders in the days to come.

Let me ask you a few questions: Have you blocked those sites on the Web that might prove a temptation to you? Do you have filtering software? Is your computer in a place where it can easily be seen by others? Do you make it a rule not to stay alone in the office after hours, when temptation might be greatest? Are you accountable to someone for your computer use?

If you struggle in this area, please get help and find someone to be accountable to.

"Be self-controlled and alert. Your enemy the devil prowls around like a roaring lion looking for someone to devour" (1 Peter 5:8). "Resist the devil, and he will flee from you" (James 4:7).

Practicing Patience

We in ministry often find ourselves frustrated. The plans we have made, the dreams we have dreamed, seem to take forever in coming to fruition. Even when it comes to ourselves, we wish we were smarter and more consistently effective. When we are making progress, results don't come as quickly as we would like. In short, we in ministry lack patience, and patience is a fruit of the Spirit (Galatians 5:22).

Consider some related admonitions—"Suffering produces perseverance" (Romans 5:2); "but you, man of God, pursue . . . endurance" (1 Timothy 6:11); "run with perseverance the race marked out for us" (Hebrews 12:1); "the testing of your faith produces patience" (James 1:3, NKJV).

We cannot live frustrated and rushed. There is a time to slow down and let patience win the day. I know—easier said than done. We can pray for patience.

"And we pray this in order that you may live a life worthy of the Lord and may please him in every way: bearing fruit in every good work, growing in the knowledge of God, being strengthened with all power according to his glorious might so that you may have great endurance and patience, and joyfully giving thanks to the Father, who has qualified you to share in the inheritance of the saints in the kingdom of light" (Colossians 1:10-12).

Overcoming Weariness

Remember that old saying "What do you do when your get up and go has done got up and went?"

Well, maybe not, but when I was a kid growing up in Arkansas, I heard that phrase a lot. It refers to someone who has a lot to do but lacks the energy or motivation to get it all done.

Have you ever felt like that? If you haven't, I promise you—you will! Let me share some simple solutions to overcoming weariness:

1. Remember your church is God's church.
2. Don't put so much emphasis on the immediate—it's the long run that counts.
3. If you're tired, take some time off. You only complicate things when you burn the candle at both ends.
4. Please do not take yourself so seriously. Mellow out and just relax.
5. Identify your stress point. It might be something totally unrelated to your church life. It could be family-related.
6. Determine not to live in isolation. Call a colleague.
7. Examine your "true" relationship with your Lord. Is it mechanical or relational?
8. Laugh! When was the last time you just had fun?
9. It is not just about you. It is about an audience of One—and you know who that is. It is not about someone on your deacon or leadership board!
10. Prioritize—Do the most important thing first.

So, my colleague . . . get up and go! You can do it!

"Let us not become weary in doing good, for at the proper time we will reap a harvest if we do not give up" (Galatians 6:9).

One Church, Different Nationalities

I was once given the opportunity to speak in two Indian churches in the New York City area. It was a blessed but very interesting experience.

The churches were packed. In one, the worship was contemporary, and in the other, traditional. The first church had a real international feel. The second could very easily have been in India. The ladies, dressed in saris, sat to my left. The men, dressed in suits, sat to my right.

As I left that beautiful experience, I could not help but think of the diversity of our nation when people gather for worship on a given Sunday morning. Same God, same gospel, same Spirit, but very different styles. I have preached in Chinese, Japanese, Korean, Hispanic, and now an Indian church—to name a few—in the United States. And I have always been amazed at the variety.

Today, we may have language barriers to our fellowship, but one day those obstacles will be removed, and people from every tribe and nation will join hearts and hands as one great big family. What a day that will be!

Have you attempted to get to know your colleagues of different nationalities? You will need to take the lead. It would be a valuable education for you to see how they face their challenges and how, from time to time, you might blend your worship experiences.

"After this I looked and there before me was a great multitude that no one could count, from every nation, tribe, people and language, standing before the throne and in front of the Lamb" (Revelation 7:9).

Your Divine Calling

"God was pleased through the foolishness of what was preached to save those who believe" (1 Corinthians 1:21) and "I make myself a slave to everyone, to win as many as possible" (1 Corinthians 9:19).

In other words, God uses a wide variety of clergy to see His will fulfilled.

Most of you will never have a radio or television ministry. You may never become well-known outside your circle of influence. But it is within that circle of influence that God allows you great authority and opportunity.

No one else can do what you do or serve where you serve. You are uniquely in the right spot to bring glory to God.

So, when your people comment on something one of the "big names" has said, or say to you, "Why don't you do it the way they do it?" don't get upset. Just know in your heart that God has you where He wants you, and because of that, God expects a harvest of love and compassion for those you serve.

"But the wisdom that comes from heaven is first of all pure; then peace-loving, considerate, submissive, full of mercy and good fruit, impartial and sincere. Peacemakers who sow in peace raise a harvest of righteousness" (James 3:17-18).

The Price of Sin

There is no place in the Bible more telling about man's rebellion than the confrontation God had with Adam and Eve in the Garden of Eden. The consequences of their sin, like ripples in a stream, have touched all humankind. They attempted to hide, but were unsuccessful. They couldn't—and we can't.

Moses warned, "And you may be sure that your sin will find you out" (Numbers 32:23). Even in a time of grace, sin brings with it a very high cost.

Thousands of churches have been wounded for all time because of clergy who set their own rules and lived below reproach. We have all paid a high price for their sin. "When you sin against your brothers in this way and wound their weak conscience, you sin against Christ" (1 Corinthians 8:12). Can you imagine how much more effective the church would be if we all lived by the admonition of Paul in Ephesians, chapter 5—"but among you there must not be even a hint of sexual immorality" (v. 3)?

My colleague, I've talked about this a lot, but I don't think I can overemphasize how important it is that those who represent Jesus Christ live lives of highest integrity and purity. We must remember that we are not powerless over sin. As we're told in Galatians 5:24, "Those who belong to Christ Jesus have crucified the sinful nature with its passions and desires."

"For we know that our old self was crucified with him so that the body of sin might be done away with, that we should no longer be slaves to sin—because anyone who has died has been freed from sin" (Romans 6:6-7).

Surrendering Your Plans to God

Like anyone who makes plans, there comes a time when you have done all you can do and must leave the results to God. That's what I've done with my assignments. I have done all I can do—prayed a lot of prayers, anticipated the unexpected—and now, surrendered the results to our Lord.

I think that is pretty good advice for any activity you are planning, as are the words from Jeremiah: "'For I know the plans I have for you,' declares the LORD, 'plans to prosper you and not to harm you, plans to give you hope and a future'" (Jeremiah 29:11).

Our God is still God, and we have the opportunity to let Him do marvelous things in our lives and ministries. I have thought for a long time that most of us live below God's waterline for our ministry. He has wonders in mind for us. Are we equal to the challenge?

Get on the same page with our Lord's ideas and plans for you. "Lead me, O LORD, in your righteousness . . . make straight your way before me" (Psalm 5:8).

I wish for you every morning a fresh glimpse of our Lord's expectation, and courage to live by faith as He surrounds you with His favor.

"In his heart, a man plans his course, but the LORD determines his steps" (Proverbs 16:9).

Be the Best You Can Be

I played tennis a long time ago. I was not as good as my cousin, James Dobson, who was on the Point Loma University tennis team, but I could hold my own. I also played golf over the years in 100-stroke territory. I surely didn't have superstar status in either sport, but I loved to compete. I just liked to play, to do the best I could. And when a game was over, I would agonize about a missed shot or a botched putt. Silly, but true.

If I had compared myself to the superstars, I would have quit a long time ago, but I didn't. I just strived to be the best I could be. Point?

You are who you are, making the most of the gifts and opportunities God has given you. Just be yourself, do the best you can, keep improving, study, love people, be positive, guard your heart, and don't compare yourself to anyone! Be the best you can be. You don't need to be a superstar, but you do need to be at your best for your Lord. Agree?

"Who is wise and understanding among you? Let him show it by his good life, by deeds done in the humility that comes from wisdom" (James 3:13).

Being Happy

There was a story in the *Christian Post* reporting on a survey by the University of Chicago. The survey found clergy as the top job for satisfaction among American workers: 87 percent of the pastors surveyed reported they were very satisfied. The exact quote was: "Pastors—perceived to be some of the most under-appreciated and on-demand workers in America—are actually the happiest and most satisfied in their jobs."

Now get this! In addition to being the most satisfied, pastors also out-ranked other American workers as being the happiest (67 percent). It was interesting to note that doctors and lawyers did not make the list of the top 12 most satisfied or happiest. At the bottom of the "happy" list were garage and service station workers (13 percent) and roofers (14 percent).

What makes pastors the happiest workers in the land? Do you think it has anything to do with why other professions are happy, or could it be because we are uniquely called, and in fact, our job is really not a "job" as such. Could it be because we give to people and help them find the Lord?

Are you happy—if so, why? Are you satisfied—if so, why? If not, why not?

The dictionary defines happiness as "a state of well-being and contentment." Is that how you would define it? Just something to think about.

"But godliness with contentment is great gain" (1 Timothy 6:6).

Investing in Others

The gospel is all about an investment that God made in the human race: "For God so loved the world that he gave . . ." (John 3:16). "Greater love has no one than this, that he lay down his life for his friends" (John 15:13). Life is full of investments!

From time to time, every one of us needs to move away from our safety net and walk in the village where needy people live. We must experience life as it is for the people we serve.

More and more, I am observing a tendency for the clergy to play it safe, to walk a journey that is protected. You will never make a investment in people that is risk-free. Nearly every time you engage someone in need, you stand the chance of failure, rejection, betrayal, or discouragment. But that is the blessing of "risky" serving. You may not succeed every time, but once in a while your efforts will reap dividends.

One Saturday I spoke at a men's conference in Bend, Oregon. When I finished my presentation, I came face to face with men whose lives I had invested in many years ago. I couldn't recall their names, but I remembered the investment. In other words, I collected a genuine return. What a blessing!

You can play it safe like the one-talent man did (Matthew 25:14-29), or you can take a chance and see what God can do. Risk it, my colleague. Risk it!

"His master replied, 'Well done, good and faithful servant! You have been faithful with a few things; I will put you in charge of many things. Come and share your master's happiness!' " (Matthew 25:23).

Your Personal Bible

If you are like me, you treasure your personal Bible. I have lots and lots of Bibles. People give me the latest "model" all the time, but I have one Bible that I use every day. It's very old, it's dog-eared, the spine is coming loose, and I know my way around in it. In fact, it has been recovered three times.

This morning I notice that in my Bible are a note from a pastor I recently helped and a couple of business cards from clergy looking for resources. There are sermon notes clipped to the inside back cover and a Ten Commandments card. There are also a *Way to Salvation* pamphlet that I use when explaining to others how to find Jesus and, from *Experiencing God*, a piece of paper with the "Seven Realities of Experiencing God" on it. On nearly every page, a verse is underlined or a note is written in the margin.

But the most precious of my "in-my-Bible" possessions is a yellowed, fragile picture of my great-grandparents, who prayed for four generations of their family every day. I was a part of that fourth generation. The picture is a gentle reminder to me that I am a product of the love and prayers of many people—and so are you!

When was the last time you just leafed through your "special" Bible and remembered? Take a tour of your Bible today.

"For the LORD [and His Word] will be your confidence" (Proverbs 3:26).

Finding Your Niche in Ministry

Finding your niche is important. Have you found yours in ministry?

One Sunday I had the opportunity to preach at one of the most successful Cowboy Churches in America. It was so interesting. The architecture, the dress, the rodeo arena, the cattle grazing beyond the parking lot, the music, the atmosphere—all these things went together to create a "Cowboy Church." The pastor is a former rodeo performer and racetrack chaplain who felt a burden for those who might not fit the norm of another church.

Montgomery, Texas, is not a very large place, but those who have been loved and fed by the Lone Star Cowboy Church flocked into the two services. I even preached in jeans and cowboy boots. It was a real blessing.

How about you, pastor? Have you found your niche? What is your niche? If you could pack it all up today and start fresh, what would the church you serve look like? Perhaps it's right where you are. Hope so!

I know for a fact that a lot of us who have struggled at one place and succeeded at another most likely found our comfort zone in that new place.

I value and love my niche—how about you? The scripture says, "I have become all things to all men so that by all possible means I might save some" (1 Corinthians 9:22). When I hear some of my colleagues say, "I'm like a fish out of water at this place," it saddens me. Have you found your niche?

"But may the righteous be glad and rejoice before God; may they be happy and joyful" (Psalm 68:3).

Pursuing Excellence

The apostle Paul admonished the church at Corinth to aim for perfection (2 Corinthians 13:11). In other words, do your best, be your best, hope for the best.

The pursuit of excellence is a repeated story in the sports world. Reporters often write about:

1. Preparation
2. Recruitment
3. Performance
4. Coaching
5. Teamwork
6. Players at skilled positions
7. Study of the playbook
8. Second effort
9. Testings and challenges
10. Minimizing the turnovers
11. Will to win

And the list goes on.

Sounds familiar, doesn't it, my colleague? The thing we have going for us is that, in our *big games*, there are no losers. You are a player/coach on the winning team in a struggle for the hearts and souls of all mankind. We may not succeed on every play, but one day when the final whistle blows, we'll know "we are more than conquerors" (Romans 8:37).

"Those who have served well gain an excellent standing and great assurance in their faith in Christ Jesus" (1 Timothy 3:13).

Loving What You Do

I celebrated a "really big" birthday a while back. It was a fun day filled with both joyful and embarrassing moments. During the celebration, Jean Daly, the wife of our Focus on the Family president, asked me about the motivation behind my many years as a pastor to pastors. I later shared my answer with the entire group—and it is what I pray for you as you go about your responsibilities as a shepherd. It can be expressed in three words: LOOK, LOVE, and PRAY.

- LOOK forward to every new day.
- LOVE what you do.
- PRAY for God's blessing according to His will.

Some days I am uncertain about the outcome, but I never dread the experience. I love what I do! Let me offer you just a bit of wisdom gleaned from the years I have served our Lord and the church He loves:

If what you are doing is not a call from our Lord, then it will soon become just a job—and, I might add, a thankless job. Remember, it is God's church, and the people are His people. Pray daily that God will renew in you His unique call and will for your life.

" 'Come, follow me,' Jesus said, 'and I will make you fishers of men' " (Mark 1:17).

Peace from God

"Glory to God in the highest, and on earth peace, good will toward men" (Luke 2:14, KJV). That, of course, was the message heralded by the angels some 2,000 years ago on the occasion of our Savior's birth. Several years later that same Jesus would speak of peace: "Peace I leave with you; my peace I give you. I do not give to you as the world gives. Do not let your hearts be troubled and do not be afraid" (John 14:27). His words were addressed to a group of His followers who were troubled, and rightly so.

Jesus told His disciples, as He tells each of us, that there is peace for those of us who love Him, seek Him, and obey Him. We experience this peace as we spend time with Him and surrender to His will in love. We find this peace as we become more intimately involved with the Prince of Peace (Isaiah 9:6).

Peace is not the result of higher church attendance, a raise in compensation, or a successful sermon (even though all of these help a lot). That's because the peace our Lord described is permanent and personal, not fleeting or conditional.

I trust this simple message finds you at *peace*. He is your peace.

"The LORD gives strength to his people; the LORD blesses his people with peace" (Psalm 29:11).

Issues of the Heart

James gives us some guidance related to issues of the heart: "God opposes the proud but gives grace to the humble" (James 4:6). Also, "Submit yourselves, then, to God. Resist the devil, and he will flee from you. Come near [confess] to God and he will come near to you" (James 4:7-8).

Our defense from things that damage the influence of the church and our extended ministries includes: intimacy with God, a loving family, right relationships (colleagues, constituency, and leadership), adequate rest, honest accountability, a meaningful ministry, an attitude of joy and thanksgiving, constant prayer, and a vigilant spirit. We just can't take chances. Guard your heart, my colleague.

"Righteousness guards the man of integrity, but wickedness overthrows the sinner" (Proverbs 13:6).

Making the Most
of Our Hours

One morning, in our staff devotions, I asked our Pastoral Ministries team what they would do if God said to them, "I am giving you one more hour today to do with as you wish." The responses ranged from finding a quiet place and just relaxing to prayer and Bible study to spending a quality hour with family. What would you do if you had one more hour given to you? Church business? In my heart, I hope not—but the question is yours to answer.

In Matthew's gospel, Jesus uses the word *hour* a lot. Remember, Jesus told His disciples in Matthew 10:19 that He would, in the right hour, give them the words to say. And in a moment of great sorrow, He asked them why they could not keep watch with Him for one hour (Matthew 26:40). When He was talking of the end times, He said, "The Son of Man will come at an hour when you do not expect him" (Matthew 24:44).

A lot can happen in one hour. It makes you wonder if we are using the hours He has given us productively.

I have said from time to time on especially busy days, "Man, I need 25 hours today." I wonder what I would do with one more hour. Would it just be sand through an hourglass? When you stop to think about it, every one of our hours has been "ordained" for us (Psalm 139:16).

Are you making the most of the hours granted you?

"Each day is God's gift. It's all you get in exchange for the hard work of staying alive. Make the most of each one! Whatever turns up, grab it and do it. And heartily! This is your last and only chance at it, for there's neither work to do nor thoughts to think in the company of the dead, where you're most certainly headed" (Ecclesiastes 9:9-10, MSG).

Earthquakes

The "earthquakes" that many of us experience in the ministry should not come as surprises, but most of the time they do.

And there are always the aftershocks. Can you relate?

I really dislike earthquakes. I went through several of them while living in California. You can prepare for a tornado or hurricane, but the moving of the earth can be really scary. I have learned this about earthquakes: (1) They are unexpected. (2) You cannot control them. (3) Everyone has their own story to tell related to their experience. (4) You can be prepared for them, but you're never really ready. (5) They happen quickly, and then you pick up the pieces. Sound familiar?

We in the ministry face tremors nearly every day. The magnitude of what we face runs the gamut from minor to major. How we handle these times can change the face of our assignments forever. How do we deal with the things we cannot control? Some of you may be going through, or are about to go through, your own "earthquakes." What should you do?

1. Be very aware of your surroundings.

2. Do not face these happenings alone.

3. Make advance plans with your leadership.

4. Know that God knows. Trust Him!

5. Do not let the issue fester.

6. Remember—it is not the end of anything.

7. Learn from the challenge.

8. Help everyone you can.

9. Begin immediately to repair the damage.

10. Keep your head up. Your people need to see you courageous.

"There will be . . . earthquakes" (Matthew 24:7).

Finding Rest

I have never had a sabbatical—have you? I've often wondered what it would be like to have 4 to 12 weeks off to just recharge, refresh, and reevaluate my ministry. One problem we face in the church is short pastorates. We often don't make it to the seventh (sabbatical) year. That was not my problem. It was that no one ever offered me a sabbatical.

How about your day off? Dr. Arch Hart and I agree that your day off should be Thursday or Friday, not Monday. Your adrenaline level is low on Monday, right? You bring more to your day off later in the week, but we have a difficult time convincing clergy of that.

The key word, however, is *rest*—not so much how and when you get it, but that you do rest. The pastors I work with who are running on fumes, feeling depleted and calloused, are those who just can't find the time to rest and regroup. Jesus needed to do this. "He went up into a mountain apart to pray" (Matthew 14:23). And remember the words of Jesus to the disciples when they were so inundated with needy people that they themselves didn't even have time to eat? "Come with me by yourselves to a quiet place and get some rest" (Mark 6:31). Those words are meant for you, my colleague. Get some rest!

"Work six days, doing everything you have to do, but the seventh day is a Sabbath, a Rest Day—no work" (Deuteronomy 5:13-14, MSG).

Feeling Comfortable
in God's Presence

When do you feel most comfortable in the presence of God? When you're walking through His creation, moved by His handiwork? When you have failed and seek His forgiveness? Or, how about when you least expect it—when the road ahead seems endless and you are facing an insurmountable obstacle? It could be when you are with your kids or grandkids, in a moment of quiet interaction, when listening to a beautiful song, or doing whatever it is that draws you close.

I have felt wonderfully close to my Lord at times. But at other times I've felt estrangement when I have allowed selfishness, ego, or flesh to take the central place in my life.

Are you in a comfortable place with our Lord today? The scripture says, "Come near to God and he will come near to you" (James 4:8). How?

- Confess the "stuff" in your life.
- Surrender your anxieties and fears.
- Develop a quiet place to meet Him each day and just be still and listen.
- Talk with Him about everything in the morning and in the evening.

Remember, He loves you unconditionally even when He seems otherwise engaged. And He wants you to be comfortable in His presence, just like you want your children to feel comfortable with you.

The prayer our Lord prayed for His disciples is a prayer He continues to pray for you: "I in them and you in me" (John 17:23).

Facing Failure

Years back, I suffered a failure of sorts. I don't mean to be melodramatic, but a dream I had—a "God thing," I thought—just did not work out. It was like a beautiful baby that was born, lived a little while, then just died. It was nobody's fault really, but in the end, it was a disappointment for some and no big deal for others. I was humbled by the failure, tempted not to try again.

Have you ever failed at something into which you put your best efforts? Had a dream vanish right before your eyes? Watched a "sure thing" go up in flames? It hurts, doesn't it?

There is something about a loss or failure that takes your breath away. It makes you feel that perhaps you're not as strong as you first imagined. But for the survivor, there will always be another challenge and something inside that says, "My God and I—we can do it! Let's try again!"

We can't let failure get the best of us, my colleague. We have to get up and try again. As I say so often, "The dream never dies, just the dreamer." Dream on!

"I am the LORD, the God of all mankind. Is anything too hard for me?" (Jeremiah 32:27).

Investing in Men

I have a theory that many men are opting out of the church altogether, or living on the fringe of the fellowship. Leon Podles writes, "A basic fear in men has resulted: church threatens their masculinity." The Barna Research Group reports, "While 90 percent of men believe in God, only a third (or less) of them attend a church." David Murrow, author of *Why Men Hate Going to Church,* says, "A lack of male participation is one of the surest predictors of church decline." He goes on to say, "If you want a healthy church for the long term, attract men. This was Jesus' strategy. It still works today."

I can't overstate how important it is that you invest in men. Your investment will in time reap a bountiful harvest for the kingdom. Walking into the lives of other men with a masculine approach to Christlike living will make a difference. Pastor—you hold the key!

Men need a challenge. Muslim men know they are locked in a battle between good and evil. We must encourage men in the body of Christ to step up and engage the evil one before we suffer one more defeat.

"Jesus called them, and immediately they left the boat . . . and followed him" (Matthew 4:21-22).

The Importance of Humility

I often deal with clergy who, because of too much power and too little accountability, take liberties with their assignment and, in the end, hurt people. The list of offenders is endless, and it continues to grow as Christian leaders set themselves above a standard we are all called to maintain. Clergy colleagues are often knocked off their lofty, self-imposed perches because they will not allow anyone to tell them no or monitor their financial dealings.

Paul writes, "It is by grace you have been saved . . . it is the gift of God—not by works, so that no one can boast. For we are God's workmanship" (Ephesians 2:8-10). That's really who we are—God's workmanship.

It is tiresome to hear so many ministers talk about what they have done. Solomon wrote, "The lips of the righteous know what is fitting, but the mouth of the wicked only what is perverse" (Proverbs 10:32). Again, "Reckless words pierce like a sword, but the tongue of the wise brings healing" (Proverbs 12:18). One more: "He who guards his lips guards his life, but he who speaks rashly will come to ruin" (Proverbs 13:3). So much is said and so much sadness surrounds careless men and women who, to make themselves look good or successful, verbally diminish others. We will be judged by our words. I know it's a fine line between praising and boasting, but all our boasting should be about Him!

"Do not think of yourself more highly than you ought" (Romans 12:3).

Pride Goes Before Destruction

Are you ready for some further thoughts on humility? Here goes. I have been with some very high-profile Christian leaders who have jockeyed for position, have been demanding, and have made the mistake of "thinking too highly of themselves." I also hear a lot of boasting as I travel the country. "I did this," "we did that," "I spoke here"—probably more "I" than is called for. There is a tendency to elevate some in our profession to an almost godlike position.

I wonder if we in ministry can ever have the luxury of thinking too highly of ourselves. How can we ever look at our successes as something we have done or achieved? The truth is, we are all servant-shepherds. Some have been given a larger pasture in which to work, but in the final analysis, we have all been called to feed the flock of God.

One national magazine referred to a well-known clergyman as "America's Pastor." When I read that, I thought about most of you. You are really "America's Pastor" because you visit hospitals and sit across from the brokenhearted. You struggle to make ends meet. You care about your people. You take what you do seriously, but not yourself. I have seen a lot of our colleagues fall because of pride. Walk humbly, colleague.

Remember, "Pride goes before destruction, a haughty spirit before a fall" (Proverbs 16:18).

A Seamless Transition
Between Pastors

One Sunday I attended a church service where a good friend of mine was preaching for the first time since he had retired exactly one year before. The church's transition to a new pastor appeared to have been seamless.

I left the church thinking, *I wish all pastors and their congregations could make a transition like that.*

How? Here are some ideas:

- Love your people. Tell them you do. Love begets love.
- Communicate! Be open with those you lead. No surprises.
- Commend others. Brag on the people you serve with.
- Be available. Most of you do not need to wear a CEO label. Be a shepherd.
- Live above reproach. Do not give naysayers ammunition to use against you.
- Lead spiritually. Be one who lives a life of righteousness and holiness.
- Don't let offenses fester. Deal with contention directly and quickly.
- Act like you're having fun. In other words, don't be downcast.
- Celebrate God's call in your life. Others will notice.

Set the table so that when it's time for a transition, it will be a happy and positive thing.

". . . so that those who oppose you . . . have nothing bad to say about [you]" (Titus 2:8).

God Will Sustain You

At the United States Olympic Training Center in Colorado Springs, I visited an exhibit titled "Praxis Athletes" by an artist named K. Lazarides. The paintings were all abstracts of famous Olympic athletes without names attached. There were gymnasts, runners, lifters, skiers, cyclists—you name it. In the mix of the paintings was a framed quote that caught my eye: "*Praxis* is not only to try and to give up, but *praxis* is also to penetrate, to fight, to win and to lose, to kneel down, to get up, to stimulate and to accept struggle and fight until the last breath." It really reflects the Olympic spirit—it also calls to mind the commitment you must make to the challenge you face in life and ministry. That "never give up" spirit personifies who you are in Christ.

It reminds me of the challenge and promise our God issued to Joshua as he took the mantle of leadership from Moses: "Have I not commanded you? Be strong and courageous. Do not be terrified; do not be discouraged, for the LORD your God will be with you wherever you go" (Joshua 1:9).

Having an Accountability Colleague

One of my greatest blessings is conversing with clergy worldwide, which leads to my question for you: How are you doing with accountability—genuine accountability?

- Do you meet regularly with a colleague?
- Do you really engage one another?
- Do you use the Shepherd's Covenant guide (www.parsonage.org)?
- Do you pray for one another?

You need your accountability colleague—your colleague needs you! I realize accountability relationships are fluid, but they are very worthwhile. If you are having a tough time finding someone, select a pastor in town who has an assignment similar to yours and ask him to join you for a coffee break. It is amazing how productive those times can be. Honest, the members of the clergy that most often find their ministries in jeopardy are those who have no accountability. So how are you doing?

"A man of many companions may come to ruin, but there is a friend who sticks closer than a brother" (Proverbs 18:24).

Living in Freedom

I deal with so many pastors who have the privilege of freedom but do not live in freedom. They are so bound up in unrealistic expectations, pressure they put on themselves, success issues, uncertainties regarding their call, and anger at their congregations, their spouses, and even their God.

There was a time when I lived like that. I look back on all of the frustration I experienced and do not want to see you, or any of your colleagues, go through those feelings unnecessarily.

Oh, I know ministry is tough and the demands are great, but there is no reason for any of us to live life with a chip on our shoulder or a knot in our stomach. That is not freedom. That is bondage! Remember it is God's church—the people we serve are God's people. I forgot that from time to time and it caused me pain.

I want you to live in freedom, not bondage. I want you to enjoy the assignment you have, not fight against it. I want you to be able to say to a young person feeling God's call on his or her life, "It will be worth it." I want you to say with Paul, "I have kept the faith" (2 Timothy 4:7).

Just remember . . . it is one thing to have freedom and yet another to enjoy it! "Now the Lord is the Spirit, and where the Spirit of the Lord is, there is freedom" (2 Corinthians 3:17).

Being a Shepherd

Some time ago, I ran across a quote from one of the up-and-coming young pastors in America discussing his role as a shepherd. When asked, "Should we stop talking about pastors as 'shepherds'?" this pastor responded, "Absolutely. That word needs to go away. Jesus talked about shepherds because there was one over there in a pasture he could point to. But to bring in that imagery today and say, 'Pastor, you're the shepherd of the flock,' no. I have never seen a flock. I've never spent five minutes with a shepherd. It was culturally relevant in the time of Jesus, but it's not culturally relevant anymore."

I thought his response was irreverent, probably because I disagree with it. In fact, I found it to be arrogant. Maybe it just struck me wrong, or I didn't understand where this prominent pastor was coming from. Anyway, it bothered me because I do see you as a shepherd of the flock, especially those of you in the small- to mid-range churches who do not have a lot of help. I have written about this before because I think "pastor" and "shepherd" share many of the same characteristics.

You as a shepherd must live as an example to the believer "in speech, in life, in love, in faith, and in purity" (1 Timothy 4:12), but also as a protector, provider, and servant. I know it sounds like a lot, but great responsibility has been given to you that goes beyond administration, planning, and preparation. Your flock must see you as someone who cares about them on an interpersonal level.

"When he [Jesus] saw the crowds, he had compassion on them, because they were harassed and helpless, like sheep without a shepherd" (Matthew 9:36).

Having a Servant's Heart

God's Son invested in that which was His own, "but his own did not receive him" (John 1:11). Even our Lord did not win them all, but He invested in everyone. He took the chance—and so should we. Today, who do you need to encounter?

Proverbs 3:27-28 in *The Message* reads: "Never walk away from someone who deserves help; your hand is *God's* hand for that person. Don't tell your neighbor, 'Maybe some other time,' or, 'Try me tomorrow.'" Great advice for one with the servant-shepherd's heart!

What a marvelous time to serve as an undershepherd in our Lord's pasture. You have an unmatched opportunity to speak of the love of God and the transformation that can take place in a person's life through Jesus Christ.

"Be shepherds of God's flock that is under your care, serving as overseers—not because you must, but because you are willing, as God wants you to be . . . And when the Chief Shepherd appears, you will receive the crown of glory that will never fade away" (1 Peter 5:2, 4).

Stand behind the cross, my colleague. Remember it is not about you, but about the One who saved you and called you. It is about those you serve and the mighty truth of God's Word.

"And if Christ has not been raised, our preaching is useless" (1 Corinthians 15:14).

Wickedness and Judgment

Violence is an attitude that permeates our society: grown men fighting one another at their sons' Little League games, a father assaulting a teenage referee in a soccer game, a deacon threatening a pastoral staff member. There's a kind of "get even" mentality that finds its way into every corner of our relationships—even the church. One of my most embarrassing moments as a pastor was my involvement in a church league basketball game brawl. It was terrible!

Why do we do these things? The answer: wickedness of the human heart. "The heart is deceitful above all things and beyond cure. Who can understand it?" (Jeremiah 17:9). Unless our hearts are changed by a relationship with Jesus, we will continue to hurt one another.

There will be a time when, like all men, we will stand before the awesome Judge of the universe and account for our behavior. Only then will we know genuine and complete justice. Unfortunately, the church does not talk much about judgment anymore, and because of that, a generation of people is going through life uninformed and unforgiven. That is a shame, because judgment is an integral part of the gospel. Pastor, preach the whole gospel— not just the parts people want to hear. A dying world is in need of God's saving grace.

"For it is time for judgment to begin with the family of God; and if it begins with us, what will the outcome be for those who do not obey the gospel of God?" (1 Peter 4:17).

Preparing to Address
Your Congregation

I know this may sound odd, but when this next Lord's Day is completed, what will your ratings be? I am not attempting to be facetious, just trying to get your attention.

Every time we stand before a group of people to present, we are being rated. Have we adequately prepared, been diligent in study and prayer, imagined the needs of those in the pews? Are our egos in the proper place? Are our hands clean and hearts pure? If that's the case, then from our Lord we will receive a "10."

Let me ask you some hard questions about your spiritual life:

- Do you feel a quiet time apart from your sermon preparation is essential?
- Can you think of an example of an unmistakable voice, direction, or impulse that was God's presence?
- Do you ever wonder what God is thinking while you're presenting?
- How do you react to a crisis moment? Do you immediately surrender it to the Lord or do you attempt to handle it yourself?
- Is it easier for you to say "I'm sorry" on a personal level or on a spiritual level?

Paul wrote, "In the presence of God and of Christ Jesus . . . I give you this charge: Preach the Word; be prepared in season and out of season; correct, rebuke and encourage" (2 Timothy 4:1-2).

Passing It Down

I often think about the people who have contributed to my life and ministry. Most of them have passed on now, but their memories remain vivid. How about you? Can you identify those in your life who have enabled you to reach your present position?

Another question: Into whose life are you contributing? Paul wrote "To Titus, my true son in our common faith. . . . In everything, set them an example by doing what is good. In your teaching, show integrity, seriousness and soundness of speech" (Titus 1:4; 2:7-8). In other words, invest in the younger generation as others have invested in you.

I believe that every young pastor needs a mentor, and every experienced pastor should become one. But just what is mentoring? Leadership expert Bobb Biehl has authored a booklet with Jerry MacGregor and Glen Urquhart titled *Mentoring—How to Find a Mentor and How to Become One.*

In it, Biehl says, "Mentoring is making available the mentor's personal strength, resources and network (friendships/contacts) to help a protégé reach his or her goals." The important aspect of mentoring is not using a protégé to accomplish the mentor's goals. Rather, it is a process by which the one being mentored becomes all that he or she should be.

Would you like to be a mentor? Do you need a mentor? I believe great fulfillment can come to any of you who choose to invest in the life of another. Bobb Biehl reminds us that "Mentoring is not a complex subject, but in our opinion, it is the single most important element in the advancement of Christian leadership for the twenty-first century."

"And the things you have heard me say in the presence of many witnesses entrust to reliable men who will also be qualified to teach others" (2 Timothy 2:2).

Experiencing Highs and Lows

I imagine some in the clergy might feel like holding a boycott sometimes. Some are saying HELP ME! Some might even feel like calling it quits—don't do it! Whatever you do, don't make any major decisions regarding your ministry or your church on a Monday. Wait until Thursday, when you are thinking more clearly. With your assignment come the highs and lows, the ebbs and flows.

Talk to the Lord about your feelings. Think about the positive side of the ministry. Get out of the house, do something fun, and laugh out loud. Find a colleague who has been through your challenges, who can help you put things in perspective. According to the words of Paul, "If God is for us, who can be against us?" (Romans 8:31).

In my Bible, I carry a prayer written by Martin Luther King Jr. that reads, "And now unto him who is able to keep us from falling and lift us from the dark valley of despair to the bright mountain of hope, from the midnight of desperation to the daybreak of joy, to him be power and authority for ever and ever, amen."

"I call on the LORD in my distress, and he answers me" (Psalm 120:1).

Spending Time
with the Lord

All of us face busy, stressful times. Too many events in a short period of time, people depending on you, and to be honest, not really knowing if you can satisfy all of those expectations. Sometimes, I don't think I can face another airport—but I do. Just like you, we do the best we can with what we have where we are.

I hope your schedule is manageable. If not, find a quiet place, look for perspective, and do the most important things first. But most of all, spend time with your Lord. The "C" in our G-R-A-C-E concept is "Constant Safeguards." Part of that means guarding your time and putting the proper value on everything you do.

Remember when Jesus and His disciples were so busy that they didn't even have time to eat? Jesus said to His disciples, who were attempting to meet so many needs, "Come with me by yourselves to a quiet place and get some rest" (Mark 6:31). Even in the midst of ministry, Jesus felt it necessary to stop for a while. Likewise, you need to stop for a while. If you haven't done so lately, you had better do so soon. Spend some quiet time listening to what the Lord has to say to you.

"The lions may grow weak and hungry, but those who seek the LORD lack no good thing" (Psalm 34:10).

Understanding Contention

Do you wonder why sometimes your people—for seemingly no reason—create an atmosphere of contention and division in your church? Or why one of our colleagues would sacrifice his ministry for a few moments of sensual pleasure?

What takes place in the minds and hearts of people who know God but are still controlled by evil desires and appetites? I'm not naïve enough to be totally surprised, but it still amazes me what some people do to create pain and loss in the lives of others. Doesn't it make you wonder?

Here are some of the reasons I believe people act like they do:

1. Self-deceit: "The heart is deceitful above all things" (Jeremiah 17:9).
2. Self-centeredness: "Each of us has turned to our own way" (Isaiah 53:6).
3. Pride: "Pride only breeds quarrels" (Proverbs 13:10).

Our hope is through the cross of Christ—"Where sin abounded, grace did much more abound" (Romans 5:20, KJV).

As pastors, we must think about what we do, what we say, and how we react. Remember, we are "created to be like God in true righteousness and holiness" (Ephesians 4:24).

Moving Forward

In Isaiah we read, "Forget the former things; do not dwell on the past. See, I am doing a new thing! Now it springs up; do you not perceive it?" (Isaiah 43:18-19).

I am afraid some of us do not "perceive it." Please do not fall into that trap. Consider ways to move forward:

1. What is the number-one challenge to your ministry today? How can you resolve that challenge? Who can assist you?
2. What is the number-one challenge facing your family at this moment? What can you do about it? Should you take the initiative?
3. Is there a weakness in your ministry that you need to work on? Is there a strength that you need to maximize? When should you begin?

I promise you, if you think through these simple questions, it will change your life, your ministry, and your attitude about everything. I'm rooting for you!

"For the foolishness of God is wiser than man's wisdom, and the weakness of God is stronger than man's strength" (1 Corinthians 1:25).

Having a Heart for Widows and Orphans

The world of the missionary has changed a lot. Missionaries spend shorter periods of time on the field and have shorter furloughs. With today's technology, they can access material and stay in touch with the world as never before.

But what has not changed is their heart for the least, the lonely, and the lost. One area of missions that I am very moved by is service to widows and orphans. Sure, there are those getting wealthy on the backs of orphans—but not all are! Many ministries to the poor and the orphaned operate with the highest integrity.

I wonder if we in the U.S. have emphasized the option of adoption as much as we should. Every church should have adequate information on adoption to hand to its people. Here are a few ideas to help your church learn more about orphans and adoption.

- Appoint a few of your congregants with a heart for children to research and find the best ministries with the highest standards.
- Invite representatives of those ministries to speak to your people about what's happening today in the area of adoption.
- Encourage your people to get involved with an organization that finds families for kids who are languishing in "the system" both here in the U.S. and abroad.

Children around the world are longing for a forever family. Shouldn't we in the ministry be a voice for those who cannot speak for themselves?

"Religion that God our Father accepts as pure and faultless is this: to look after orphans and widows in their distress and to keep oneself from being polluted by the world" (James 1:27).

The Most Important People

Some years ago, my dad passed away. He had grown old, and suddenly one day, he just died. It was a pivotal moment for me. As an only child, I had to step up and assume the role as head of the family.

I think about my dad just about every day. He was a part of a generation of clergy who, for some reason, thought the church was more important than family. He was a great dad in that he gave me everything I ever wanted, but he failed as a father because, as I was growing up, he didn't have time for me. Maybe you had the same experience—whether your dad was a pastor or not.

The reason I tell you this is to remind you of your role as husband, father (or wife, mother), and spiritual leader of your home and family. I don't want you to have any regrets. I know it's trite, but the most important people in your congregation are your spouse and children.

At home, talk about things other than the church. We never did that. Take time to establish memories aside from church activity. I don't remember many of those times. And whatever you do, model love before your children for your spouse. Tell your family members often how much you love them . . . even your adolescent children.

"How great is the love the Father has lavished on us, that we should be called children of God! And that is what we are!" (1 John 3:1). That's what I'm talking about—"lavished" love.

Doing Everything for God's Glory

We know when we have done our best, even when the results are not there. And then there are times when we just sit back in amazement at how God has worked through our feeble efforts. In other words, we must keep our successes and our failures in perspective, especially if we do everything to His glory and honor.

All of us prepare, plan, and pray for our activities. Sometimes they are successful, but other times, the results are not so great. Do you think for one moment that God looks upon you, His child, as someone who has performed better or worse than others? Of course not. He is thrilled with the successes of His children. And He offers comfort to those who struggle. We should do the same for one another.

So, it doesn't matter if you won or lost this past weekend. Hold your head up high. Remember Whose team you are on and for Whom you do what you do. It's all about perspective. If you have planned, prepared, and prayed . . . God's church will triumph.

"Do your best to present yourself to God as one approved, a workman who does not need to be ashamed and who correctly handles the word of truth" (2 Timothy 2:15).

Making Decisions with Confidence

You know the story of Abraham and his obedience to the call of God on his life and mission (Genesis 12). The thing I find intriguing is that Abraham's mission was a mystery to him. Yet, he packed up and followed God's direction—and he was 75 years old.

When given the choice of the best land, Abraham gave it to Lot and took what was left. He was rewarded for his decision.

Today, I deal with so many who think they must know each step to take before making a decision. And when they do make a decision, they feel it must be "the best one." Not so—God still asks us to live by faith and to bloom where we are planted.

I know there are those reading my words right now who are in the throes of making a decision. They have analyzed all the angles to death and still find themselves undecided.

There are two things I see that worked in Abraham's favor: First, he built an altar to the Lord wherever he was. He was obedient. He worshiped. Second, he entered into a covenant with his God. They made sincere promises to each other. God said to His servant, "Do not be afraid, Abram. I am your shield, your very great reward" (Genesis 15:1). God was faithful.

So, my colleague, you will be faced with many decisions. Be faithful, be obedient, be courageous. Make your decision—and move on with confidence.

"But I trust in you, O LORD; I say, 'You are my God'" (Psalm 31:14).

Loving Your People

Love begets love. When you love your people genuinely, they will love you back.

Over the years, that fact has been proven to me again and again. From many whose names I could not remember, and faces I could not identify, have come words of thanks and blessings for my loving them and standing in the gap for their families and marriages.

I'm not tooting my own horn. I am just responding to a dangerous trend I see in the church—where the pastor wants to be served and stands aloof from the people of his pasture. I promise you that years from now—no, weeks from now—your people will scarcely remember the sermons you preached. But I promise, they will never forget the love you showed to them and the joy you expressed at being called their pastor.

Love your people. They will love you back—I promise!

"It is right for me to feel this way about all of you, since I have you in my heart" (Philippians 1:7).

Living a Life of Praise

There are times in our busy schedules when we have some down moments that make praising God difficult, and for a while, we may "forget His benefits." How?

(1) By failing to live a life of praise. "Let the redeemed of the LORD say so" (Psalm 107:2, KJV). Be filled with praise that begins and ends each day with, "This is the day the LORD has made; let us rejoice and be glad in it" (Psalm 118:24).

(2) By creating a negative environment for others. We need to live in such a way that we bring hope to the lives of those we meet along the journey. As His shepherds, we must leave people encouraged.

(3) By treating casually the greatest gift of all—God's gift of His Son, Jesus. We must never lose the focus of our message: "How great is the love the Father has lavished on us, that we should be called children of God!" (1 John 3:1). People need to know how blessed they are—so do you.

In Psalm 107:1, the psalmist writes, "Give thanks to the LORD, for he is good; his love endures forever."

There's No Promotion
from the Pastorate

A few years back, I returned to California to preside at a memorial service for a beloved physician I had been privileged to pastor. My former church was without a senior pastor and I felt the freedom to respond to the family's invitation.

As I stood before people I had loved and cared for during a very important part of my life, I thanked God for the opportunity He had given me to walk with them through the valleys, rejoice with them on the mountaintops, and share a piece of their lives through good times and bad.

I looked into the faces of former parishioners who had come to know Christ through the foolishness of my preaching and had looked to me for guidance in times of perplexity. I had pointed them toward Christ and they had embraced Him and found the peace that passes all understanding. I also came face-to-face with those who, during my absence, had lost their dearest loved ones. It was evident by the look in their eyes that, in many ways, life for them would never be the same.

But do you know what I felt most as I addressed those who had come to offer comfort to a grieving family? I felt again that there is no promotion from the pastorate. We may go on to other things, but we will never go on to better things. Be a shepherd, my colleague; be a shepherd.

"And of this gospel I was appointed a herald and an apostle and a teacher" (2 Timothy 1:11).

The Wisdom of
Veteran Ministers

As I listen again to Focus on the Family radio interviews I had conducted with veteran ministers and leaders such as Richard Halverson, W. A. Criswell, Howard Hendricks, Bruce Wilkinson, Chuck Colson, Jerry Bridges, Luis Palau, Jack Hayford, and James Dobson, I can't help but be impressed with their depth of wisdom and maturity.

In their interviews, they do not revert to gimmicks or "fad talk." As they comment on subjects like holiness, forgiveness, sovereignty of God, family, and political involvement, they do so from years of training and experience, but also from the mind of God. I am moved both by their knowledge and humility, and I'm reminded once again how important it is for all of us to have a mentor—someone we admire who will interact with us when we are troubled, challenged, or arrogant. Someone who, because of their vast experience, can see the bigger picture.

Do you have someone like that? If not, I encourage you to find a mentor with experience you may not have. Someone who will be honest when he sees you going down the wrong path. Someone who can advise you when you don't know what to do. Someone who is wise and experienced.

"Give me wisdom and knowledge, that I may lead this people" (2 Chronicles 1:10).

Be a Welcoming Church

Visiting a new church is a daunting experience for many people. Here are some suggestions for taking the edge off for new attendees: (1) Encourage your greeters to engage people in conversation. Make sure they know where the restrooms and drinking fountains are. (2) Where possible, seat visistors next to a family that is positive and excited about the church. (3) Encourage them to attend a Sunday school class or small group. (4) Don't have them stand to be introduced. (They could be from a neighboring church.) (5) Have a member of the greeting committee call them personally by Monday evening, and a pastoral staff person by Friday. (6) Make sure they receive a letter from the pastor filled with information about the church, especially activities for teens and children. (7) Have the pastoral staff positioned at the doors to shake hands with everyone. You may have only two or three weeks to connect with new attendees. In most cases, if you don't connect then, you never will.

"Greet the friends there by name" (3 John 14).

Pressures on Clergy Children

Beverley and I often reflect on the lives of our children and grandchildren and ask, "Where did the years go?" Life is on fast-forward these days, and the values we teach and the traditions we set must compete with all the other influences in the world. That is why the words of Joshua are so appropriate for our generation: "As for me and my household, we will serve the LORD" (Joshua 24:15).

Children of the clergy are not exempt from real-world pressures. In fact, as my experience in the Pastoral Ministries department at Focus on the Family proves, they are at great risk. Satan would like nothing more than to weaken the fiber of the clergy home by causing division and turmoil. We must be on the alert for his cunning attacks.

I urge you to celebrate with your children. Honor them, love them, teach them, and discipline them. While we respect your most precious calling—to lead the church—we also encourage you to serve as an example to your children.

"Train a child in the way he should go, and when he is old he will not turn from it" (Proverbs 22:6).

Emphasizing the Cross

I know it is impossible to maintain full-scale evangelistic momentum all the time, but it is not impossible to sustain an ongoing sense of urgency for lost souls. Think about those who will not spend eternity with Jesus.

As I stood at Ground Zero in New York City, I was angry and confused, but with much compassion for the families whose innocent loved ones were ambushed. I also wondered about the eternity of those who were lost. As I surveyed the destruction, I saw a huge cross of remnant metal beams standing tall and triumphant in the midst of all the confusion. It was then that I was reminded that the "old rugged cross" does make a difference. In truth, it is the only thing that will never change. Do you talk about the old rugged cross very often?

"May I never boast except in the cross of our Lord Jesus Christ" (Galatians 6:14).

Caring for Those We Serve

We are many things in the ministry, and one responsibility we must not overlook is the care and nurture of those we have been called to serve. It is not easy.

Jesus stood in the synagogue one day and read words from the prophet Isaiah. He announced the call His Father had assigned Him and, subsequently, has passed on to you and me: "The Spirit of the Lord is on me, because he has anointed me to preach good news to the poor. He has sent me to proclaim freedom for the prisoners and recovery of sight for the blind, to release the oppressed . . ." (Luke 4:18).

In other words, He accepted His responsibility to walk in the village of life and care for those with needs, who were in bondage, who were being held captive.

As ministers of the gospel, we are called to do the same. Have you considered the best way to care for your people? Are you proclaiming freedom for those imprisoned in sin? Do the people who sit in your pews know about "Jesus Christ and him crucified"? It's a solemn responsibility. Please think about it.

"But God demonstrates his own love for us in this: While we were still sinners, Christ died for us" (Romans 5:8).

Meaningful Scriptures
for Ministry

Scripture has much to say to those of us who serve in the ministry. Here are several that are particularly appropriate reminders of how we should think and act. Take a few moments to think about how they apply to your ministry.

"Set an example for the believers in speech, in life, in love, in faith and in purity" (1 Timothy 4:12).

"Watch your life and doctrine closely" (1 Timothy 4:16).

"Remember your leaders, who spoke the word of God to you. Consider the outcome of their way of life and imitate their faith" (Hebrews 13:7).

"Obey your leaders and submit to their authority. They keep watch over you as men who must give an account" (Hebrews 13:17).

"Now we ask you, brothers, to respect those who work hard among you . . . Hold them in the highest regard in love because of their work" (1 Thessalonians 5:12-13).

"The elders who direct the affairs of the church well are worthy of double honor, especially those whose work is preaching and teaching" (1 Timothy 5:17).

"Preach the Word; . . . correct, rebuke and encourage—with great patience and careful instruction" (2 Timothy 4:2).

"As Jesus went on from there, he saw [one] named _____ [put your name in the space] . . . 'Follow me,' he [said]" (Matthew 9:9).

If You're Going to Make News, Make Good News!

When I was a kid growing up in a pastor's home, my dad was always in the news. He would be fighting an evil like casinos on the Mississippi River or promoting some event. Those times were both frightening and exciting. He fought the mob so strongly that our lives were potentially in danger. He was even chaplain for the St. Louis Cardinals when Stan Musial was a star. I was proud of him.

In the past few years some of my megachurch colleagues have been in the news representing good causes like feeding the hungry and defending the institution of marriage. Nice going! But there have also been troubling reports about noted televangelists whose lavish lifestyles have caught the attention of government officials.

A while back, four news stories crossed my desk. The first was about an evangelist who was arrested on a murder charge while he was preaching. They discovered his wife's body in a freezer. Another told of a preacher who was convicted of aggravated menacing for waving a gun and cursing at a lady who cut him off in traffic.

And then there were two stories related to pastors' wives. One woman shot her husband to death and was convicted of voluntary manslaughter. Another, the copastor of a popular megachurch, was involved in an altercation with a flight attendant.

So, what's the point? You, who have influence, should make good news. Don't draw attention to yourself in such a way that calls your ministry into question or diminishes the message you preach. If you're going to make news . . . make good news!

"In the same way, let your light shine before men, that they may see your good deeds and praise your Father in heaven" (Matthew 5:16).

Supporting Each Other

It is appropriate that we ministers support and appreciate each other. Who better than a colleague to understand our challenges and stresses? Who better than another ministry family to relate to the pressures our loved ones encounter? Who better to appreciate the battles required for guiding a congregation than someone else who faces them? Who better to realize what is at stake than one who shares the same calling?

Any time is a wonderful time for you and your family to tell a comrade in the faith how grateful you are for his or her commitment to carrying the message entrusted to us by our Lord. By simply making a phone call or sending a note of affirmation, you might encourage another minister in your community. Better yet, get together face-to-face.

We are all on the same team, playing for the same coach, and engaged in a titanic struggle with evil. We will not win the battle alone, but only as we join our hearts and talents in a mighty show of mutual faith and admiration for each other.

"Therefore encourage one another and build each other up, just as in fact you are doing" (1 Thessalonians 5:11).

Joy Suckers—Dealing with the Tough Ones

Dealing with the tough stuff can make you wonder if the God who calls you really understands the challenges you are facing. And then, of course, you remember: He is God and He knows.

If you have been in ministry very long, you have run head-on into "joy suckers." I talk about the "joy suckers challenge" in many of my speaking assignments. That's because if you don't learn how to deal with joy suckers, you stand a good chance of becoming calloused or reclusive, neither of which is good for a shepherd.

A joy sucker is someone who is determined to create either discouragement or hardship for your ministry. Joy suckers take on all shapes and sizes, but most often, they are negative in their outlook, disappointed with their family, in need of attention, or enamored with their own power. Somewhere along the way, they have been allowed to get away with unacceptable behavior. Because they are not happy people, they are determined that others should not be happy either. So, they are critical, fault-finding, and contentious. Close your eyes for a minute, and you will see every joy sucker you have ever served. Painful, isn't it?

If you have seven or eight joy suckers in a small- to medium-sized congregation, it can cause the fellowship to become dysfunctional as well. So, how do you deal with the tough stuff that can make even the strongest pastor flinch?

(a) You try to understand the cause of the negative spirit. Why do these people act the way they do? (b) You consider family situations. (c) You gauge their level of spirituality. (d) You monitor their influence in your church. Is there a big family connection? (e) Have you done all you can to talk through the concern with them? (f) Do you pray for them? (g) Do they have a history of this kind of behavior? (h) What will it cost you to confront them? (i) Does leadership understand your challenge? (j) Is the contention severe enough to render your ministry ineffective?

Every church has joy suckers, and we all must develop our own method of dealing with them. If you let them run free, your church will never be all that God intends and your ministry will be defined by negativity.

"Now it is required that those who have been given a trust must prove faithful" (1 Corinthians 4:2).

Togetherness: The Value of a Teammate

I enjoy watching the Ryder Cup. If you're a golfer, you know the format, but in case you do not, here it is: The United States team is pitted against a team of European golfers. They have a variety of specific matches that pit one two-man team against another two-man team. The final day, each American golfer goes head-to-head with a European. It is a total team effort.

Okay, enough about the game of golf. For me, the most interesting thing about the Ryder Cup is the unselfish nature of each team member. Those who are not playing cheer for those who are. Those who are playing together do all they can for their partner to ensure their success. Those who win are applauded. Those who lose are applauded. For each team, it is an exercise in togetherness. It is great!

So, you probably know what I am going to say next. What would it be like if *we*, who are on the "clergy team," developed a mind-set that we are going to do all we can to help one another succeed? That would result in exceptional pastors, but no one would be a prima donna. Those who have a lot would help those who have little. Those with a great deal of experience would mentor those who are inexperienced. And on and on it would go.

The end result: Communities across North America would see the unity of their spiritual leaders, and, in time, they would model that unity. Acts chapter 2 would jump off the pages of the New Testament and become reality. What if? What if?

I love the spirit of Acts chapter 11 where, in a time of crisis, it says, "The disciples, each according to his ability, decided to provide help for the brothers living in Judea. This they did" (Acts 11:29-30).

An Eternal Bailout

Please do not think me naïve, but yesterday, as I was watching the news and hearing the word *bailout* over and over, I was reminded of the greatest bailout of all time: the price Jesus paid for our freedom, security, and *salvation*. Paul wrote to the Romans, "You see, at just the right time, when we were still powerless, Christ died for the ungodly" (Romans 5:6). Please notice the words *right time* and *powerless*.

John echoed Paul's words: "God has given us eternal life, and this life is in his Son [Jesus]. He who has the Son has life; he who does not have the Son of God does not have life" (1 John 5:11-12). It's an eternal bailout if there ever was one. Yet, a lot of people reject God's offer.

I'm telling you, my colleague, what is happening in our world today gives you a perfect opening to preach a life-changing salvation message. Go for it!

"This is how much God loved the world: He gave his Son, his one and only Son. And this is why: so that no one need be destroyed; by believing in him, anyone can have a whole and lasting life" (John 3:16, MSG).

A Willingness to Leap

Recently I had the opportunity to teach at the Billy Graham Training Center at The Cove. It was a genuine privilege. Who would have thought that a rebellious kid from Arkansas would have a chance like that to prove God really does direct the paths of His children?

As I looked around that magnificent place and observed the many reminders of how God has used Mr. Graham and his team to reach out to a troubled world, I was humbled by the reality that God can use people like you and me to carry out His redemptive purposes.

What every one of us needs is a dream, a team, and a plan to move forward. We need to become the leaders that God intends for us to be. Will you accept God's design for your ministry? Will you pay the price to become the leader God has ordained you to be?

There are so many definitions of leadership. I have a new one. "A leader is one with a God-given dream, vision, or project and uses his or her gifts to recruit people and resources to achieve goals."

I know we all take different routes along the leadership journey, but every leader must constantly have before him something that is risky but worth the effort. Be a leader! I promise you, people will respond to your challenge.

"Now finish the work, so that your eager willingness to do it may be matched by your completion of it, according to your means" (2 Corinthians 8:11).

The Struggle with Morality

A nationwide survey by the Barna Research Group indicates that Americans have redefined what it means to do the right thing. Researchers asked adults which, if any, of eight behaviors with moral overtones they had engaged in during a given week. The behaviors included exposure to pornography, using profanity in public, gambling, gossiping, engaging in sexual intercourse with someone to whom they are not married, retaliating against someone, getting drunk, and lying.

While there's no room to go into details here, according to George Barna, who directed the survey, the results reflect a significant shift in American life. "We are witnessing the development and acceptance of a new moral code in America. The consistent deterioration of the Bible as the source of moral truth has led to a nation where people have become independent judges of right and wrong, basing their choices on feelings and circumstances. It is not likely that America will return to a more traditional moral code until the nation experiences significant pain from its moral choices."

Pastor, these are the people you minister to, the people in your community. I encourage you to look beyond the doors of your church to the masses who are perishing. I encourage you to think about how you can best minister to people who have lost their moral direction, who don't believe in absolute truth, who do what is right in their own eyes.

"People will be lovers of themselves, lovers of money, boastful, proud, abusive, disobedient to their parents, ungrateful, unholy, without love, unforgiving, slanderous, without self-control, brutal, not lovers of the good, treacherous, rash, conceited, lovers of pleasure rather than lovers of God" (2 Timothy 3:2-4).

In Your Labor . . . Trust Him!

"Come to me, all you who are weary and burdened, and I will give you rest. Take my yoke upon you and learn from me, for I am gentle and humble in heart, and you will find rest for your souls. For my yoke is easy and my burden is light" (Matthew 11:28-30).

I am blessed by the way Warren Wiersbe describes Matthew chapter 11. John the Baptist knew his ministry was over, and he wondered if Jesus really understood what was at stake. In other words, "Jesus, do you think you have what it takes?" Jesus replied, "Trust me! It will be all right."

I know that a lot of you who read these words wonder, as John the Baptist did, "Am I making any difference?" Is it worth the toll it is taking on me and my family? Am I where I can do the most good? But, as Jesus made clear to His prophet, "Your work is not in vain. You have not failed. I will reward you. Just trust me!"

I say to you, my colleague, take some time to get away with your Lord. Walk with Him. Talk to Him. Tell Him anything. Watch how He works and learn from Him the new lessons He has for you. You will develop a new pace for living, a revived sense of worth for your mission, and a deeper appreciation for the One who called you. Just stay close to Him. Trust Him. And, as Warren Wiersbe writes, "Surrender to Christ's loving yoke and you will experience His perfect rest." In other words—trust Him!

"Let him who walks in the dark . . . trust in the name of the LORD and rely on his God" (Isaiah 50:10).

Meeting Men in the Village

Several times in this book I've talked about the importance of reaching men because I believe it's critical to the health of both the church and the family.

A while back I spoke at a men's conference in a forest of towering redwoods in California. I have spoken at scores of men's events, but this one had a unique feel to it. Two words highlighted our time: *surrender* and *legacy.*

Surrender. So many of those I met struggled with addictions, unforgiveness, broken dreams, and shattered families. Many of them were at the point of choosing their own path or surrendering to the power of God for a solution. "Humble yourselves, therefore, under God's mighty hand . . . Cast all your anxiety on him because he cares for you" (1 Peter 5:6-7).

Legacy. How these men influence their children and spouses will determine how the spiritual baton is passed from one generation to the next. "So the next generation would know . . . even the children yet to be born, and they in turn would tell their children" (Psalm 78:6).

It was an awesome sight to see bikers, ex-cons, drug addicts, and yes, just normal guys choosing the God alternative over their own.

My question: How much time do you spend one-on-one with men in your congregation? I'm not just talking about those on your leadership team, but men who sit in the pews on Sunday—even those who are on the fringe and don't often attend church. It would be interesting to know if your men have ever had a quality conversation with their pastor.

I promise you, my colleague, if you would give part of one day each week to meet individually with the men under your care, the understanding of their challenges, doubts, and insecurities will change the way you lead your church. It will also enhance your appreciation for who they are and how they can improve the effectiveness of your congregation. Caution: If you make this effort, you will run into some dead ends and disappointments, but you will also find great blessing.

"I looked for a man among them who would . . . stand before me in the gap" (Ezekiel 22:30).

You Can't Please Everyone

All of us in Christian work receive our share of criticism, and, personally, I have always been a little thin-skinned. But working with pastors, I have become much tougher.

Our Lord said, "Woe to you when all men speak well of you" (Luke 6:26). For most of us, there's no danger of that! We must realize that challenges to our opinions are as much a part of the ministry as affirmation. We need to get tougher, not take ourselves quite so seriously, and when we believe our ideas are God's ideas, take a risk!

You can never please everyone, but we are all on the same team and will be spending eternity together. Let's not forget that.

"In everything set them an example by doing what is good. In your teaching show integrity, seriousness and soundness of speech that cannot be condemned, so that those who oppose you may be ashamed because they have nothing bad to say" (Titus 2:7-8).

Having Honest Dialogue

We are different. Being in ministry makes us different. We have different schedules, unique stresses on our families, and more unrealistic expectations placed on us than many others. Sometimes we dump too much on our spouses about the problems we are facing, and at other times we hold everything inside. We need, where possible, to take the "worry load" off our mates, talk with a colleague instead, and trust God at all times. "Pour out your hearts to him, for God is our refuge" (Psalm 62:8).

How are you and your family doing? When was the last time you and your spouse just took a walk or sat down over a cup of coffee to have a conversation totally related to her (or him)? Here are a few questions that will help you get in touch with what's going on with your spouse:

How are you feeling?

Are you fulfilled?

Are you sensing pressure from the church community to do or fill a role you are not prepared for?

Are you getting enough of my time?

Are your gifts being utilized?

Do you have a close friend you can confide in?

If you could change one thing about your situation, what would that be?

I admit that asking these questions takes some courage and willingness to engage in honest dialogue. But don't you think it might be worthwhile?

"Wives, understand and support your husbands by submitting to them in ways that honor the Master. Husbands, go all out in love for your wives. Don't take advantage of them" (Colossians 3:18-19, MSG).

The Most Important Message

We cannot depend on personal crises or scary events in the world to drive men and women into the church, or even to Christ. The only thing that will accomplish that goal is for mankind to realize they are lost without Jesus. Foxhole conversions are few and far between. The most effective way to turn people's hearts to God is through the genuine witness of those who have embraced our Lord and who, with childlike excitement, share that good news (Mark 16:15).

Each Sunday gives us clergy the opportunity to encourage our people to live lives of faith and courage, to engage their friends and family in meaningful conversation about the value of being born again (John 3:7). Is there a more important message? I think not.

An elderly pastor once quoted an old saying to me: "Don't forget, son. The light that shines brightest at home can be seen farthest away!" The light of your local church ministry should shine so brightly that the world is influenced by its vision. Pastor, encourage your people to be light in a dark world.

"You are the light of the world. A city on a hill cannot be hidden. Neither do people light a lamp and put it under a bowl. Instead they put it on its stand, and it gives light to everyone in the house. In the same way, let your light shine before men, that they may see your good deeds and praise your Father in heaven" (Matthew 5:14-16).

Having the Courage of Elijah

I don't think I would have been comfortable being King Ahab. The Bible says in 1 Kings, chapter 16, that the king "did more evil in the eyes of the LORD than any of those [kings] before him" (v. 30). It also says King Ahab "did more to provoke the LORD . . . to anger than did all the kings of Israel before him" (v. 33). He must have really been something.

Now, just imagine that you were Elijah, the prophet, and that you had been chosen to confront this evil person with a word from the Lord that would displease him very much. That assignment would not be a walk in the park, would it?

Well, my friend, the assignment that Elijah accepted is similar to the task that our Lord has for you. You, as a kind of Elijah, have been consigned by our Lord to defend righteousness and confront evil. As the servant of God, it is your assignment to take a stand.

Every day presents us with challenges—things we can take a stand for or against, issues that might not be too popular with some in the community, topics that might even stir up our congregants. Will you take a stand, even if your words and actions displease people? Will you have the courage of Elijah to speak truth even if you become a target for people's hostility?

As pastors we have to do what's right rather than what's popular. I pray God will give you the courage.

"Who will rise up for me against the wicked? Who will take a stand for me against evildoers?" (Psalm 94:16).

Protecting Your Family

My wife, Beverley, was a pastor's wife for more than 30 years. During those three decades she exhibited myriad emotions as she went about her role as a wife, mother, and involved laywoman.

In the early years of our ministry we served a church that was unschooled in its treatment of the pastor and his family. A lot of unrealistic expectations were placed on Bev. Plus, congregants often made references to former pastors and their families, and they commented on everything, from how she dressed to her attendance at church functions. We were pretty young and inexperienced at that time, so we just accepted the situation as part of the pastoral territory. But as we matured in the ministry and assumed responsibility with larger congregations, we learned this kind of thing would take its toll on us if we didn't set some parameters.

We talked it over and, in time, came up with the following guidelines to protect Bev and our children. I share them with you for your consideration.

- A family-before-ministry schedule should be considered a safeguard for your home rather than a detriment to your ministry.
- Your home should be *your* sanctuary, not a gathering place for the congregation (unless, of course, that's what you want). You should have the liberty to shut the doors and pull the shades of your house for uninterrupted privacy.

- The fact that your children are PKs does not make them fair game for the gossip of curious church folks. Your family, not the constituency, should determine what role each person in your home will embrace in church.
- Guard your days off, and take vacations. Don't jump for the telephone every time it rings. Monitor the calls and respond only to real emergencies. When possible, try to get away from the house for most of your downtime.
- You should set the tone for the whole family. Make it plain to the church leadership and congregation that your family is your priority, and they should be treated with the same respect and courtesy as any family in the church community.

Take my thoughts for what they are worth. These guidelines worked well for us. I hope you will think a little bit more about your home and each individual who lives there.

"A [pastor] . . . must manage his children and his household well" (1 Timothy 3:12).

Take Time to Look Around

When I see the beauty of nature, I think of God the Creator, and the words of a song come to mind: "Ah, sovereign Lord, you have made the heavens and the earth by your great power and outstretched arm. Nothing is too difficult for you."

And then there are the words of the psalmist: "When I consider your heavens, the work of your fingers, the moon and the stars, which you have set in place, what is man that you are mindful of him, the son of man that you care for him?" (Psalm 8:3-4).

To think that, above and beyond all of this beauty, God cares much more for you and me! He wants us to slow down and let Him show us His love, to feel His touch on our shoulder and to hear His voice softly call our name. When we live such frantic lives, not only do we miss the beauty of His handiwork, but we also miss the still small voice of His direction for us. Slow down, my colleague—look around. Listen . . . be still, and you will be amazed at God's limitless concern for you and what you do.

"Be still, and know that I am God" (Psalm 46:10).

The Little Black Book:
A Lesson in Forgiveness

You know you should forgive, but sometimes it just seems impossible. You know what I mean. A church member makes life miserable for you and your family. And eventually, the conflict leads to your leaving a place you have loved. Life has not been the same since, and that feeling of betrayal burns like a hot coal in the pit of your stomach. *The remedy: forgiveness.*

Maybe for you it has been more of a political issue. Your projected road to the top has been detoured by a denominational leader. You just didn't measure up to his expectations, and you found the road blocked. You have gone on, but your spirit was broken and your dreams shattered. Nobody else really knows about it, but inside, there is sadness. *The remedy: forgiveness.*

Perhaps it's a more personal conflict. Your father never gave you the kind of approval and love you needed. You reached for it, but there was little or no return. Maybe a spouse or a child has not contributed to your ministry the way you had hoped. In fact, your progress was stalled because, as others viewed your family, they realized you were not a team. You go on, but there's an angry attitude that permeates your spirit. *The remedy: forgiveness.*

In my work as a pastor to pastors, I have seen evidence in the lives of too many of our colleagues that they carry around a "little black book" in their hearts that is filled with the offenses against them. The little book has almost become a security crutch. It represents people to blame, unacceptable circumstances, and excuses for ineffective ministry. Many of our clergy friends have become paranoid, fearful, bitter, and at times, hopeless because they have been unable to deal, and ultimately cope, with the injustices they have suffered. *The remedy: forgiveness.*

That little black book will become a millstone around your neck unless you make it a steppingstone to total healing. The remedy *is* forgiveness.

"Bear with each other and forgive whatever grievances you may have against one another. Forgive as the Lord forgave you" (Colossians 3:13).

Assessing the Health
of Your Congregation

So, if it's not size but health that counts, what about the health of your church? May I suggest a few guidelines for assessing the health of a congregation of any size?

Biblically Based. Do your congregation members have a clear understanding of what they believe and substantial information to assist them in defending their faith? Is there a discipleship training program?

Mutually Concerned. Do your people genuinely care for one another? Is there a system in place that informs your congregation when people have needs, and a prayer chain to respond to those needs?

Socially Concerned. If you do not have a small group ministry, do you have a Sunday school program that provides adequate time for your people to break bread together? Church is fellowship as much as it is a formal worship service.

Community Saturated. Are you aware of the day-to-day decisions being made in your community that affect the school system, social programs, and overall moral climate of the city you serve?

Financially Stable. The church that is fiscally responsible can weather any situation. Every pastor and governance board should insist on maintaining a certain dollar reserve, and do everything possible to avoid ministry paralysis through an unrealistic building or property debt. People must be taught by example to give and to give cheerfully.

Clearly Defined Vision. Every church needs to know who it is, what its calling is, and how it will be directed to meet the challenge of the future. If not, many small, and even larger, churches will simply exist to support an institution.

Positive Outlook. Please do not allow yourself to fall into a "poor me, small us" mentality. Small-mindedness is contagious. See yourself as God sees you—full of potential and planted for a purpose.

I'm sure there are many other good health indicators for churches of any size. I urge you to consider the ones I have listed, then add your own ideas to the mix. One thing I know, Christianity needs you to find a way to make your ministry meaningful and to help change the way pastors and laypeople alike look at the church of Jesus Christ. I am rooting for you!

". . . and to present her to himself as a radiant church, without stain or wrinkle or any other blemish, but holy and blameless" (Ephesians 5:27).

Doing It Right . . .
Preaching, That Is

Majestic outcomes occur when the divine tool of preaching is used properly. So, approach your pulpit with awe and anticipation that God will make a difference in the lives of those who hear His Word proclaimed. Too often, too many of us do not grasp this sword with both hands and wield it with skill.

Dr. Stephen F. Olford firmly believed that great preaching must be expository preaching, which he defines as "the historical, grammatical and contextual examination and presentation of Scripture, in the power of the Holy Spirit, with a homiletical pattern and an evangelical purpose." In his booklet *Preaching the Word of God*, Dr. Olford constructs a method of biblical exposition based on the model of Jesus as He opened the Scriptures to His companions on the road to Emmaus:

The Reading of the Text of Scripture. Your people need to hear the actual words of the Bible. We should never underestimate the power of the Word of God to change lives on its own. Further, being able to recite the Scriptures from memory provides an added benefit because it underscores your personal conviction regarding the importance of knowing God's Word.

The Revealing of the Truth of Scripture. The biblical expositor is to restate the truth, showing its relevance to the Lord Jesus. For, ultimately, the mosaic of all revelation comes together in Jesus Christ. Four hermeneutical principles enable the preacher to unlock the treasures of Scripture:

1. Illumination: Request insights from the Author of the Bible.

2. Contextual Interpretation: Never interpret a verse in isolation from both its immediate and larger context.
3. Clarity: Use verses that are clear to gain understanding of those that are difficult or ambiguous.
4. Grammatical-Historical Method: Understand the meaning of the words as they were employed by the authors and in the historical situation which produced the writing.

As H. G. Mackay has reminded us, "Accuracy is essential in the ministry of the Word. It is a solemn thing to misquote the Almighty!"

The Relating of the Thrust of Scripture. It is a biblical principle that all truth has an application to life, and the application of divine truth always ministers personally and profitably. The biblical expositor must present the thrust of Scripture in such a way that its relevance to character and conduct is both indisputable and irresistible.

Charles H. Spurgeon wrote, "Never play at preaching, nor beat about the bush; get at it, and always mean business." We have a tremendous honor and privilege to speak for our Lord. We also have a great responsibility to do it right.

"Preach the Word; be prepared in season and out of season; correct, rebuke and encourage—with great patience and careful instruction" (2 Timothy 4:2).

Who Would Have Imagined?

Recently I visited my old high school in University City, Missouri. I loved my high school years. I was an average football player, a below average wrestler, and an above average mid-distance runner. Oh, and I was an average student.

As I sat and remembered those years, it dawned on me how differently things have transpired than most people would have imagined. After all, at one reunion I was voted the one with the most unlikely profession!

Isn't it wonderful how God has a way of creating vessels of usefulness out of things that appear too broken to mend?

I don't know where this message finds you today. You may be playing on the first team without a care in the world—or you may be riding the bench, wondering if your game will ever be good enough.

Well, first of all, you're on the team. Thank God for that fact, and celebrate it. Second, God knows your gift mix and He has wonderful plans for you. Third, you must be ready. Stay in shape. Listen to the coach and cheer for your teammates. And if you're on the first team, don't gloat; just encourage those who might be struggling to find their place.

On my short trip back along memory lane, I paused and thanked God for opening up a world for me that most would have never thought possible. Most of all, me!

"Take a good look, friends, at who you were when you got called into this life. I don't see many of 'the brightest and the best' among you, not many influential, not many from high-society families. Isn't it obvious that God deliberately chose men and women that the culture overlooks and exploits and abuses, chose these 'nobodies' to expose the hollow pretensions of the 'somebodies'? That makes it quite clear that none of you can get by with blowing your own horn before God. Everything that we have—right thinking and right living, a clean slate and a fresh start—comes from God by way of Jesus Christ. That's why we have the saying, 'If you're going to blow a horn, blow a trumpet for God'" (1 Corinthians 1:26-31, MSG).

Who Prays for You?

The prayer of the intercessor cannot be restrained from the palaces of kings, the hovels of the poor, the homes of pastors, or the rooms of troubled teens. Intercessory prayer penetrates even the most formidable strongholds of pain, sickness, discouragement, and challenge.

I wonder why, with all of this power at our disposal, we do not pray more or seek to encourage others to pray for us. Paul wrote to Timothy, "I urge, then, first of all, that requests, prayers, intercession and thanksgiving be made for everyone" (1 Timothy 2:1). And the prophet Samuel said, "As for me, far be it from me that I should sin against the LORD by failing to pray for you" (1 Samuel 12:23).

Of course, there are times when we feel frustrated in prayer. We are only human. But we should never deny that the prayer of the intercessor is powerful and projects faith and love. The psalmist says, "Be still before the LORD and wait patiently for him" (Psalm 37:7). We must never doubt God's timing.

Picture two rooms separated by a wall. In one room, there is a person in need, and in the next, there is God. As an intercessor in the hallway, you can see each of them. The wall might be sin, unbelief, sickness, a spirit of bitterness, or discouragement. But you, the intercessor, can figuratively reach through a doorway, take the hand of God and the hand of man, and put them together. That is why the great men and women of prayer say the prayer of intercession is the greatest of all prayers.

Who do you pray for? Who prays for you, my friend? I have a colleague who prays for me every day by name. I am blessed. What an awesome gift.

I love you, pastor. I pray for you. I value you more than you will ever know. As he did Peter, Satan wants to sift you like wheat, but I have prayed for you that your faith will not fail.

"I pray that out of his glorious riches he may strengthen you with power through his Spirit in your inner being, so that Christ may dwell in your hearts through faith" (Ephesians 3:16-17).

Majesty in the Moment

As I've mentioned before, nearly every day as I leave the office, I behold a beautiful sight to the west—the majestic landscape of the Front Range of the Rocky Mountains. Most notable is Pikes Peak, which inspired Katharine Lee Bates to write "America the Beautiful." Because I witness this wonderful piece of God's creation so often, there are times when I take it for granted.

Sometimes the works of God become commonplace, but He wants us to remember Him. The psalmist wrote, "The heavens declare the glory of God; the skies proclaim the work of his hands. Day after day they pour forth speech" (Psalm 19:1-2). David was aware of God's handiwork. Daily he recognized the awesome power of the One who could create a universe and also care for each of His children.

So I also think of you, my colleague—whether you have labored in His vineyard for decades or you are just getting started. What a magnificent and "fearfully and wonderfully made" (Psalm 139:14) creation you are.

There must be times in your journey, though, when you wonder if God knows your burdens: a prodigal child, an empty marriage, a cumbersome assignment. We all go through moments of wondering where He is. Even when we can't see Him or when we've taken Him for granted, "by day the LORD directs his love, at night his song is with me" (Psalm 42:8).

The Peak, as Coloradans call it, has so many varied personalities—from snow-packed to barren, from cloud-covered to a brilliant array of colors and hues—but it is still Pikes Peak, a constant day to day.

Each day for you will not always be the same. There will be times of sunshine and shadows. Laughter and tears. Success and failure. But the one constant looms larger than anything else: Our glorious Lord, who towers above creation, loves you unconditionally. He is aware of your surroundings, and if you look carefully, you will see His unmistakable attention given to you, your family, and your ministry. Whatever you do, please never take that for granted.

"Give thanks to the God of gods. *His love endures forever*" (Psalm 136:2).

Let It Begin in Me

To be honest, I have great concern about the church in America today. In my travel and contact with pastors, denominational leaders, and concerned laypeople, I have observed a spiritual drought in our land. We pray, but we do not change. We "fight the fight" and go through the prescribed motions. But we don't actually initiate the deep change within ourselves necessary for spiritual renewal.

Praying is only one part of the equation for spiritual renewal and a rebirth of vitality in the church. According to 2 Chronicles 7:14, humility and repentance must also be present.

I believe God hears our fervent cries for revival in the land, but I also believe that answered prayer comes as a result of obedience to the will of God. Disobedience brings judgment—obedience brings great blessing. As leaders, are we setting the proper example of personal obedience?

I realize it is impossible to deal with a subject as complicated as the rebirth of the church in a few words. But I am certain of one thing: The ingredients of rebirth are found in three words from Scripture: humility, prayer, and repentance.

I pray that spiritual renewal might begin in me.

"If at any time I announce that a nation or kingdom is to be uprooted, torn down and destroyed, and if that nation I warned repents of its evil, then I will relent and not inflict on it the disaster I had planned" (Jeremiah 18:7-8).

When Is Revival Needed?

Charles G. Finney once offered a list to help determine when a church needs a revival. The list from his revival lectures is timeless. He believed revivals are needed when these conditions prevail:

- Lack of love: "When there is a lack of brotherly love and Christian confidence among professors of religion, then revival is needed."
- Disunity and division: "When there are dissensions and jealousies and evil speakings among professors of religion, then revival is needed."
- Worldliness: "When there is a worldly spirit in the church, then revival is needed."
- Sin in the church: "When the church finds its members falling into gross and scandalous sins, then revival is needed."
- Controversy and disagreement: "When there is a spirit of controversy in the church, then revival is needed."
- Wickedness controls society: "When the wicked triumph over the churches and revile them, then revival is needed."
- Sinners are careless: "When sinners are careless and stupid, then revival is needed."

Do you see any of these conditions in our churches and society? I sure do.

"People will be lovers of themselves, lovers of money, boastful, proud, abusive, disobedient to their parents, ungrateful, unholy, without love, unforgiving, slanderous, without self-control, brutal, not lovers of the good, treacherous, rash, conceited, lovers of pleasure rather than lovers of God—having a form of godliness but denying its power" (2 Timothy 3:2-5).

Prayer, the Key to Revival

Seldom have great spiritual awakenings come to pastors, churches, or countries without intercessory prayer. Before an awakening in India near the turn of the twentieth century, John Hyde, a praying missionary, asked Christians these questions to stimulate faithfulness in prayer for revival:

- Are you praying for quickening in your own life, in the life of your fellow workers, and in the church?
- Are you longing for greater power of the Holy Spirit in your life and work, and are you convinced you cannot go on without this power?
- Will you pray that you may not be ashamed of Jesus?
- Do you believe that prayer is the great means for securing this spiritual awakening?
- Will you set apart one half hour each day as soon after noon as possible to pray for this awakening, and are you willing to pray till it comes?

Real revival restores an individual and a church to spiritual health and well-being. For an individual, genuine revival enables him to live out his faith in the daily details of life. Such a renewal brings a church from subnormal, barely-making-it Christianity to a supernatural empowerment, a sense of anointing, and the awareness that it is a unique organization owned and energized by God.

Revival stirs a congregation. It challenges and empowers us to live out the radical demands of Christianity in every phase of life, inside and outside the church.

"Be joyful in hope, patient in affliction, faithful in prayer" (Romans 12:12).

"Devote yourselves to prayer, being watchful and thankful" (Colossians 4:2).

You Might Be a Pastor If . . .

I am sure you've heard "You might be a pastor if . . ." jokes many times. Things like: You might be a pastor if . . . you find yourself counting heads at a sporting event. You would rather talk to people with every eye closed and every head bowed. You had a dream that while you were speaking no one was listening, and then you realized it wasn't a dream. You have a difficult time explaining to your kids just exactly what a pastor does. You're leading the church into the twenty-first century, but you don't know what you're preaching on Sunday. You've ever wanted to "lay hands" around a deacon's neck.

I think you get the picture. Every assignment has its challenges, but it seems these days those of us who serve the church have been especially stretched.

Some time ago, I wrote a prayer with you in mind. I prayed this prayer over you and your colleagues this week. I will continue to do so.

"Dear God, thank you for these you have called to lead your church. I pray for them . . . That the demands on their time will not threaten their intimacy with you. That they will give adequate attention to their own families as they seek to guide those within their congregations. That they may find a colleague to join them in fellowship and prayer for one another and their community. That their preaching and teaching will not be tepid, but courageous and purposeful. That the people they lead will respond to their passion for truth and righteousness, and follow them with great enthusiasm. That their congregations and our nation will wake up and realize that Your call in their lives cannot be ignored. And finally, as they continue their journey, that they do so with joy, patience, purity, and faith, and that they be allowed to finish strong, with no regrets. One more thing, Lord: May they feel this day affirmed and valued. Amen."

"And this is my prayer: that your love may abound more and more in knowledge and depth of insight" (Philippians 1:9).

Fringemen

If I were you I would focus in on two or three men in your congregation who need some extra TLC. Have coffee with them or just drop by for a chat. Men on the fringe were often my target in ministry—those who could easily slip out of sight and not be missed by anyone. Men who have been hurt by the church or used by a pastor who influenced their families in an unscrupulous way.

Build confidence in these "fringemen." Help them to see you don't want to "use" them, but simply be their friend. Let them talk. Just listen. I submit that the greatest economy in your church is its ministry to men. If you reach the men, you will save the families.

"Right Relationship" is the "R" in G-R-A-C-E. Investing in men is one way to establish a relationship that will last a lifetime. Who can you identify as a fringeman to concentrate on? Pick three or four.

"And the things you have heard me say in the presence of many witnesses entrust to reliable men who will also be qualified to teach others" (2 Timothy 2:2).

Be Thankful for Who God Has Made You

I remember hearing a phrase years ago by an old gospel singer—"Just remember, God don't make no junk." It was made in reference to a person feeling down on himself.

This feeling of worthlessness can come and go. But if we're not careful, we will minimize God's creation and His investment in our lives and ministry. I want you to take a few moments and just give God thanks for who you are—thank Him for your talent, your personality, your voice, your mind, your ability to learn and project your thoughts into sermons. Thank Him for those moments when He gives you insight into other people's challenges and, with a word, you are able to make their lives different. Thank Him for a gentle spirit that allows you to be still and listen to His direction for your next steps.

Whatever you do, please do not hang your head and bemoan your lot. Think of those many ways God has used you, blessed you, anointed you, and chosen you for a "miracle moment."

Enjoy this day with those who mean so much to you, and thank our Lord for making you unique. Like a wide-eyed child, celebrate God's creativity.

"If anything is excellent or praiseworthy—think about such things" (Philippians 4:8).

Are We Having Fun Yet?

Are you having any fun? Maybe I sound like a broken record reminding you over and over to take an occasional break, but I've found that a lot of pastors need reminding. If you don't schedule times for fun, you will miss something very special. So, some suggestions:

- Unless you're taking a road trip or an extended vacation, don't take it all at once—spread it out!
- Make your day off count, or add a day of vacation to your day off. It will seem like a minivacation.
- Ask your children, if they are still at home, what they would most enjoy doing on a day with you. If they're grown and live nearby, they'll still want to spend a day together.
- For the next few months, plan a regular "take a walk," "eat some ice cream," or "ride a bike" date with your spouse. Then see what happens.
- Do something you have wanted to do but just haven't taken the time for. For instance: go fishing, work on your car, or go to a ball game.

Do you get my point? If you don't *plan* for fun, you may not have any. Do something impromptu for a change. The "C" in G-R-A-C-E means constant safeguards! Having fun is one of those safeguards. You know what that means? It means you look forward to joyful times and to laughing out loud. Now please, go have some fun.

"A merry heart maketh a cheerful countenance" (Proverbs 15:13, KJV). "A merry heart doeth good like a medicine" (Proverbs 17:22, KJV).

Loving God's Way

Who is your biggest fan?

And how would your spouse answer this question? Husbands and wives should be each other's biggest fans.

What does that mean? It means we pray for each other. We protect each other. We show genuine compassion for each other. We strive to be a part of the solution to a problem, rather than an obstruction. Also, it is crucial that we cheer for each other.

I remember a time not long ago when I was speaking at a conference with some very high-profile religious leaders. Beverley could tell I was nervous and that this engagement was important to me. I delivered my message and gave it my best. As we were walking out of the convention hall, Beverley slipped her arm through mine, looked at me, and said, "I was proud of you tonight." I can't tell you how much that meant to me. The one who mattered most had affirmed me.

Take a few minutes to look at the last few weeks through a relational lens. Did you affirm your spouse and your children regularly? Did you look for the positive in each of them rather than the negative? Did you take the time to ask, "How are you doing?" Did you, by your words, actions, and deeds, express unconditional love? Did you live your faith as an example?

Let us seek to love one another as God has loved us. When we do, we'll find that we've become the biggest fan our loved ones have ever had.

"A new command I give you: Love one another. As I have loved you, so you must love one another" (John 13:34).

Sharing in His Daily Creation

When you face a traumatic moment, be it a close call or near-death experience, a change takes place. I can't explain it completely, but there is a profound sense that what you have been through cannot be treated casually. There is a renewed commitment to your work, a deeper love for your family. There is a heightened realization that each day is a gift—that we live and die at the mercy of a loving God, the One who is truly the author and finisher of life. I pray I never lose the feeling of gratitude I have right now for life, my family, and the ministry He has called me to.

Each day is a gift, my friend. Please do not mistreat it, deny it, or waste it. It's amazing to know our God has invited each of us to share in His daily creation. It is in seeking to please Him and live in obedience each day that we find fulfillment and great joy.

"We obey his commands and do what pleases him" (1 John 3:22).

A Passion for Unity

As I observe the church, one thing that concerns me is the fragile nature of the word *unity*. It does not take much to divide a congregation, eliminate the effectiveness of the pastor, and stunt the church's growth and influence within the community. The Hartford Institute for Religion Research conducted a study of more than 14,000 U.S. congregations. The study found that 51 percent of them have had a serious conflict in the previous three years. The study also indicated that lingering conflict is associated with declining vitality and membership.

Until we make unity one of our highest priorities as pastors and people, we will continue to send a negative signal to the watching world. They will avoid us.

Several years ago, Stan Toler and I wrote *The Minister's Little Devotional Book*. In it, we tell the story of a church that was having great success. They were performing miracles and great numbers of people were turning to the Lord. Then problems surfaced. The church treasurer ran off with the money. The leaders in the congregation kept upsetting one person or another. One of the associates always acted impulsively and immaturely. Finally, the situation became so unbearable that many of the faithful moved to another city to worship. Sound familiar? It should. It was the first church—comprising the people who had most recently been with Jesus!

Someone once said, "Tying two cats' tails together does not necessarily constitute unity." So what does? Please consider the following as you seek to unify your congregation and maintain peace within your fellowship:

Bridle the tongue.

Don't break a promise.

Let praise be the rule, not criticism.

Value people more than programs.

Make joy and laughter a priority.

Communicate openly and fairly.

Attack gossip and backbiting with the truth.

Accept one another's differences.

I talk with pastors and their staff members regularly, and I find that far too often their mind-set is about winning—having their own way regardless of the consequences. That mind-set leads only to bitterness, separation, and destruction. It is high time that the world sees us practice what we preach.

Live by the prayer that Jesus prayed for us: "I have given them the glory that you gave me, that they may be one as we are one: I in them and you in me. May they be brought to complete unity to let the world know that you sent me and have loved them even as you have loved me" (John 17:22-23).

Thank You for All You Do

I want to express to you pastors and you who are on staff my heartfelt appreciation for all you do for the cause of Christ. God's Word as paraphrased in *The Message* says:

"So proclaim the Message with intensity; keep on your watch. Challenge, warn, and urge your people. Don't ever quit. Just keep it simple" (2 Timothy 4:2).

"Appreciate your pastoral leaders who gave you the Word of God. Take a good look at the way they live" (Hebrews 13:7).

"Be responsive to your pastoral leaders. Listen to their counsel. . . . Contribute to the joy of their leadership . . . Why would you want to make things harder for them?" (Hebrews 13:17).

"Keep a firm grasp on both your character and your teaching. Don't be diverted. Just keep at it" (1 Timothy 4:16).

I love you and pray for you. Our world would be a much darker place if it were not for your faithfulness and loving Christlike example. Don't ever give up!

"Honor those leaders who work so hard for you. . . . Overwhelm them with appreciation and love!" (1 Thessalonians 5:12-13).

Where There Is Forgiveness, There Is Hope

I've written before about being compassionate when preaching against abortion. Don't get me wrong. I am against abortion with every fiber of my being. But I am a pastor. And being a pastor places unique demands on my attitudes.

Sometimes we get so caught up in condemning certain sins, such as abortion or homosexuality, we forget that the idea is to point people toward redemption. I beg you, the next time you preach and teach on the subject of *any* sin, tell your congregation that sin is wrong. But don't forget to tell them that God offers forgiveness for those who live under the dark shadow of guilt. Express hope by adding gentleness to your preaching. Tell them that coming to God is the answer to the crushing anguish they carry. Tell them that they do not need to carry this burden any longer. View yourself not only as a stalwart against sin, but also as a physician for the soul.

"I tell you that in the same way there will be more rejoicing in heaven over one sinner who repents than over ninety-nine righteous persons who do not need to repent" (Luke 15:7).

The Significance of Your Music

As I travel the country, one thing that I see dividing congregations and setting pastors and people at odds with one another is music. It forces me to agree with what many church experts are saying: Music will define your church's ministry. Like it or not, the style of worship music you choose will impact who will join you in serving the Lord.

Several years ago, pastor Rick Warren of Saddleback Church in Mission Viejo, California, described the cultural factors he felt we need to understand if we are to have effective ministries. After discussing America's low-commitment nature, its multiple-choice tendencies, and the shift from a family-centered to a marketplace culture, he made the following remarks:

"I believe music style is the single greatest positioning factor in the local church, even more than preaching style. It determines whom you attract. Tell me your style of music, and I will tell you whom you're reaching and whom you will never reach. The moment you define your music, you position your church."

He went on to relate that at first Saddleback tried to appeal to all musical tastes, "from Bach to rock." That approach alienated everyone. So they took a survey of what radio stations attendees listened to. Because 97 percent listened to a certain style, that was the style they adopted for the church.

Warren explained, "Imagine a missionary going overseas and saying, 'I'm here to share the good news, but first you must learn to speak my language, learn my customs and sing my style of music.' We'd call that strategy for failure! Yet many churches in America do just that. Our culture has changed, but we insist on using the same language, programs, customs and musical style we used in the 1950s."

The key to success, of course, is your ability to convince people that the music style chosen for your church is best for all. Like you, I wish it were easier. I wish we could please everyone who attends our churches. But most of the time, that's just not possible.

As you evaluate the personality of your congregation and the music best suited to its tastes, needs, and objectives, you will have to make a difficult choice and live with the consequences—and, I hope, the blessings.

"Speak to one another with psalms, hymns and spiritual songs. Sing and make music in your heart to the Lord" (Ephesians 5:19).

Patience Is a Virtue

I am not a patient person. I get antsy if the car in front of me moves too slowly when the light changes. I think the toaster should toast faster and the water should boil sooner. I have never been one to say, "Oh well." I love the Nike slogan that encourages people to "Just do it."

Are you a patient person? It's biblical, you know. The Bible says, "Therefore, as God's chosen people, holy and dearly loved, clothe yourselves with compassion, kindness, humility, gentleness and patience" (Colossians 3:12). Patience is a virtue. I need to pray about that.

I wish I were more patient—it would save me a lot of problems with others. In fact, life would be so much more enjoyable if we were all more patient.

So . . . what say ye? Shall we work on it? How? Take a deep breath, put the issue in perspective, and just say, "Oh well." Let's see how the week goes.

"But we glory in tribulations also: knowing that tribulation worketh patience" (Romans 5:3, KJV).

Giving God Control

Have you ever had that "going around in circles" feeling? You know, when you finish the day and you wonder, "What just happened?"

Pastors really don't like to be out of control, do we? We get pretty uncomfortable when things don't work out the way we had planned. When people don't respond as we had hoped, we should ask ourselves, "Do we really need to be in control?"

Proverbs says, "Many are the plans in a man's heart, but it is the Lord's purpose that prevails" (19:21). "In his heart a man plans his course, but the LORD determines his steps" (16:9). Do I ever relate to that! You can't control what you can't control.

Maybe the problem is that we take ourselves too seriously. Oh, I know that we must take what we do seriously, but do we need to live so burdened? I don't think so! When was the last time you had a really good laugh? Laughter begets laughter. Solomon wrote, "There is . . . a time to weep and a time to laugh" (Ecclesiastes 3:1, 4).

We need to see every day as a gift, as I've said before. Live life to the fullest, but remember how frail we really are. Lighten up a little! And again, always remember Who is really in control.

"But the plans of the LORD stand firm forever, the purposes of his heart through all generations" (Psalm 33:11).

What to Expect in a Christian Counselor

When it became necessary to refer one of my parishioners to a professional Christian counselor, the following guidelines were most helpful to me. Perhaps they will help you as well. A good counselor is:

Someone who can be trusted to keep confidentiality. It is very important that parishioners who have been referred do not hear their stories from the pulpit some Sunday or in a gathering of community Christian leaders.

Someone who is a good listener. People go to a counselor to be heard. It is so critical that they be given a hearing rather than a sermon by the counselor.

Someone who will not turn the client into a counselor. Occasionally, counselors spend more time revealing their own weaknesses (especially sexual ones) or reflecting on their own problems than focusing on the needs of the counselee. This should not be.

Someone who has integrity and experience. Just because a Christian counselor visits a pastor seeking clients does not mean he/she is qualified. Before you recommend anyone to a counselor, please check credentials and experience. Don't just take a card from your desk drawer and use it as an easy out.

Someone who is adequately educated by a reputable school. I know degrees and accreditations can be misleading. But for the most part, you can tell a great deal about Christian counselors by where they received their training and did their internships.

Someone who is affordable. You should not expect any counselor to render services free of charge, but you should expect them to work with you and those you recommend to: (1) terminate the series of counseling sessions in a normal time, (2) provide a sliding scale for those who cannot pay full fees, (3) be up-front about any insurance coverage available.

Someone who tracks with you theologically. This will vary from person to person, but you should try to recommend therapists who agree with, or are at least sensitive to, your theological position. You do not want to be doing damage control with your parishioners over biblical teachings.

Someone who is diligent. Make sure your parishioners are treated with the utmost respect, that "honest" counseling and therapy are going on, that the 50-minute meetings are well-organized, that good records are kept, and that the purpose of the meetings is realized.

Someone who is a team player. The healing community (physician, psychologist, minister, etc.) must work together and not be threatened by one another's opinions. As a pastor, I want any counselor who sees my people to work with me, talk with me when permissible, and not be threatened by my input in our mutual parishioner/client relationship.

Someone who is faithfully available. All parties involved should be able to reach the counselor and expect a timely response. If someone is taking the counselor's calls, then the client should be aware of this and feel comfortable with the stand-in.

I am sure you are very careful whenever you turn your flock over to someone else. The thoughts above are just my own. But they are the steps I followed as I prayed for total healing in the minds and hearts of those who trusted me not to lead them astray.

"I know, my God, that you test the heart and are pleased with integrity" (1 Chronicles 29:17).

Counsel in Times of Crisis

One Thursday morning as I was preparing for an event in Cheyenne, Wyoming, there was a breaking news report on the television channel I was watching. President Bush was holding a press conference to address the economic crisis in our country. He really didn't say very much of comfort to anxious Americans. In addition, newspaper headlines across the country warned of a staggering economy. Added to that were reports of disasters from hurricanes to earthquakes to train wrecks in various states.

Unless you have endured a natural catastrophe, visited the site of a devastated area, or had your savings wiped out, it is impossible to know what those who have been affected by such disasters are going through.

This weekend you will most likely stand before your people, some of whom have experienced crises. What do you say to them? How do you help them cope with their fears? I'm sure you have thought about this, but one of your major responsibilities is to comfort and guide your people. How should we as Christian leaders deal with any crisis? How do catastrophes affect the way you go about your day-to-day activity? How do you encourage your people? Tell them…

1. Don't panic. Our faith is in God, not in money or things. We have all been in these tight spots before, and we will survive this challenge. Be patient.

2. Encourage one another. We, as believers in Christ, have a marvelous opportunity in times of crisis to show where our foundations are strongest.

3. Be wise. Make the best decisions you can to minimize losses. Keep your credit card debt low. Save instead of spend, and turn to trusted counsel.

4. Increase your faith practices. Don't miss church. Sing, worship, pray, read, and assemble. Be in places where you will feel protected, not threatened. "Give thanks in all circumstances" (1 Thessalonians 5:18).

5. Remember that God knows your situation. He cares. Do not fret. Paul writes, "May the Lord of peace himself give you peace at all times and in every way" (2 Thessalonians 3:16).

There is a great angst in our country right now. But our God is still in control. Your people may need a reminder this week.

"I will proclaim the name of the LORD. Oh, praise the greatness of our God!" (Deuteronomy 32:3).

So Do Not Worry

Life is uncertain and short. The psalmist agonized over the brevity of life, comparing each day to a handbreadth and man's life to a breath (Psalm 39:5). He concluded that his only secure hope was trust in the Lord. He was right!

Many of the people you serve are probably facing uncertainty. The events of the past may have left them wondering if the bad guy too often wins. The psalmist, too, wondered about this. But he wrote, "I have seen a wicked and ruthless man flourishing like a green tree in its native soil, but he soon passed away and was no more. . . . Observe the upright; there is a future for the man of peace" (Psalm 37:35-37). Our security then is this: If we are a people of peace, God will provide for our future.

I am so impressed by men and women like you who have stared evil in the eye without blinking and led your people with a sincere faith, affirming the assuring words of Jesus to not worry. The psalmist knew that there would be desperate times—the earth itself might give way, waters rage, mountains quake. He even referenced the uproar of nations. But his conclusion was that even if all these things happen, the Lord Almighty is with us. God is our fortress (Psalm 46). He is the rock you stand on. He is the source of your courage and boldness. He's why you can say, "Do not worry!"

"Do not worry about your life. . . . Who of you by worrying can add a single hour to his life? . . . Do not worry about tomorrow, for tomorrow will worry about itself. Each day has enough trouble of its own" (Matthew 6:25, 27, 34).

Christist with Skin On

Two phrases in Isaiah 9:6 really jump out at me—*Wonderful Counselor* and *Prince of Peace*. Jesus is truly the difference between light and darkness. He can turn sadness into laughter, and He can break the chains of bondage (Isaiah 9:3-5). But He has also gifted you with the wisdom to be a counselor to those seeking guidance and an instrument of peace to those who are troubled. Like the old saying goes, "Sometimes I just need someone with skin on."

You are that one! You reflect the characteristics of Christ. He gives you great wisdom to help your people through circumstances that seem too broken to mend. He also gives you the courage to be His channel of peace. As St. Francis prayed, "Lord make me an instrument of your peace." That is you!

There is probably a person under your pastoral care who could use some gifted counseling or tender direction. Think about that person, and be "Christ with skin on" to him or her before next Sunday.

"Dear children, let us not love with words or tongue but with actions and in truth" (1 John 3:18).

Making Difficult Decisions

Sometimes in our careers, we have to make very big decisions. To be honest, the process ties me in knots.

I know some will say, "Hey, you're a big boy. Just buck up and do what needs to be done." In fact, I'm sure I have said that to others. If I could find them, I would apologize for having been insensitive.

So, how do you make major decisions in your life and ministry?

May I share with you my process and see what you think? Here goes:

- Be rational. Once you know a decision must be made, begin by using the "pro and con" test. What's good—what's not so good?

- Where confidence can be guarded, talk it over with sensible, sensitive, spiritual people. Paint the scenario and give them time to weigh the complexities of the issue. See it through fresh eyes.

- Be careful to consider the whole of the organization and your family, not just the immediate pressures or an individual's feelings. What will the future be like—not just tomorrow?

- Pray as you go—be constant in prayer. As you're driving, shaving, or walking, talk it over with your Lord. He is with you. Acknowledge Him.

- Don't play the "appease" game. Avoid the short-term solution that will only complicate things in the future. Concession made at the sacrifice of principle is never good.

- Make the right choice. You have prayed, you have consulted, and you have come to a conclusion. Now, by faith in God and yourself, do what is right.

- Whatever you do, have leadership on your side. If you want to be a human sacrifice, that is your choice, but it is much better to make all major decisions with folks standing with you.

Remember the words Moses spoke to Joshua: "The LORD himself goes before you and will be with you; he will never leave you nor forsake you. Do not be afraid; do not be discouraged" (Deuteronomy 31:8).

Dealing with Change

As you know, from one week to the next, the landscape of your congregation can appear very different. Even though folks say change is good, and most of the time it is, no one ever said it's easy. Change is constant, change is tough, and change can be managed. The word *manage* is the one that is tricky.

I was thinking about how I have dealt with major changes in my life, and, of course, the first word that comes to mind is *panic*—"How will we get through this?" But when reality sets in, you have to put things in *perspective* and continue to live *consistently* as a person of faith. *Surrender* the situation to God, who knows the end from the beginning. Do all you can to *minimize the negative consequences* of the change. Find godly people and take seriously their *counsel*. Keep your head up. Stay as *positive* as you can. Remember, people are watching and depending on you. Be *thankful* in all situations (1 Thessalonians 5:18) and be *expectant*. God has an answer. Change is coming, that is for sure. So manage it well!

"To the faithful you show yourself faithful, to the blameless you show yourself blameless, to the pure you show yourself pure. . . . You, O Lord, keep my lamp burning; my God turns my darkness into light" (Psalm 18:25-26, 28).

Reasons Not to Skimp on Sleep

Getting your good night's sleep could be one of the smartest health priorities. Too little or poor sleep can affect your cardiovascular, endocrine, immune, and nervous systems. Between 50 and 70 million Americans suffer from a chronic sleep disorder such as insomnia or sleep apnea.

According to news.yahoo.com, research has shown:

- Insufficient sleep appears to tip hunger hormones out of whack. Leptin, which suppresses appetite, is lowered, and ghrelin, which stimulates appetite, gets a boost.
- When you're sleep-deprived, you're more apt to make bad food choices, resulting in a diet higher in cholesterol and saturated fat. Women are especially affected.
- Those getting five or fewer hours of sleep each night are 2.5 times more likely to be diabetic.
- Women who sleep five or fewer hours per night are 45 percent more likely to have heart attacks.
- Blood pressure may also increase as a consequence of insufficient sleep.
- Nearly 20 percent of serious car-crash injuries involve a sleepy driver, and that's independent of alcohol use.
- Older folks who wake up at night and are drowsy during the day are more likely to fall due to being off balance.
- Adults, adolescents, and middle-schoolers plagued by lack of sleep report more symptoms of depression and lower self-esteem. Also, more behavior problems are seen in these kids.
- There is approximately a 15 percent greater risk of dying for those who routinely get five hours or less of sleep per night.

It should be obvious by now that sleep is important for all of us. Are you getting enough sleep?

"I lie down and sleep; I wake again, because the LORD sustains me" (Psalm 3:5).

What Men Need

As you prepare your sermon this week, remember the emotional and spiritual condition of many of the men who'll be sitting in your congregation.

Some of them will be dealing with a variety of issues, such as pornography, unfaithfulness, a loveless marriage, or being a dad to another man's children. Others will feel uncomfortable in God's house because they have been pressured to be there. Some will be suffering from the "father wound" they have carried for years. Some will be on the fringe, close to walking away from the church entirely.

In many ways, you will be like a coach this Sunday. Through much prayer and study, you will be preparing your men and their families for life's next "inning." Please do not browbeat your men. Love them. Honor them.

The Focus on the Family booklet *The Pastor's Role in Establishing an Effective Men's Ministry* notes:

- Men need a safe place where they can discover that someone understands them and that they are not alone.
- Men need a clear, compelling vision of biblical manhood they can take hold of.
- Men need time with other men to effectively process their manhood.
- Men need practical how-tos with which they can taste success. They need ways to implement, in a bite-sized manner, what they hear.
- Men need male cheerleaders—other men to admire their efforts and cheer their successes.
- Men need a sacred moment where they know they've become a man.
- Men need a positive relationship with Jesus Christ.

There is great economy in a vital message to men. When you, pastor, make this a priority, you will find a new sense of purpose, exhilaration, and meaning about what you do.

"To do what is right and just is more acceptable to the LORD than sacrifice" (Proverbs 21:3).

Your Witness

Some pastors I know are hesitant to let people know they are members of the clergy, while others flaunt it to the point of embarrassment.

One of the most impressive ways to share your witness is by the way you treat people. Just show a bit of interest in people that you meet in restaurants or supermarkets.

Another is by inserting God into your conversation with people, for example, "I will pray for you" or "It really seems like God was looking out for you." Or, when you visit your parishioners in the hospital or nursing home, don't leave without making a contact with someone who does not attend your church. Some of the most effective ministry is to those who do not have a pastor.

There are so many ways we as clergy can make Christ known without being overly aggressive. A touch, a smile, a kind word, a listening ear, an honest compliment, a small act of caring—all of these can be a witness.

"I will tell of the kindnesses of the LORD, the deeds for which he is to be praised, according to all the LORD has done for us" (Isaiah 63:7).

There Are Some Things
We Shouldn't Forget

In Philippians 3:13-14, the apostle Paul encourages us to forget and press on. But that doesn't mean we should forget the lessons we have learned from our mistakes. Sometimes, I'm reminded of mistakes I've made in dealing with people or in my management of the church. Forgetting those times would not allow me to use them as a steppingstone to something better. I know Paul is saying you shouldn't beat yourself up for things in the past or be discouraged because things didn't work out the way you had hoped. But most of us improve as Christian leaders when we refuse to sweep things under the rug.

What was the most important lesson you learned recently? I would guess you learned that lesson from a difficult moment. Don't forget it!

I learned a painful truth in 2008 about my workaholic lifestyle. It caught up with me, and my health will never be the same. It was the result of too many late nights, early mornings, plane connections, and speaking engagements added to never wanting to say "no," believing that a 70-year-old can do the same things he did in his 40s or 50s. In honest self-evaluation, I realized that I brought this on myself—a lesson I don't want to forget.

Be honest with me . . . no, with yourself! What happened in the past year that God used to challenge you, to mature you, to equip you? As you remember those times, are you not reminded to move to a higher level? Do not forget those tough conversations you had with your kids or your spouse. Do not forget those moments when stubbornness led you to force your will on another, or that scary moment when you were tempted and almost yielded.

I'll forget many things, but some lessons I always want to remember.

"I remember my affliction and my wandering, the bitterness and the gall. I well remember them, and my soul is downcast within me. Yet this I call to mind and therefore I have hope: Because of the LORD's great love we are not consumed, for his compassions never fail" (Lamentations 3:19-22).

Finish the Race with Enthusiasm

Every four years, when the summer Olympic Games roll around, I become engrossed in sports that I have not heard anything about since the last games. Sports like double trap shooting, judo, fencing, canoeing/kayaking, and badminton don't usually make headlines outside the country winning the gold medal. The players may never be heard from again, but their gold medals are forever a source of pride for their countries.

In this example is a great lesson for folks like you and me: to "run," as the writer to the Hebrews expressed, "with perseverance the race marked out for us" (Hebrews 12:1). Or to persevere, as James expressed: "Blessed is the man who perseveres under trial, because when he has stood the test, he will receive the crown of life" (James 1:12). Paul exclaimed in his farewell address, "If only I may finish the race and complete the task the Lord Jesus has given me" (Acts 20:24). And again, he admonished Timothy, "If anyone competes as an athlete, he does not receive the victor's crown unless he competes according to the rules" (2 Timothy 2:5).

When God called you, He did so with the full expectation that you would be a winner, not a whiner. That you would finish the race with joy, not drop out along the way. Paul looked back on his life and ministry saying, "I have finished the race, I have kept the faith" (2 Timothy 4:7). He was eligible for the prize . . . the crown.

So are you, my colleague, but you must fight the good fight—finish the race—and no matter what, keep the faith! You may never receive a gold medal, but if you remain faithful, the Righteous Judge will award you something much better: His approval, His recognition, His blessing. So be prepared: The finish line lies before you! Go for it! And do it with enthusiasm.

"Everyone who competes in the games goes into strict training. They do it to get a crown that will not last; but we do it to get a crown that will last forever" (1 Corinthians 9:25).

DEVOTIONS

·

FOR

·

SPECIAL

·

DAYS

New Year's Day: A Prayer for the Coming Year

I am not much for resolutions, but as I examine my life each new year, I determine to do better at what God has called me to do. With the world in such chaos, your role as a spiritual leader is more significant than ever before. Let's all vow to be better. How? Look forward, not backward. Forget, and move to the next level of obedience and challenge. Brush off the failures and setbacks of the past year. Learn from them and, like Joshua, hear God saying, "Be strong and of good courage; do not be afraid, nor be dismayed, for the LORD your God is with you wherever you go" (Joshua 1:9, NKJV).

Sometimes we underestimate the hand of God in our lives. We can act like orphans and feel we are all alone, but that is never the case.

And now, my prayer for you and your colleagues as you all enter a fresh, unblemished new year:

Dear God, our heavenly Father, thank You for my colleagues who serve You so unselfishly. Father, I pray for my brothers and sisters that they be ever more sensitive to the moving of Your Spirit in their lives. Help them to live with great expectation, standing on tiptoes of faith, as they survey the vast panorama of Your opportunities. May they have a renewed interest in Your Word, and a hunger to spend quality "first-of-the-day" time with You. May they—we— know it is from those times that we gain our strength to follow Your direction.

Please, Father, may they be instruments of peace—first in their own homes, and then elsewhere. Keep them free from jealousy and envy. And, Father, challenge them to guard their hearts. May they find reward for their labor. Amen.

"We continually remember before our God and Father your work produced by faith, your labor prompted by love, and your endurance inspired by hope in our Lord Jesus Christ" (1 Thessalonians 1:3).

Sanctity of Human Life Sunday: Preaching Compassionately

In our book *They Call Me Pastor*, Neil Wiseman and I wrote, "When you raise your voice to speak with such tenacious authority about the evils of abortion, be sure to lower that same voice to speak with great compassion to those who have been damaged by sin, assuring them there is healing, forgiveness and mercy. . . . Tell them that coming to God is the answer to the crushing anguish they carry."

A veteran minister who had been a pastor for nearly a lifetime said, "I never deal with any sin without getting a tear in my eye. A tear of sadness for the consequences I see in a sinner's life. A tear of joy that no sin is too great for a Savior to forgive. And a tear that God, by grace, kept me from the same sin." Never preach against abortion without a tear in your eye.

I do urge you to preach against this evil, but to listen to your message through the ears of the most needy in your congregation. Do you offer them hope? Are you communicating Christ's boundless love? It might surprise you to know how many of those who come and go through your church doors—both men and women—carry the pain of an aborted child.

The fight for life is an ongoing battle. Even if you do not feel comfortable addressing the issue of life from the pulpit, I pray you are finding ways to assist your congregation in remembering that we are "fearfully and wonderfully made." God has something in mind for every one of His creations—those that have been born and those who are yet to be born.

"My frame was not hidden from you when I was made in the secret place. When I was woven together in the depths of the earth, your eyes saw my unformed body. All the days ordained for me were written in your book before one of them came to be" (Psalm 139:15-16).

Valentine's Day: Reaffirming Our Love and Support

February 14 gives us a chance to reaffirm our love and support for our spouses. Have you made any special plans to recognize the contribution your spouse has made to your life and ministry on Valentine's Day?

Here are some thought-provoking questions for you to consider and perhaps talk about with your husband or wife:

When/where did you first meet?

What was the subject of your first conversation?

What did you do on your first date?

How did you/he propose marriage?

Where did you go on your honeymoon?

What was the highlight of your first ministerial assignment?

What do you usually disagree about?

Did you ever agree on how many children you would have?

What is his/her favorite dish?

When was the last time you paid your spouse a heartfelt compliment?

When you have free time, what do you most enjoy doing together? (Perhaps you could include that in your day tomorrow.)

Please take some time just to be together and laugh out loud. If you have some negative stuff going on, this would be a great time to do what it takes to live peacefully together.

"Though one may be overpowered, two can defend themselves. A cord of three strands is not quickly broken" (Ecclesiastes 4:12).

Lent: A Time of Personal Examination

The Lenten Season should be much more than planning for a big crowd and festive weekend. It should also be a time of preparation for your heart, your attitude, your message, and your relationship with the risen Christ. The apostle Paul wrote, "For I resolved to know nothing while I was with you except Jesus Christ and him crucified. I came to you in weakness and fear, and with much trembling. My message and my preaching were not with wise and persuasive words, but with a demonstration of the Spirit's power, so that your faith might not rest on men's wisdom, but on God's power" (1 Corinthians 2:2-5).

As a pastor, I used the days from Ash Wednesday to Easter Sunday to call my people to a time of personal examination. Every service, including midweek, had an Easter theme that would draw people along the road to Jerusalem, to the foot of the cross, and into the celebration of the empty tomb.

During the Lenten Season, I would ask our congregation:

1. Who among us has someone to forgive?
2. Who among us has a blockage that would keep the Holy Spirit from moving freely in his or her life?
3. Who among us has allowed their relationship with the risen Lord to stagnate?

What if, during this time of preparation, you guided your people to a new plateau of intimacy with Jesus? The celebration of Easter can hold great significance, especially to the new believer. I pray that your Easter activities will be underscored by the Spirit's power.

"Everyone who has this hope in him purifies himself, just as he is pure" (1 John 3:3).

Palm Sunday: Preaching Liberation

Jesus rode into Jerusalem on that memorable Palm Sunday as a liberator. As He approached the city, He wept over it (Luke 19:41). He was crying because He knew the fickle nature of people. He cried because they had missed the point. He had not come to them to be a rescuer or a miracle worker. He had come to be their Savior. They totally misunderstood the reason for His visitation (Luke 19:44).

Though many of those He loved did not understand why He had come, Jesus' role was set in stone centuries before in Isaiah 61: "The Spirit of the Sovereign LORD is on me, because the LORD has anointed me to preach good news to the poor . . . to bind up the brokenhearted, to proclaim freedom for the captives and release from darkness for the prisoners" (verse 1). He read from the Old Testament scroll in Nazareth (Luke 4:18-19) and concluded, "Today this scripture is fulfilled in your hearing" (Luke 4:21).

Jesus' words are so relevant on Palm Sunday—"If you . . . had only known . . . what would bring you peace" (Luke 19:42). Will the people in your pews understand the urgency of the message He proclaimed and the great compassion He has for them? During Holy Week, I urge you to preach liberation from sin, addiction, fear, pain, loneliness—you name it. Jesus is the greatest liberator the world has ever known, and He is available to your people. I assure you, they will be open to the message of freedom, receptive to the possibility of deliverance. Sin and evil have been overcome by the mercy of a loving Lord. Preach freedom, my colleague! That is the Easter message!

"Blessed is the king who comes in the name of the Lord!" (Luke 19:38).

Monday: Power

On Monday, Jesus chased the moneychangers out of the temple (Mark 11:12-17) and taught a lesson over a cursed fig tree (Matthew 21:18-22).

So much of who Jesus was, as well as the nature of man, was revealed in the course of one week.

What will it take to ignite the church and our people? What will it take to experience a Palm Sunday kind of excitement in which our congregations are filled with praise and our lives are vibrant with enthusiasm about the resurrection reality?

You can be a catalyst if during the next few days, your messages are bold and your joy contagious. Challenge your people to lift "Holy Hurrahs" and give God credit for all things. Urge them to give witness to their faith and live with a sense of victory in a world of sorrow.

In short, you hold the key, my colleague—through your very countenance you can let your flock see how blessed you feel to have an Easter message to deliver and eternal hope to anticipate.

"As it is written, How beautiful are the feet of them that preach the gospel of peace, and bring glad tidings of good things!" (Romans 10:15, KJV).

Tuesday: Confrontation

On Tuesday, Judas betrayed his teacher (Luke 22:3-6); Jesus was in conflict with the Herodians, the scribes, and the Pharisees (Matthew 21:23–23:39); and the conspiracy against Christ continued (Mark 14:1-2).

As we approach the climactic moments of Easter, how are you doing—spiritually, emotionally, physically? Are you "all together" as you face the challenges of this week? You need to be if you are going to do right by yourself, your people, and your God during this most important time of the year. You have a few days to prepare your people, look deep within your own spirit, and anticipate the climactic event. There is no greater event than the celebration of our Lord's resurrection. May I suggest a working day off to "live" the Easter story?

Find a quiet place and begin by reading through the Gospels' account of Easter week. Each day has documented significance with the exception of "silent" Saturday. In your mind, see the disciples as they journey up the hill to Jerusalem. After you have followed Jesus to the cross, concentrate on His seven last words. Imagine the circumstances that surround each phrase. Then pray for those who will assemble for Holy Week services. Pull the mantle of the Holy Spirit around you and let Him anoint you for the task ahead.

Finally, secure a copy of an Easter film. It might be *The Passion of the Christ*, or *The Robe*, or *The Gospel of John*. Sit back and soak in the sounds and sights of that unbelievable event. If you have been to the Holy Land, it might make sense for you to get out your pictures and relive your experience.

The better prepared you are to interject yourself into Passion Week, the better your people will relate to the awesome sacrifice that was made for them and the miracle of the resurrection.

I remind you that there will be people in your services who have never bowed their knee at the foot of Jesus. Please give them a chance to witness the transformation that comes when a person finds Jesus as his or her Savior.

Jesus said to His disciples, "As you know . . . the Son of Man will be handed over to be crucified" (Matthew 26:2).

Ash Wednesday: Together

"As Jesus was sitting on the Mount of Olives opposite the temple, Peter, James, John and Andrew asked him privately, 'Tell us, when will these things happen? And what will be the sign that they are all about to be fulfilled?' Jesus said to them: 'Watch out that no one deceives you. Many will come in my name, claiming, "I am he," and will deceive many. When you hear of wars and rumors of wars, do not be alarmed. Such things must happen, but the end is still to come. Nation will rise against nation, and kingdom against kingdom. There will be earthquakes in various places, and famines. These are the beginning of birth pains'" (Mark 13:3-8).

The disciples must have been troubled by Jesus' words. There wasn't much good news in His message. We don't hear much good news today, either, and people are troubled. As we look around us, we see so much uncertainty—spiritual wickedness in high places, war and rumors of wars on practically every continent, moral decay at every level, and a mind-set that seems to say, "What does it matter anyway?" But are things hopeless? By no means! You see, Easter is the time of the year when we are reminded of who Jesus really is—that the One who turned our darkness to light 20 centuries ago is the same yesterday, today, and forever (Hebrews 13:8). We need not hang our heads in defeat because there is One who has already secured our victory (1 Corinthians 15:57). We can look forward—and upward—to the One who is alive, who defeated sin and death and Satan . . . and who lives and reigns forevermore. He is still the One! His name is Jesus!

"Peace I leave with you; my peace I give you. I do not give to you as the world gives. Do not let your hearts be troubled and do not be afraid" (John 14:27).

Maundy Thursday: Passion

According to the Gospels, Thursday was busy—from the preparation for the Passover (Luke 22:7-23), to the last meal Jesus and His disciples shared (Matthew 26:21-24), to the garden where Judas betrayed Jesus (Matthew 26:47-50), to the arrest, Peter's denial (Luke 22:60-62), and the appearance of our Lord before the high priest (Matthew 26:57-66).

However you choose to celebrate Easter, it will be a time of remembering. You will feel the emotion of that last supper when Jesus—His heart broken—observed His faithful brothers and washed their feet. You will remember His sadness when He went away to pray while those He would leave behind to lead the church slept. You will be reminded of that awful moment when one of His trusted disciples sold Him out for a paltry sum. You will recall the spectacle of the trial, the mocking of the crowd, and the haughty trade of Jesus for a criminal. And how can you fail to remember the journey to the cross and creation's reaction as Jesus endured agony and death?

When I first viewed Mel Gibson's *The Passion of the Christ*, I was mesmerized by the film. When it was over, I walked alone in the Colorado evening and just talked to my Lord. I remember saying to Him, "I don't ever want to hurt You—You have suffered so much." I was reminded as I took my walk that Easter that the events of Jesus' death and resurrection were real—not fiction, not a church pageant, not the figment of one's imagination. It was real! Your people need to understand that and experience His presence.

"When evening came, Jesus arrived with the Twelve. While they were reclining at the table eating, he said, 'I tell you the truth, one of you will betray me—one who is eating with me.' They were very saddened, and one by one they said to him, 'Surely not I?'" (Mark 14:17-19).

Good Friday: Suffering

In Mark 15, Luke 23, and Matthew 27, we follow Christ from early morning through the evening: from Pilate, to the cross, and then to the tomb.

In reading through the accounts related to the last week of our Lord's earthly life, my eyes caught anew two passages from the Gospel of Mark. The first is in chapter 14, when Jesus was arrested. He seemed frustrated when He said, "Am I leading a rebellion that you have come out with swords and clubs to capture me?" (v. 48). "Then everyone deserted him and fled" (v. 50). He must have felt very lonely. He knew what He would face in the next few hours—He would confront His darkest hour alone.

The second word Jesus uttered while on the cross was: "My God, my God, why have you forsaken me?" (Mark 15:34). Loneliness. It was His destiny to suffer the humiliation of the cross alone. The cup He had to drink alone was the wrath of God upon the world's sin. It was the fulfillment of the prophecy that cried, "On him [was] the iniquity of us all" (Isaiah 53:6).

It was not unlike His tearful entry into Jerusalem a few days earlier when He basically said, "If only you could see how much I love you." But they could not. Rejection of one's love is the height of loneliness. As He was nailed to that cross, it was the weight of a world's sin on His shoulders that was crushing Him, the reality that He who knew no sin was made to bear the sin of all mankind. We serve a resurrected Lord, not a suffering Savior. Understood. But before that triumphant morning, there was the agony of the cross. We must never forget that.

"One of the soldiers pierced Jesus' side with a spear" (John 19:34). "Without the shedding of blood there is no forgiveness" (Hebrews 9:22).

So the suffering of Christ was reality—real pain, real blood, real loneliness, and real betrayal. It is all a part of the Easter miracle. I urge you to preach it!

"But he was pierced for our transgressions, he was crushed for our iniquities; the punishment that brought us peace was upon him, and by his wounds we are healed" (Isaiah 53:5).

Saturday: Who Crucified Jesus?

According to Matthew, the chief priests and the Pharisees went to Pilate and asked him to secure Jesus' tomb so that the disciples wouldn't "steal the body and tell the people that he has been raised from the dead" (Matthew 27:64). Meanwhile, it was the Sabbath and the Scriptures say little about what the followers of Jesus were doing. We can imagine that they were in shock, asking many questions. We're still asking questions today. Here's one.

Who crucified Jesus? This was a question so many people argued when Gibson's *The Passion of the Christ* was released. The answer from Scripture is simply stated in Isaiah 53: "Smitten by God, and afflicted . . . He was wounded for our transgressions. . . . The LORD has laid on Him the iniquity of us all" (Isaiah 53:4-6, NKJV). The Bible names God as the One responsible for the earthly death of Christ.

Oh, I know you can state the fact that sin killed Jesus, or the betrayal of Judas, or the jealousy exhibited by the scribes and Pharisees, or spineless Pilate. But the fact remains that Christ's crucifixion was in God's plan even before the foundation of the world. It was because God loved us so much that He sacrificed His Son. So here is a commentary on a loving God and the crucifixion:

1. Our condition: "All have sinned and fall short of the glory of God" (Romans 3:23).
2. The consequences: "The wages of sin is death" (Romans 6:23). Sin separates us from God forever.
3. God's passion: "God demonstrates his own love for us in this: While we were still sinners, Christ died for us" (Romans 5:8).
4. Love demands a response: Fortunately there is hope for all who respond to God's love. Confess—believe—accept (Romans 10:9).

Easter Sunday: Alive Forevermore!

On Easter Sunday, the women visited the tomb (Luke 24:1-8), the disciples gathered (John 20:2-10), and the resurrected Lord appeared (Matthew 28:5-10). He is risen!

It is Easter. Resurrection Day! We have the silence of a Saturday to contemplate its meaning, and then, like a sunrise or the beauty of a freshly blooming garden, it is Easter!

In truth, there is a time for everything. Solomon's words ring loudly to all of us this Easter season: "a time to be born and a time to die" (Ecclesiastes 3:2). That one phrase sums up the human predicament. We will all, in His time, move from this world into eternity.

Yet, what about the afterlife? Is that not one of the major messages of Easter? What if we gain the whole world in life, but lose our souls in death? To the believer in Christ, "Death has been swallowed up in victory" (1 Corinthians 15:54). Paul wrote, "And if Christ has not been raised, your faith is futile; you are still in your sins. . . . If only for this life we have hope in Christ, we are to be pitied . . . But Christ has indeed been raised from the dead" (1 Corinthians 15:17, 19-20).

It is estimated that 40 percent of those who will sit in your sanctuary on Easter do not have a personal relationship with the resurrected Lord. You have an unprecedented opportunity to offer life to those who live in death: "I am the resurrection and the life. He who believes in me will live, even though he dies; and whoever lives and believes in me will never die. Do you believe this?" (John 11:25-26). What a privilege to show these lost souls the way to eternal life. Your people need to remember that Easter was and is for them.

"The angel said to the women, 'Do not be afraid, for I know that you are looking for Jesus, who was crucified. He is not here; he has risen, just as he said. Come and see the place where he lay. Then go quickly and tell his disciples: " 'He has risen from the dead and is going ahead of you into Galilee. There you will see him" ' " (Matthew 28:5-7).

The Day After Easter: Comfort

Fresh out of the tomb, Jesus began to comfort those who loved Him most. He saw Mary crying at the entrance to His grave and comforted her. "I have seen the Lord!" (John 20:18), she told the disciples. In one of my favorite biblical narratives, Jesus walked with two of His followers on the Emmaus Road. When they recognized Him, their hearts burned within them (Luke 24:32). He ate with His disciples and showed them the scars in His hands and feet. He comforted Thomas, "Stop doubting and believe" (John 20:27). Thomas was overwhelmed.

Then there was that marvelous moment on the beach when Jesus fixed their breakfast while Peter and his comrades were out fishing. In that life-changing moment, He reinstated the one who had denied Him three times. In simple words, He commissioned Peter to "follow me." The fisherman never looked back. In the time before the Lord ascended into heaven, He encountered hundreds of people. The reality of the resurrection would in time take over the world. Amazing what can happen in just a few days! From loneliness to exceeding great joy.

Well, Easter has come and gone. We know the story. We have been confronted with resurrection power. Now what? The church is in many ways impotent, but the power that amazed Jesus' disciples the week following Easter is just as powerful today as it was then. Will we recognize it? Paul wrote, "I want to know Christ and the power of his resurrection" (Philippians 3:10). How about you? The aftermath of Easter is more powerful than ever!

Professional Assistants Day: Honoring Your Assistant

They know stuff we don't, can make the system work when we would be confused, and keep schedules and plan events efficiently. But like a lot of good things, we too often take what they do for us for granted. We shouldn't do that. What will you be doing to honor your assistants? You know, don't you, that they could write a book about your church—and probably you.

Sue and I have worked together nearly 37 years. She has been invaluable to my ministry and is now part of our family's life. It's kind of like having two wives (in the proper sense). But I have survived this long, and I see no reason to change a good thing. Both Sue and Beverley, my wife, say that I'm not the easiest guy to work and live with—but they have really been patient.

So, we should thank all of those who commit their lives to serving the body of Christ by serving those who lead His church. Again, colleague, how do you plan to tangibly honor your assistant?

"In Joppa there was a disciple named Tabitha . . . who was always doing good and helping the poor" (Acts 9:36).

Pentecost: Renewal

Pentecost is an important moment in history for the Jews. It is also the birthday of the church for Christians. In the second chapter of Acts, Peter preached a marvelous message of hope and redemption. At its conclusion, the people asked, "What shall we do?" (Acts 2:37). Peter responded, "Repent and be baptized, every one of you, in the name of Jesus Christ" (v. 38).

Warren Wiersbe writes, "The Spirit came, not because the believers prayed, but because the day of Pentecost had come, the day appointed for the birthday celebration."

Our God gifted the first-century church with power, unity, compassion, coping skills, and a spirit of optimism. There was something contagious about that humble band of believers. People not only recognized a difference in those called Christians—they were intrigued by that difference.

Do you observe Pentecost Sunday? Do you help your people understand the dynamics of that special day? Do you as a pastor yearn and pray for a repeat of Pentecost in your midst? More than emotion, more than showmanship, more than style, more than just something good—it was an evidence of God's power. The best!

What would it be like to experience, as a pastor and people, the anointed power of the Holy Spirit in your place? It can happen, you know! "Be filled with the Spirit" (Ephesians 5:18).

It is appropriate that, as clergy, we use this Pentecost as a starting point for a significant renewal in our own lives, as well as in our congregations. "The promise is for you" (Acts 2:39).

National Day of Prayer: Never Stop Praying

The prayer that we all turn to at this time of year is found in 2 Chronicles 7:14 and concerns the dedication of the temple. Solomon had prayed a beautiful prayer in 2 Chronicles 6:14-40, and the Lord responded by filling the temple with His glory. He also made a promise: "My eyes and my heart will always be there" (2 Chronicles 7:16). This promise was a follow-up to a directive He had given Solomon and the people to call on His name, humble themselves, pray, seek His face, and repent. Those were the conditions for the healing of the land and forgiveness. In other words, God said, "It's up to you."

If we want the Lord to send revival, we need to practice what we pray. As Christians, stop fighting each other. As pastors, seek to rid congregations of sin within the leadership. Be humble. Realize that, without God, we are really nothing. Repent of pride, selfishness, and arrogance. Ask Him what He wants for us. Sometimes, rather than just pray 2 Chronicles 7:14, we need to put it into practice and just be obedient. Don't ever stop praying!

"If my people, who are called by my name, will humble themselves and pray and seek my face and turn from their wicked ways, then will I hear from heaven and will forgive their sin and will heal their land" (2 Chronicles 7:14).

Mother's Day: Honoring Moms

A pastor's wife once told me what she would like most from her family. Do you know what it was? A love note! That's right—a love note! I encourage you, my colleague, to take a moment to write your thoughts to the wonderful wife and mother who contributes so much to your ministry and life. Let her know how you feel. Let your children, in their own words, also express to their mom just how much they love her and why.

Caution: In your worship service will be many women whose experience is painful—abortions, broken marriages, prodigal children, widowhood, infertility. So be prayerful and sensitive as you approach your Mother's Day sermon. Let the Lord guide your words and your message so that you don't cause more pain to those who may be hurting. There are so many challenges we face as the clergy in setting the proper feel and putting the right emphasis on Mother's Day. But you can do it.

Paul wrote to Timothy, "I have been reminded of your sincere faith, which first lived in your grandmother . . . and in your mother . . . and . . . now lives in you" (2 Timothy 1:5).

Memorial Day: Your Legacy

With Memorial Day upon us, I was thinking about the legacy we as clergy will leave and the overall impact our ministries will have on those we have served.

While reading about the death of Moses in Deuteronomy chapter 34, I was impressed by the following: "He buried him in Moab . . . but to this day no one knows where his grave is" (Deuteronomy 34:6). What was he—120 years old? He still had good eyesight and evidently was strong, but yet he died.

Think about it. They couldn't even find his grave, but they would not forget his deeds. Read on—"Since then, no prophet has risen in Israel like Moses . . . who did all those miraculous signs and wonders the LORD sent him to do in Egypt" (Deuteronomy 34:10-11).

The point: Even if you are a Moses, it is not so important where you are buried after you have passed on as it is how you are remembered for what you did while you were alive. Our assignment is to live life to the fullest, accomplish all that God has instructed, and then let someone else handle the burial details.

And so on this holiday, we pause to remember the lives and contributions made by those we have loved and still do. It's not so much about the grave as the person. "Precious in the sight of the LORD is the death of his saints" (Psalm 116:15).

Father's Day: Three Things for Fathers to Emphasize

There are approximately 64.3 million fathers in our nation. An estimated 26.5 million of those dads are married with children under the age of 18—millions who have the priceless opportunity to influence their children and direct their lives.

The challenge comes, however, when a dad decides how involved he will be in his children's lives. That decision is priceless.

Here are three things for fathers to remember:

1. Fathering must be intentional. Parenting of any value does not leave the results to chance. Dads must take seriously the development of their family.

2. Fathering must be patient and loving. Dads need to be involved. That means we are called to show love in such a way that our children can model our behavior. Showing love to their mom is a great start—loving them is priceless.

3. Fathering must be spiritual. For a child to properly develop as a whole person, he or she needs a dad with biblical values, and one who puts into practice his faith. Statistics prove that families with godly dads have better results. Bottom line: Dads are priceless! Encourage the men in your congregation to be involved fathers.

"And, ye fathers, provoke not your children to wrath: but bring them up in the nurture and admonition of the Lord" (Ephesians 6:4, KJV).

Independence Day:
Happy 4th of July

There's a popular song sung by Lee Greenwood titled "God Bless the USA." Some of the lyrics go like this:

> *And I'm proud to be an American*
>   *where at least I know I'm free . . .*
> *And I'd gladly stand up next to you*
>   *and defend her still today.*

This song will be sung a lot over Independence Day weekend. Are you proud to be an American? I know I am.

Oh, there are things I am not so proud of. I agonize over the issue of same-sex marriage. Why would we, as a nation, ever want to destroy the institution of marriage defined as a union between a man and a woman? I worry about the easy availability of pornography over the Internet. I see its hold on so many men and women—even in the clergy. I wish our laws in America were stricter. I still can't believe that abortion is legal and that it is such a powder keg of opinion. Why is it that the school requires parental consent to give a child a painkiller, but the same child can get an abortion without notifying a parent? I see racism growing in America. If we would only take seriously Dr. King's "I Have a Dream" speech, but folks still seem to make many decisions based on the color of one's skin. I wish politics in our country were not so dirty. The science of getting elected has become more about what's wrong with a person than what they believe. It bothers me that there are so many people in poverty, that we import so much oil, that church attendance is declining, and that our education system is lacking.

But I'm proud to be an American because I can say what I just said, and you can say what you want to say. That as a country we care for others who are less fortunate. And that we do have a faith-based heritage and a democracy that gives all men and women an opportunity to become what they want to be. I'm blessed by the fact that our United States House and Senate open their sessions with prayer, and that we support our troops who serve in harm's way. I'm proud when we sing our national anthem and offer a pledge to the flag. I love it that we have a National Day of Prayer and print "In God We Trust" on our currency. I am proud to be an American because it is my country and I have inalienable rights as its citizen. I can vote, and so can you. And it would be a shame if we did not take advantage of our freedom. This Independence Day celebrate your freedom. Be proud to be an American. I know I am.

"Live as free men, but do not use your freedom as a cover-up for evil; live as servants of God" (1 Peter 2:16).

Back to School: It's Crunch Time

When I was pastoring, school would usually begin the first Tuesday after Labor Day. The following Sunday would be a really big day. In fact, preparation for that Sunday would begin weeks in advance.

The choir would be back together after taking the summer off. Every Sunday school teacher would contact each child in his or her class. I would be excited to have the church family back in their places. It was really like a homecoming. And, most times, attendance would be up. Offerings would be above average, and as a pastor—like a proud father—I liked having the whole bunch back home again.

But now, things are different. School begins "whenever," and families seem more fragmented than they used to. Excitement takes on a different tone, and for many pastors, the first Sunday back is just like any other.

Pastor, between now and January 1, you will have the greatest opportunity to reach the greatest number of people. But you must consider several things if you and your leadership are to succeed. Here they are:

Enthusiasm—You must be positive and expectant.

Game plan—What do you have in mind for your people? What new twist will you insert in your playbook?

Teamwork—Is everybody on board? Is your leadership team engaged?

Divine assistance—Sometimes a "hail Mary" pass is not just lucky—it is the hand of God enhancing hard work and preparation that pays off. God knows!

Persistence—Even if it doesn't look that good on the scoreboard, you know when you have done your best.

"He commanded us to preach to the people and to testify that he is the one whom God appointed as judge of the living and the dead" (Acts 10:42).

Labor Day: Honoring Workers

Labor Day is dedicated to the social and economic achievements of American workers and to the strength and prosperity of our country as a result of them. Labor Day was first celebrated on September 5, 1882. It recognizes the contribution of the American rank and file, which make up the greater percentage of your congregation.

These are the people who support your church budget, teach your children, sing in your choir, witness to others, and respond to the challenges the church faces.

These are the people you can count on when "all is not well." And even when there is no pastor to carry on, they persist through prayerful faithfulness.

These are the people who will be called on to, with God's grace and guidance, lift the church out of its present doldrums and find a pattern of living and worship that excites those who are on the fringe.

Just as we cannot take for granted the American worker, neither can we take for granted those stalwart members of our church body who show up every Lord's Day full of expectation and hope. Recognize them this Sunday, my colleague. Honor and thank them for all they do. If it were not for them, our task would be impossible.

". . . a workman who does not need to be ashamed" (2 Timothy 2:15).

Clergy Appreciation:
A Few Questions

The intent of clergy appreciation month is not to put you on a pedestal, but to create awareness among the laity of your value and the divine nature of your call. You fill a spot in society that is essential and valued. Your people should not look for ways to exalt you, but to celebrate God's special assignment for you. Here are a few common questions about Clergy Appreciation Month:

1. Why is Clergy Appreciation Month so important? It recognizes the call of God in the lives of men, women, and couples to full-time Christian service. It is to call to the attention of the American public the contribution their spiritual leaders make in our society.

2. What are some of the challenges and struggles unique to pastors and their families? Today the challenges are greater than ever. So many pastors are undercompensated, and their ability to give full time to their assignment is often complicated by financial stress. But the greatest struggle remains one of management and balance. How does a busy, in-demand pastor give the proper time to his family and marriage and meet the expectations of the congregation?

3. What are some of the greatest needs of pastors? In my sermons to laypeople, I stress several things all pastors need: (1) Congregations who are united and who serve together in love. (2) Freedom to dream. A pastor without a dream is a pastor who is treading water or settling for the ordinary. (3) Prayer.

Now, whether or not anyone gives you special recognition this month, please know that you are appreciated and the work you do is important. We at Focus on the Family love you and pray for you. Our world would be a much darker place if it were not for your faithfulness and Christlike example.

"Now we ask you, brothers, to respect those who work hard among you, who are over you in the Lord and who admonish you. Hold them in the highest regard in love because of their work. Live in peace with each other" (1 Thessalonians 5:12-13).

September 11: Remembering

When I think back to that September morning, it still seems surreal—watching a tiny-looking plane fly into one of the Twin Towers, followed by explosions, panic, and casualties. It seemed like a high-budget movie. Yet, it was not a movie. It was real, and a nation went into mourning. For most of us, September 11 changed everything.

Shortly after 9-11, I stood at Ground Zero, helping those engaged in the rescue and recovery efforts. I watched them remove bodies from the rubble and, in desperation, search for any signs of life. It was almost like I was standing in front of a large window taking in the moment without really being there. But I was.

The jagged skeletons of destroyed buildings, the odor of burning materials, the huge cross on an elevated platform, and the weariness in the eyes of those working around the clock are impressions I shall never forget.

Thousands of our countrymen and women have given their lives, and tens of thousands have been wounded in the attempt to liberate Iraq and protect our freedoms in America. Freedom really isn't free, is it? We are indebted to our brave military personnel.

I hope you will find a way this weekend to honor those in your congregation who serve in our nation's military, and to remember the families who lost loved ones that September morning.

The truth of all this is that life *is* uncertain. As Proverbs says, "Do not boast about tomorrow, for you do not know what a day may bring forth" (Proverbs 27:1). Approximately 7,200 people will die today in the United States. How many of them will be ready to meet their God? How many of those who died in the Twin Towers attack were ready to meet their God? That is the reality that haunts me.

"Woe to me if I do not preach the gospel!" (1 Corinthians 9:16).

Trick or Treat: Redirecting Celebrations

Halloween has become a major unofficial American holiday. Researchers at Hallmark Cards report that 65 percent of us decorate our homes and offices for the annual event. It is second only to Christmas in retail spending at about $5 billion, and it is the third biggest party day of the year in the U.S.

The treat ends there for many thoughtful Christians, however, who understand a very troubling reality. Halloween is the high holy day for real witches and pagans, not just a night of "pretend." Several hundred thousand American pagans, Druids, and witches celebrate Halloween as a holy day called Samhain (pronounced "sow-en") or Shadowfest, a 2,000-year-old Celtic festival held to honor Samhain, the lord of death. Pagans considered it to be the end of "life" (summer) and the beginning of "death" (winter).

Although today's pagans don't roam in black or bloody garb, snatching children, they nevertheless gather to sing ritual songs and chant ancient prayers, most of which were condemned by the early Christian church. Some still put out food offerings for the dead.

Halloween is still the primary festival celebrated by those who follow Satan, but most of our culture has absorbed the festival by embracing its supposedly innocent customs. In fact, modern witches, warlocks, pagans, and Satanists have long used the holiday as a "hook" to present their belief system as a fascinating, even benevolent religious alternative.

Certainly, for Christians to shun Halloween and other pagan practices is to swim against the cultural tide. But redirecting Halloween celebrations for our children and ourselves is one of the easier ways we can take a quiet stand.

"Let no one be found among you who sacrifices his son or daughter in the fire, who practices divination or sorcery, interprets omens, engages in witchcraft" (Deuteronomy 18:10).

Elections: Encourage Your People to Vote

During election years, you have the opportunity to exercise one of your most valued rights of citizenship—voting! I pray that you do, and that you encourage your congregation to as well. With so many liberal and humanist groups flooding pastors and other leaders with intentional misinformation, it is important for pastors to know the activities they can legally undertake and those that could have an impact on their church's tax-exempt status.

Under current guidelines, pastors and churches are allowed to address any issues or ballot measures specifically. But they must avoid openly favoring one candidate over another, or endorsing one candidate over another as a representative of the church. Statements made that are clearly those of a personal citizen, and not of a representative of a nonprofit organization or church, are legal.

Make the most of voting guides that are circulated. Use your Sunday school classes as a forum for education—not debate—on the issues. Speak from your pulpit on ballot measures that affect your schools, church families, and reverence for the sanctity of human life.

It is absolutely crucial that you vote and that you urge your people to do the same.

"For rulers hold no terror for those who do right, but for those who do wrong. Do you want to be free from fear of the one in authority? Then do what is right and he will commend you" (Romans 13:3).

Veterans Day: Praying for Our Military

Do you regularly pray for men and women in the armed services? Do you write to them while they are away and recognize their attendance when they are home? I pray so!

I am burdened for the American households who surrender their family members to our military. And I am indebted to the men and women who serve us with such courage and loyalty. We must pray for them, their families, friends, and for those who have accepted a sacrifice most of us will never know. On this Veterans Day, please remind your congregation to remember our military families and the sacrifices they make.

Our Pastoral Ministries department has a great deal of contact with military chaplains across the country. I have a deep appreciation for them and a genuine compassion for their families. In many ways, these chaplains operate under certain constraints that would trouble some, but there is a real sense of camaraderie among these men and women. I value the times I have had to both learn from them and encourage them. Do you know a military chaplain—either on active duty or in the reserves? Do you pray for your chaplain colleagues in the military? Do you correspond with them? Do you take time to serve their families? Do you remember them during the holiday season?

"Endure hardship with us like a good soldier of Christ Jesus" (2 Timothy 2:3).

Thanksgiving: We Are Blessed

Thanksgiving is a time for us who lead the church to call our people to an "attitude of gratitude." It is also a time for us to remind our people that what we have is a blessing, not a given. Encourage your people to make the most of Thanksgiving. Let there be unprecedented love between you and those whom God has given you to serve. You can set the pace by:

1. Expressing your love and gratitude for your people and the assignment God has given you.
2. Making your ministry positive. In spite of the conditions around you, usher your people into the "faith life" that truly believes God is in control.
3. Challenging your congregation to give of themselves during the next six weeks. Ask each family to find a project that will edify the body of Christ.
4. Researching a way to bless a sister church in your area that is struggling.
5. Making a personal holiday calendar in advance of the season and making sure it includes plenty of time for your family.
6. Being thankful! Just think: God chose you to be a messenger of His unconditional love. What an honor!

Remember that the opportunities before you are greater than those of any previous generation of Christian leaders. I pray for you as Paul prayed—that God strengthens your heart so you will be blameless and holy in His presence. Happy Thanksgiving, my colleague!

"Enter his gates with thanksgiving and his courts with praise; give thanks to him and praise his name. For the LORD is good and his love endures forever" (Psalm 100:4-5).

First Sunday of Advent: Jesus' Light in the Darkness

As the busy Christmas season begins, many churches observe the tradition of Advent. *Advent* is a Latin word meaning "the coming." It refers to the preparation time for celebrating the coming of Jesus, the Light in the midst of darkness, symbolized by the Advent wreath. Its observance begins the fourth Sunday before Christmas.

The Advent wreath is a circle of evergreen branches laid flat to symbolize God's endless love for His people. Four candles stand in the circle—typically three purple and one white or pink—each symbolizing different meanings in different Christian traditions. Occasionally, blue candles are used to emphasize the hope found in the fulfillment of God's promise through the birth of Jesus.

One candle is lit the first Sunday, two the second, three the third, and all four on the fourth and last Sunday before Christmas. A white candle positioned in the center of the wreath, called the "Christ candle," is typically lit when Christmas falls on Sunday.

The first Advent candle reminds us that the coming of Jesus brought light into a dark world. That light still shines in the darkness, but many have been blinded to its truth. We must make that light so bright this Advent season that even the most skeptical will be able to see it.

I pray for you His joy and His peace as you enter this most beautiful time of the year.

"In him was life, and that life was the light of men" (John 1:4).

Monday: Full Disclosure

A thought came to me this week that might make the oncoming holiday season a bit more orderly. So often, the members of the pastor's family have such frantic schedules that they fail to connect or advise each other of activities in advance. Here's a suggestion:

Take a December calendar and have each family member fill in his or her responsibilities for the month. Write down each church service, Christmas party, pageant rehearsal, civic or business-related event, school play, church social—anything that has a seasonal feel to it. Post the calendar on the refrigerator door or some other well-visited location in the house. Urge each family member to look at the schedule every day so no one will be surprised by the others' duties. This will not only help clarify expectations, but it will also alleviate miscommunication and the inevitable "I didn't know" or "Why didn't you tell me?"

I know there's no perfect way to approach this month, but when all in the family have a sense of what everyone else is doing, it is a bit more tolerable. That's what I call "full disclosure."

"Many are the plans in a man's heart, but it is the Lord's purpose that prevails" (Proverbs 19:21).

Tuesday: The Meaning of Peace, Joy, and Hope

The early Christmas cards are beginning to arrive. As I sit and read them, I see phrases like "All the joy that life can bring," "Christmas is the promise of peace and hope for the world," "May the glad tidings of Christmas fill your heart with joy all year," "To wish you the peace of love at Christmas and always," "A season of hope—a promise of peace—a reminder of miracles—Christmas!" And one that states, "May Jesus be the glorious gift your heart celebrates at Christmas."

I know you receive many such greetings. Do you read the verse on each Christmas card or just the name at the bottom? The cards you receive have words like *peace, joy, glory, good tidings,* and the like—but have you ever thought how empty those words would be without the reality of Jesus' birth and His unselfish sacrifice?

I pray that your messages this Advent season will be more than just Advent words, but ones packed with substance based on the reality of a living Lord without whom there will never be peace, joy, or hope.

"A Savior has been born to you" (Luke 2:11).

Wednesday: Pace Yourself

As a pastor I usually could barely stay awake until midnight on December 31, much less ring in the new year with bells and whistles. I totally ran myself down with my excessive Christmas enthusiasm.

Other ministers talk about similar experiences. Some tell me that a feeling of mild depression hangs over them as they try to plan for the coming year. None of this should be too surprising. We could list several reasons for post-Christmas doldrums: Church attendance is usually down, offerings are low, the weather turns cold, flu season hits, bills come due.

As I look back on my Decembers in the pastorate, I wish I had saved a little more energy and enthusiasm for the winter days to come. When I existed on adrenaline, I reduced my ability to think positively and creatively—and it usually showed both at home and in the congregation.

But "new year blues" aren't inevitable. Why not be prepared this year? Pace yourself this December. Save some of your holiday enthusiasm for the weeks ahead.

"Find rest, O my soul, in God alone; my hope comes from him" (Psalm 62:5).

Thursday: Avoid Holiday Stress

I recall the stress that accompanies any holiday season in the pastorate. If you are not careful, you will miss the moments of greatest joy. Some suggestions:

1. Be sure all your family issues have been resolved. Don't enter the holidays without peace at home.
2. Arrange your calendar to accommodate time for Advent surprises. Don't miss these nonrepeatable moments.
3. Tune your heart afresh to the heart of God. Hear Him speak to you about your Advent messages. Don't be mechanical. Be open to the moments of divine revelation. Quiet your heart.
4. Find three or four people on your block who really need to know they matter. Bless them.
5. Finally, laugh a lot. Joy begets joy. Those moments you will long remember.

"Be still, and know that I am God" (Psalm 46:10).

Friday: Be Prepared

The season of Advent can and should be one of your most positive months. Keep the spirit of your congregation at a high level—preach positive, uplifting sermons. Give your people opportunity for praise and laughter. Make a special effort to engage members you have not talked to or seen for some time. Dream some new dreams in advance of the new year, and whatever you do, keep the "reason for the season" your highest priority.

During the Advent season there will be many and varied activities under your "watch." More people will be attending your services than at any other time of the year. Be ready for them: Be prepared, be friendly, be respectful, and be world-class. In other words, do what you do the very best way that you can. Be God-honoring in every respect, and as Paul wrote to the church in Colosse: "And whatever you do, whether in word or deed, do it all in the name of the Lord Jesus, giving thanks to God the Father through him" (Colossians 3:17).

Saturday: Slow Down

I urge you to slow everyone in your family down a bit as you face the events leading up to Christmas Day. How?

1. Begin early in the season to set priorities for each family member.
2. Mark out evenings on the calendar that are solely family time.
3. Establish a list of people or families who would benefit by your special attention at this time of the year.
4. Talk about the reason for gift-giving and establish a guide for buying presents.
5. Decorate early. Make the holiday season last with an unhurried attitude.
6. At the dinner table read Scripture and stories that reflect on the miracle of Christ's birth.
7. Find a way for the whole family to block out the world for some uninterrupted time together, either on Christmas Eve or Christmas Day.
8. Visit a Christmas program or presentation at some place other than your own church. See what others are doing and enjoy!

"Come to me, all you who are weary and burdened, and I will give you rest" (Matthew 11:28).

Second Sunday of Advent: Make Room for Jesus

As you light the second Advent candle, remind your people that Christmas is for everyone. Remember the loneliness of Joseph and Mary as they searched for a place for the Christ child to be born. Are we sensitive to the needs of others who may also desire a place to be loved and accepted?

As the Christ child searched long ago for a place to be born, He continues to search today for a place in the hearts of the more than six billion souls that populate planet Earth. Christmas is not just a pleasant season or a festive holiday—it represents one of the most significant events in human history. Now, more than ever, we need to emphasize "the reason for the season." Encourage your people to greet those along the way with a smile and a cheery "Merry Christmas!" We must not forget it is Jesus' birthday we are celebrating.

"Because there was no room for them in the inn" (Luke 2:7) was a sad commentary in the first century, and it continues to be so even now. We must give our Lord room to love His world.

"All the prophets testify about him that everyone who believes in him receives forgiveness of sins through his name" (Acts 10:43).

Monday: Fear Not

In announcing the birth of Christ, the angels proclaimed, "Do not be afraid." An angel was sent to Joseph with these comforting words: "Do not be afraid to take Mary home as your wife" (Matthew 1:20). But it was the words of Jesus Himself that gave man the greatest hope: "He has sent me to proclaim freedom for the prisoners and recovery of sight for the blind, to release the oppressed" (Luke 4:18). Wherever He went, He put people at ease. When they were sick or troubled or perplexed, He would encourage them. "Don't be afraid; just believe" (Luke 8:50). But it was His teaching found in John 14 that brought clarity to a lost and hopeless world: "Do not let your hearts be troubled. Trust in God; trust also in me. . . . Do not let your hearts be troubled and do not be afraid" (John 14:1, 27). He was the divine liberator. Jesus looked the enemies of sin, death, and loneliness in the eye and said, "You cannot terrorize my people anymore." Encourage your people, my colleague!

Paul said it this way: "For God did not give us a spirit of timidity [fear], but a spirit of power, of love and of self-discipline" (2 Timothy 1:7).

Tuesday: Stop and Smell the Roses

I have walked through many rose gardens and have seldom stopped long enough to smell the roses. That's pretty sad really, but it just goes with the lifestyle I have chosen. Do you stop to smell the roses? Do you take time to enjoy the simple blessings of life, or do you just rush through those times and later regret missing something very special?

My prayer for you in this Advent season is that you will not become so busy in the "Christmas Garden" that you miss the sights and sounds that make it so meaningful. In spite of the demands of the season, you must take time to soak in the joy called Christmas.

How? Start by taking time to do simple things. Drive with your family through the brightly lit neighborhoods. Take your children out for hot chocolate or pancakes as a special treat. Or just sit and listen to them. Go for a walk with your spouse and reminisce about those memories that mean so much. Or just sit in your sanctuary—alone—and plan the services around people that our Lord brings to your mind. Visit a nursing home with your staff or loved ones for a carol sing. You know, just take time to let the little things become like individual roses in a lovely garden.

Whatever you do, don't miss the beauty of this wonderful time of the year. From the Word of the Lord, "In repentance and rest is your salvation, in quietness and trust is your strength" (Isaiah 30:15).

Wednesday: Love, Peace, and Hope

Through the years, I've found that three words epitomize the season of Advent: *love, peace,* and *hope.* In the midst of turmoil the world over, these words are timely reminders of God's intent for all mankind in sending His only Son as the Savior.

LOVE: "For God so loved the world . . . God did not send His Son . . . to condemn the world, but that the world through Him might be saved" (John 3:16-17, NKJV).

PEACE: Jesus said, "Peace I leave with you, My peace I give to you. . . . Let not your heart be troubled" (John 14:27, NKJV). The angels announced His birth with the promise of peace and goodwill toward every man (Luke 2:14, KJV).

HOPE: He came with a message of deliverance. He confronted people who were sick or lonely, and appeared with the promise of better things. Paul said, "It is not just in this life we have hope but because of Him we have everlasting hope" (1 Corinthians 15:19-20). Great news!

These words never grow old and have a place in every Christmas message. Preach it, my colleague! Preach it in love!

Thursday: Gifts to Give Our Lord

For so many, the reason for the season is really not the reason for the season. It is more about "doing Christmas" than it is celebrating the Lord's birth.

If you had to look back across the years and identify one Christmas gift that stands above all the others, what would it be? My guess is it would not be some expensive something as much as it would be a gift of special meaning—something that you treasured even though its value to another might be minimal. The fact that it was from someone who loved and honored you is what made the present meaningful. The same is likely the motivation for your gift-giving.

In the Christmas story, the Magi "opened their treasures and presented him with gifts" (Matthew 2:11). What is it that we present to our Lord as we celebrate with our families and congregations? I was thinking about that biblical phrase, "They opened their treasures." What would that mean to you? What treasure would you offer our Lord at this Advent season? Perhaps . . .

- A renewed commitment to your call.
- Your promise of daily interaction with the Father as His child.
- A commitment to guard your heart and to flee those things that might negatively entrap you.
- A more sensitive commitment to the lost, those for whom Christ died.
- Perhaps a disciplined and vigilant attitude toward a healthy lifestyle. You are a temple that must be protected.
- A realization that your spouse and your children need more attention than any others in your congregation.
- A humble spirit that will not allow envy or pride to dominate your thinking or actions.
- Loving Him back.

To me, and I hope to you, that would characterize genuine gift-giving. Your treasure becomes His gift. "Thanks be to God for his indescribable gift!" (2 Corinthians 9:15).

Friday: Caring for Widows and Orphans

While reading in James, I realized that at this time of the year, widows, single parents, and children in fractured homes deserve a special effort from you and your congregation on their behalf. My years as a pastor showed me that the holidays are difficult for so many because they have no one with whom to share significant moments.

Why not look through your church records and identify those who could use some extra attention? Then determine who from your congregation might adopt some of those individuals or families on your list. Identify elderly widows or widowers who might need some practical help during this season and ask your Sunday school classes to adopt them. Have the congregation buy gifts for children whose parents are serving overseas during the Christmas season. Encourage your congregation to reach outside the church to the children of prisoners through Angel Tree, a ministry of Prison Fellowship. There are many ways to serve the "widows and orphans" among us. Be creative and get your people involved.

James writes that the "religion that God our Father accepts as pure and faultless is this: to look after orphans [the fatherless] and widows [single parents] in their distress" (James 1:27).

Saturday: Respecting Your Spouse

One of the things about the Christmas season I remember as a pastor was the toll it took on my wife. There were years Beverley could barely wait for December 26th. Why? Because we worked her almost to death.

I think back to those days and the round of seasonal parties I dragged her to, not to mention the decorating, shopping, and planning for the in-laws' arrival. And, of course, there were the school programs. Whew! I know what you are saying: "What's the big deal? That's what we do every year!" I know, but do you enjoy all of the busyness? Does your spouse? Sometimes I feel like it was not the Grinch that stole Christmas—but the church.

I believe there is a limit to what should be expected of your spouse, and I am just waving the flag on his or her behalf.

Here are some suggestions:

1. Give your spouse private time to do Christmas things without worrying about dinner or kids—his or her night out!
2. On your day off, just the two of you take on the season and have fun while doing the "Christmas thing."
3. Make one night family decorating night with the entire family putting up the tree or helping with the lights.
4. Make baking a family event. Let the kids do their magic, and you wash the pots and pans.
5. Take the kids and go shopping for your mate. Even wrap the presents together.
6. Give him or her the gift of knowing that after the Christmas excitement, all of you can get away for a few days—away from the phone and church expectations.

Wishful thinking? Not really. A lot of this is up to you. I challenge you to make it different this year. Be creative.

"Many women do noble things, but you surpass them all" (Proverbs 31:29).

Third Sunday of Advent: Peace

As you light the third candle in your Advent wreath, remember the great message delivered by the angels to the shepherds: "Glory to God in the highest, and on earth peace" (Luke 2:14). The prophet declared, "For to us a child is born . . . and he will be called . . . Prince of Peace" (Isaiah 9:6).

Our Lord taught us to pursue peace. "Blessed are the peacemakers, for they will be called sons of God" (Matthew 5:9). In our churches, are we identified as peacemakers? I ask you, why are so many of our churches gripped by contention and bitterness when we should be beacons of light, people of peace in a troubled world?

The Prince of Peace now lives among us. He's the epitome of peace, and yet the world He died to save is full of war, poverty, sickness, and hate. Remember, on this third Sunday of Advent, we are expressions of that peace. Are we truly peacemakers? Speak peace, my colleague. We must preach the peace our Lord preached.

"Suddenly a great company of the heavenly host appeared with the angel, praising God and saying, 'Glory to God in the highest, and on earth peace to men on whom his favor rests'" (Luke 2:13-14).

Monday: An Opportunity
to Share Christ's Message

We know Him as Lord and Savior because we have a personal relationship with Him. But the majority of our world is as lost to the truth of the Messiah as those John wrote about: "The light shines in the darkness, but the darkness has not understood it" (John 1:5). Our responsibility is to cooperate with the Holy Spirit in such a way that all men might know the "light of life."

What a marvelous opportunity you have been given during this Advent season to paint a picture of the One who has come. Isaiah proclaimed, "For to us a child is born, to us a son is given . . . And he will be called Wonderful Counselor, Mighty God, Everlasting Father, Prince of Peace" (Isaiah 9:6). Just think what that means to people who are searching for something—anything—that will bring them the peace and assurance of a Father's attention that will never cease. What a message!

Please, my colleague, give Jesus life through your preaching and ministry. You will be blessed.

"As you go, preach this message: 'The kingdom of heaven is near'" (Matthew 10:7).

Tuesday: Spreading Goodwill

Regardless of denominational affiliation, all pastors face similar challenges, and none of us can succeed in isolation. Our theologies may clash at times, the form of worship can be different, the traditions have been formed on separate journeys, but the human predicament is much the same.

How often do you "cross over" to fellowship with one whose theology and practices might vary from yours, but from whom you can gain new and meaningful insight into ministry? I am convinced that we can learn from one another.

During this season of goodwill, what better way to spread peace and love than to reach out to fellow clergy and foster new relationships that will result in a stronger church? Why not make a point of having coffee with a clergy colleague for the sake of encouragement and edification—even though you might disagree on some points.

Bottom line: We really do have so much more in common than we have differences. Call a colleague this week. Make plans to reach out to other clergy during this next year. When there is genuine fellowship, there can be unity, especially on the things that matter most, in spite of our diversity.

"There is one body and one Spirit—just as you were called to one hope when you were called—one Lord, one faith, one baptism; one God and Father of all, who is over all and through all and in all" (Ephesians 4:4-6).

Wednesday: A Family-Focused Christmas

Today I remind you that your number-one priority at this time of the year is your own family. They need to hear the story of Christmas from you, to have some quiet moments of reflection as you share with them from your childhood. Make some memories. Establish some family traditions of your own.

For many of us, the pressures of the season are so intense that our attitudes are anything but yuletide bright. And even when we are at home, we are distracted from, or even disinterested in, the events surrounding our own families. Do everything in your power to prevent Advent adversity. Be especially sensitive to your spouse. Smile a lot, sing a lot, laugh a lot, encourage and affirm a lot. Schedule time with your family so that Christmas will truly be a time of peace and goodwill rather than a bah humbug event filled with resentful feelings. Make it the most Christ-centered, family-focused Christmas you have ever experienced. If you do, I promise it will be your most memorable Christmas ever.

"Glory to God in the highest, and on earth peace to men on whom his favor rests" (Luke 2:14).

Thursday: Having the Right Perspective

How do you balance the many expectations of church and family during the holidays? Suggestion: Keep everything in perspective.

I don't remember the author, but someone wrote, "Christmas, after all, should be a time of warmth and celebration. A blazing fireplace, a brightly lighted tree, the sense of families drawing closer, the shining smiles of eager youngsters . . . but ironically, this joyous season often becomes a time of stress and dread for many." Why? Because we lose perspective.

Christmas—when put into proper perspective—is a celebration of life for God's people, a time of rejoicing and praise. We can celebrate because our Savior has come, and with Him have come freedom, hope, and peace for us all. When we lose perspective, this truth is muted.

I challenge you, my colleague, to put it all in perspective for your people this coming Advent Sunday. We are often frustrated because we take our eyes off the central figure and simply concentrate on the pageantry.

"Yet to all who received him [Jesus] . . . who believed in his name, he gave the right to become children of God" (John 1:12). Now that's perspective!

Friday: Giving Hope

Just think, you have the privilege of preaching the same message that was delivered to the shepherds hundreds of years ago—a message still relevant and life-changing.

This Christmas, a number of people who need hope will be in your church. They will not be going on trips or receiving expensive gifts. Some are lonely, depressed, or afraid. Many will have lost loved ones; others are sick. Some will have lost jobs. Some are separated from children who are also away from God. There will be those with sad hearts camouflaged by smiling faces. They all need hope! Tell them what Jesus would tell them: "I have come to offer you hope, with love and a sense of belonging. I'm here for everyone, including the lonely and broken."

Colleague, please make sure this message is clearly told and not lost in the tinsel and trappings of the season. Be bold. Preach and teach the truth with passion and transparency. Let your people know how blessed and thrilled you are to serve them, and feed them with the sustenance of Scripture. Emmanuel—God with us! Now that is what I call hope!

"But the angel said to them, 'Do not be afraid. I bring you good news of great joy that will be for all the people. Today in the town of David a Savior has been born to you; he is Christ the Lord'" (Luke 2:10-11).

Saturday: Having Joy During the Advent Season

The angel proclaimed, "I'm here to announce a great and joyful event that is meant for everybody" (Luke 2:10, MSG). The heavenly messenger was, of course, talking about the coming of the Christ child—Christmas. My question to you: Are you having any fun? Is your Christmas season filled, as it should be, with joy?

Those of us in the clergy all know that, for many of the people we serve, the Advent season is not especially meaningful, much less joyful. How can we ourselves be convinced, and help our congregations see more clearly, that this beautiful event is meant for everybody, as the angel indicated?

Some thoughts:

- Keep reminding them of the true meaning of the season.
- Discourage materialism.
- Encourage them to be involved in assisting others less fortunate.
- Practice peace—especially in the home.
- Use Christmas to establish new family traditions.
- Make worship during the Advent season a priority.
- Read the Christmas story from various translations for devotions.
- Pick one or two people as targets for friendship evangelism.
- Pray over every Christmas card given or received.

I know the ideas I suggest here are not profound, but they do offer handles for all of us to use as we observe this great and joyful event. "Be joyful always" (1 Thessalonians 5:16).

Fourth Sunday of Advent: Love

As you light the fourth candle in the Advent wreath this weekend, you will do so in remembrance of the greatest gift of all—the gift of God's love.

John wrote, "How great is the love the Father has lavished on us, that we should be called children of God! And that is what we are!" (1 John 3:1).

I would often say to my congregations at the beginning of a worship service, "God loves you today as though you were the only one in all the world to love, and that makes you very special." I really do believe that. I don't understand it, but that is the mystery of the Virgin Birth.

How do we respond to that love? There is no way to repay it, but there is a way to reflect it—to love your God with all your heart and to love His children, your brothers and sisters. Gift-giving is a tradition that captures the imagination of us all, but on this Christmas Sunday, our Lord is most interested in how we show our love to Him . . . and to our neighbors. Looking for a gift? "Love never fails."

May His love be real to you. Merry Christmas!

"The Spirit of the Lord is on me, because he has anointed me to preach good news to the poor. He has sent me to proclaim freedom for the prisoners and recovery of sight for the blind, to release the oppressed, to proclaim the year of the Lord's favor" (Luke 4:18-19).

Monday: Let Christmas Come to You

As you prepare for your Christmas service, why not plan to do something totally different? Scale some things down. Be casual. Vary your order of service. Instead of a major message, tell or read a Christmas story that underscores Christ's gift of salvation. Talk about your own Christmas experiences. Have the children come and sit at the front of the sanctuary while you tell the story. Mix up Scripture and carols. Take a moment to let families just chat among themselves about what this Christmas means to them. Laugh a lot! Laugh out loud! If the crowd is smaller than normal, gather your people near the front so when you sing it is not like a bunch of solos. Just relax . . . and let Christmas come to you!

One thing I know: You cannot control your people's habits or attendance. You simply must be ready to feed them when they are present. *The Message* reads, "Here's my concern: that you care for God's flock with all the diligence of a shepherd. Not because you have to, but because you want to please God. Not calculating what you can get out of it, but acting spontaneously" (1 Peter 5:2).

Tuesday: Being There
for Your Friends

The Christmas season not only makes us think about family past and present, but also brings to mind friends who have touched our lives through the years. We do not see them as often as we would like, but when we are together, they seem like relationships that have always been.

I am positive that, as you read this, you can think of a colleague who has gone through tough times. Perhaps there has been a failure of some sort in their ministry. Maybe their family is struggling. There might even be a pastor in your circle who has been forced to step away from his assignment because of a conflict within the congregation.

My point is a simple one: The Christmas season can be very lonely for those of us who are away from our roots. The moves we have made have taken us out of our comfort zones. What might it mean to your clergy friends if you made a call, sent an e-mail, or initiated some contact that would help them realize they are not alone, that they matter? I urge you to take a few minutes and "do the friend thing."

"A man that hath friends must show himself friendly" (Proverbs 18:24, KJV).

Wednesday: Receiving Cards

In the hurry of the season, you can easily overlook the significance of each greeting you open. You see, every card represents a person or family that you have influenced in some way.

Some of the first Christmas cards I read this week were from former church members I had helped through difficult times. As I read their letters, I rejoiced with them for the many blessings received over the past year. From others, I could read between the lines and find loss and pain.

Now that I no longer pastor a congregation, each card has a very special feel to it. These folks have invested their time and money to remember our family. I am thankful for that. In my last pastorate, there were so many people and so many cards that I took a lot of them for granted.

A suggestion: As you open your cards, take a moment to read the printed message, then visualize the family who took time to remember you. Pray for them and thank God for the privilege of having a small part in their Christian journey.

Christmas cards in many ways echo the beautiful message of the angels so long ago: "Glory to God in the highest, and on earth peace to men on whom his favor rests" (Luke 2:14).

May this Christmas season fill you with the joy of that announcement.

Thursday: How Blessed We All Are!

As a pastor to pastors, this is the time of the year when I must admit I become a little bit envious of pastors and church leaders like you. No, I am not envious of the multiple board meetings you sit through or the financial balancing act you must perform. I would never be envious of your mood swings from Sunday to Sunday, predicated on the weather, church attendance, the quality of your sermon, or a cantankerous sound system. I am not envious of the complicated expectations that require you to be all things to all people at all times. I am sure Beverley is not envious of your spouse's fish bowl existence or the many hours that call you away from your family.

But I am a bit envious—in a righteous way—of your opportunities over the next few days as a pastor. I loved the busyness of the Christmas season. I didn't resent the many hours of planning that went into the services from Thanksgiving to the new year. The sights and sounds that accompanied these days energized me.

There was always that tired but happy feeling I had as I drove home from one of those blessed holiday events, thinking how thankful I was to be called "pastor." What a treat it was to serve parishioners who prayed for my family and were filled with thanksgiving for the many ways God had touched their lives. It was a privilege to lead those wonderful folks from Thanksgiving to Christmas and into the new year. How much better could it get?

I pray you feel this way as you read these words. Let there not be one utterance of the negative as you face the most beautiful time of the year.

"Give thanks to the LORD, call on his name; make known among the nations what he has done. . . . Enter his gates with thanksgiving and his courts with praise; give thanks to him and praise his name. . . . Let us exalt his name together" (Psalm 105:1; 100:4; 34:3).

Friday: What We Offer Jesus

During Christmas all the buying and receiving of gifts has a materialistic feel to it. After all, we are celebrating the birthday of our Lord and Savior Jesus Christ. What if we were presenting gifts to Jesus? Would they consist of flat screen TVs or video games? Would our gifts be brightly wrapped treasures with little lasting value? Or would we present to Him something much more in line with His nature and His purposes?

I'm sure you already have your Christmas Sunday sermon prepared, but what if you added a little segment to it and said, "If I could offer to Jesus Christ anything this Christmas, it would be . . ."?

My list would include:

- A concentrated effort by the North American church to do all we can to eliminate hunger and poverty throughout the world. (We could if we would.)

- A return to biblical literacy by believers. A resolve to live by the truth of God's Word—not just hear it, but do it!

- That not one more North American pastor would be accused of immorality and/or inappropriate use of the church's money.

- A gift of myself to our Lord to live in such a way that He would be pleased and glorified.

"And when they had come into the house, they saw the young Child . . . and fell down and worshiped Him. And when they had opened their treasures, they presented gifts to Him: gold, frankincense, and myrrh" (Matthew 2:11, NKJV).

Saturday: What I Want for You

I'm going to tell you what I want for you this Christmas.

First of all, I wish for you a new dream—something the Holy Spirit instills in your heart that appears so impossible only God's miraculous help will bring it about.

Second, I pray you receive joy. Not just happiness, but a joy that accompanies you every day. The kind of joy that Paul wrote about to the Philippians. The joy of serving, of praying, of loving, and even joy in the challenges.

And I ask for you the luxury of a very special colleague. Someone who, along with your spouse, will hold you accountable for your spiritual, physical, and emotional health . . . and you for them.

Finally, I want for you this Christmas the unbridled affirmation of your family and their support for what God has called you to do. The unquestioned feeling from those you love most that your household is a team.

That's what I want for you this Christmas. I truly hope you get it all.

"May the God of hope fill you with all joy and peace as you trust in him, so that you may overflow with hope by the power of the Holy Spirit" (Romans 15:13).

Christmas Eve: Focusing on Jesus

As the Christ candle is illuminated, it is essential that you focus on JESUS. From the beginning, men sought to destroy God's gift of love—His Son—but they could not. Two millennia after His birth, we still serve Him, honor Him, and seek to live by His teachings.

Some thoughts for Christmas Eve . . .

- We relight the first Advent candle to remind us of Jesus' coming (John 1:4-5).
- We relight the second Advent candle to remind us to make room, both for Jesus and the needs of others (Luke 2:1-7).
- We relight the third Advent candle to remind us to pray for peace on earth and for those who live in harm's way (Luke 2:8-14).
- We relight the fourth Advent candle to remind us to recognize the greatest gift of all—the gift of divine love—Immanuel (Luke 4:18-19).
- We light the Christ candle and remember that tomorrow is Jesus' birthday (the reason for the season) and that He should be worshiped and honored above all else (Matthew 2:1-12).

"After Jesus was born in Bethlehem in Judea, during the time of King Herod, Magi from the east came to Jerusalem and asked, 'Where is the one who has been born king of the Jews? We saw his star in the east and have come to worship him' " (Matthew 2:1-2).

Christmas Day: God's Great Love

"For God so loved the world that he gave his one and only Son, that whoever believes in him shall not perish but have eternal life" (John 3:16). That is the message of Christmas in a nutshell. At just the right time, in just the right way, our heavenly Father stepped out of heaven with a baby in His arms and laid His Son in a manger. As John noted, "This is how God showed his love among us: He sent his one and only Son into the world that we might live through him" (1 John 4:9).

It is not always easy to love others. It is not always pleasant to work for peace. But what would it be like in your congregation if, as you worship together today, those in the service were challenged to "drop the charges," to rid themselves of any bitterness or anger toward others, to be compassionate and forgiving even as they have been forgiven through Jesus Christ? What if they were challenged to show God's love to one another by extending forgiveness and peace?

I strongly believe that today many under your influence would have a much happier Christmas if they would just release those they hold in debt due to broken relationships. "Live out your God-created identity. Live generously and graciously toward others, the way God lives toward you" (Matthew 5:48).

New Year's Eve: Preparing for the Challenge

I always look forward to the new year because it gives me the opportunity for a little self-examination, as well as some new thinking.

For you, the past year may have been a winner. Or maybe it has been close, but no trophy. Or perhaps it has been a tough one. No matter what last year was like, the new year looms with the promise of new horizons.

In anticipation, there is the ingredient of surrender. The Bible says, "You do not know what a day may bring forth" (Proverbs 27:1), but it doesn't say that we are to simply put our feet up and watch the world go by. We are to plan, to dream, to remember God's blessings in the past and anticipate what He has for us in the coming year.

Whatever you do, please do not wake up on January 1 without a new challenge before you. Plan for success; believe for God's blessing. Concentrate on the positive aspects of your ministry. Surround yourself with spiritual people. Study hard and be prepared. Love what you do and the people you serve. And laugh a lot. Trust God for your direction. I know it sounds simplistic, but what is the alternative? It's up to you!

My life verse continues to be the most quoted scripture in the Old Testament: "Trust in the LORD with all your heart, and lean not on your own understanding; in all your ways acknowledge Him, and He shall direct your paths" (Proverbs 3:5-6, NKJV). Happy New Year, my colleague!

"The steps of a good man are ordered by the LORD" (Psalm 37:23, NKJV).

FOCUS ON THE FAMILY®

Welcome to the Family

Whether you purchased this book, borrowed it, or received it as a gift, we're glad you're reading it. It's just one of the many helpful, encouraging, and biblically based resources produced by Focus on the Family® for people in all stages of life.

Focus began in 1977 with the vision of one man, Dr. James Dobson, a licensed psychologist and author of numerous best-selling books on marriage, parenting, and family. Alarmed by the societal, political, and economic pressures that were threatening the existence of the American family, Dr. Dobson founded Focus on the Family with one employee and a once-a-week radio broadcast aired on 36 stations.

Now an international organization reaching millions of people daily, Focus on the Family is dedicated to preserving values and strengthening and encouraging families through the life-changing message of Jesus Christ.

Focus on the Family MAGAZINES

These faith-building, character-developing publications address the interests, issues, concerns, and challenges faced by every member of your family from preschool through the senior years.

| FOCUS ON THE FAMILY MAGAZINE | FOCUS ON THE FAMILY CLUBHOUSE JR.® Ages 4 to 8 | FOCUS ON THE FAMILY CLUBHOUSE® Ages 8 to 12 | FOCUS ON THE FAMILY CITIZEN® U.S. news issues |

For More INFORMATION

ONLINE:
Log on to
FocusOnTheFamily.com
In Canada, log on to
FocusOnTheFamily.ca

PHONE:
Call toll-free:
800-A-FAMILY
(232-6459)
In Canada, call toll-free:
800-661-9800